American Ethnic Writers

MAGILL'S CHOICE

American Ethnic Writers

Volume 2

Jamaica Kincaid – Hisaye Yamamoto

Edited by
David Peck
University of California, Long Beach

Project Editor
Tracy Irons-Georges

SALEM PRESS, INC.
Pasadena, California
Hackensack, New Jersey

Most of these essays originally appeared in *Identities and Issues in Literature*, 1997, edited by David Peck. The remainder were adapted from *Magill's Literary Annual*, from *Masterplots, Revised Second Edition*, 1996, and from the following *Masterplots II* series: *Drama*, 1990; *Poetry*, 1992; *African American Literature*, 1994; *Women's Literature*, 1994; and *American Fiction, Revised Edition*, 2000. All bibliographies and lists of published works have been updated.

∞ The paper used in these volumes conforms to the American National Standard for Permanence of Paper for Printed Library Materials, Z39.48-1992 (R1997).

Library of Congress Cataloging-in-Publication Data

American ethnic writers / David Peck; project editor Tracy Irons-Georges.

    p.   cm. — (Magill's choice)

Includes bibliographical references and index.

    ISBN 0-89356-157-6 (set : alk. paper). — ISBN 0-89356-172-X (v. 1 : alk. paper). — ISBN 0-89356-184-3 (v. 2 : alk. paper)

    1. American literature—Minority authors—Bio-bibliography—Dictionaries. 2. Minority authors—United States—Biography—Dictionaries. 3. Authors, American—Biography—Dictionaries. 4. Ethnic groups in literature—Dictionaries. 5. Minorities in literature—Dictionaries. 6. Ethnicity in literature—Dictionaries. I. Peck, David R. II. Irons-Georges, Tracy. III. Series.

PS153.M56 A414 2000
810.9'920693—dc21

                                         00-059529

First Printing

Table of Contents

American Ethnic Writers

Jamaica Kincaid
(Elaine Potter Richardson)

BORN: Saint Johns, Antigua; May 25, 1949

Kincaid's short stories and novels are admired for their lyricism and for their insights into feminist and racial issues.

TRADITIONS: African American, Caribbean
PRINCIPAL WORKS: *At the Bottom of the River*, 1983; *Annie John*, 1985; *A Small Place*, 1988; *Lucy*, 1990; *The Autobiography of My Mother*, 1996; *My Brother*, 1997

Jamaica Kincaid was born Elaine Potter Richardson on the tiny Caribbean island of Antigua. The family was poor, but she recalls her early years as idyllic. As does the protagonist of *Annie John*, Kincaid felt secure as the focus of her mother's attention. With the births of three younger brothers, however, Kincaid became increasingly alienated from her mother, and with adolescence, her alienation turned to bitter resentment.

In addition to her antipathy toward her mother, there were other reasons for Kincaid to leave her Caribbean home as soon as she was old enough to do so. As she points out in *A Small Place*, on Antigua blacks were still relegated to the bottom tiers of the social structure, just as they had been in the colonial past. Black women were even more repressed than black men. In her short story "Girl," which appears in the collection *At the Bottom of the River*, the mother makes it clear to her daughter that a woman's sole purpose in life is to wait on a man and to keep him happy.

Jamaica Kincaid (Sigrid Estrada)

Determined to find her way in the world, in 1966, the seventeen-year-old young woman left Antigua for the United States. Her impressions of the different country are reflected in her second semiautobiographical novel, *Lucy*. In common with the title character, Kincaid first supported herself by working as a live-in baby-sitter in New York City. Although Kincaid took high school and college courses, in the main she educated herself by reading. Eventually she found a job on a magazine, turned out articles, and tried her hand at short stories. She was finding a new identity as a writer; in 1973, she took the name Jamaica Kincaid, in a sense inventing herself as a person. In 1978, "Girl" was published in *The New Yorker*, the first of many stories to appear there. Shortly thereafter, Kincaid married and moved to Vermont.

After an absence of nearly two decades, Kincaid returned to Antigua. Having found herself, Kincaid was now free, and in the years which followed she often took her children to visit her early home. By leaving her native island, Kincaid learned not only to understand herself but also to empathize with women who, like the protagonist in *The Autobiography of My Mother* and like her own mother, were assigned their identities in a society that permitted them no options.

Annie John
TYPE OF WORK: Novel
FIRST PUBLISHED: 1985

Annie John, Kincaid's first novel, is a story of a girl's coming-of-age. On a conscious level the protagonist is contemplating death, friendship, sexual desire, and the developments in her body; she is also experiencing a deeper need to cut herself off from her mother, even if in the process she must hurt them both. The novel is set on the Caribbean island of Antigua. As a young child, Annie John clings to her beautiful and loving mother. She likes to caress her, smell her perfume, take baths with her, and wear dresses made of the same fabric as hers. At school, Annie shows that she has a mind of her own, but at home she takes note of everything her mother says or does.

Soon, however, Annie begins to realize that human relationships are fragile. They can be dissolved by death, by infidelity, or by changes in one's feelings. At a new school, Annie finds herself abandoning her best friend, Gwyneth Joseph, for a dirty, defiant red-haired girl. At home, Annie betrays her mother's trust and love. She lies to her about unimportant matters, such as whether or not she has any marbles, and she even insults her. To some degree Annie is acting out her feelings about her parents' lovemaking and about her own sexual development. Annie is also reacting to her mother's evident embarrassment when Annie assumes a woman's identity. On a deeper level, Annie's love for her mother is so strong that only by rejecting her can she establish a space for herself and a personality of her own.

At school, Annie gets into trouble by writing under the picture of Christopher Columbus the same words that her mother had said in mockery of her father, Pa Chess. Clearly, Annie senses that there is a similarity between the colonial system, which guaranteed that blacks would remain low in the economic system, and the patriarchal family, which ensures the subordination of females. By the time she is fifteen, Annie is thoroughly miserable, loathing her mother, herself, and her existence. She becomes ill, and for almost four months she is bedridden, nursed by her mother, her father, and finally, by her grandmother, Ma Chess, who appears mysteriously and evidently effects a cure. At last, when she is seventeen, Annie is sent to England. As the ship prepares to sail, Annie and her mother weep, and Annie relents enough to wave good-bye. Now free to find her own identity, she is free to love her mother, if only at a distance.

At the Bottom of the River
TYPE OF WORK: Short fiction
FIRST PUBLISHED: 1983

Some critics call *At the Bottom of the River* a novel; others call it a collection of stories. Certainly the stories' interconnections lend a sense of continuity to this thin volume. Much of *At the Bottom of the River* is a recollection of Jamaica Kincaid's childhood on the Caribbean island of Antigua. The author captures the identity of this region and its people with remarkable accuracy in her sketches. By telling her stories largely from a child's point of view, Kincaid gracefully intermixes the outside world with her protagonist's mental world of dreams, images, fantasy, and mysticism.

The book's ten stories dwell upon racial and mother-daughter relationships. The daughter is obsessed by her mother, an overpowering love object for her. Her attempts to break from her maternal dependence are central to many of the sketches. The sketch "My Mother" recounts with great poignancy a girl's emotional odyssey from early childhood to the point of needing to loose herself from a reliance upon the mother she dearly loves. The narrative is disarmingly simple and direct. The child's dreamworld intrudes constantly upon the outside world, with which she must necessarily merge. She cries a "pond of tears" at separating from her mother. The girl's exile, expressed in the words "she [the mother] shook me out and stood me under a tree," is connected to her memory of the childhood punishment of being banished, when she had misbehaved, from her house to take her dinner under the breadloaf trees. This story is about lost innocence and the attempt to recapture it.

The sketch "At Last" considers the essence of things. The child asks what becomes of the hen whose feathers are scattered, whose flesh is stripped away, whose bones disappear. Kincaid broaches similar universal questions in "Blackness," in which she deals with the mystery of the generations, with the child who grows up to become a mother to the succeeding generation. The questions posed in this story are questions that puzzled the ancient Greek philosophers and that still puzzle thinking people everywhere.

SUGGESTED READINGS

Bemrose, John. "Growing Pains of Girlhood." *Maclean's*, May 20, 1985, 61.

Bloom, Harold. ed. *Jamaica Kincaid.* Philadelphia: Chelsea House, 1998.

Kenney, Susan. "Paradise with Snake." *The New York Times Book Review*, April 7, 1985, 6.

Kreilkamp, Ivan. "Jamaica Kincaid: Daring to Discomfort." *Publishers Weekly* 243 (January 1, 1996): 54-55.

Lee, Felicia R. "Dark Words, Light Being." *The New York Times*, January 25, 1996, C1, C10.

Natov, Roni. "Mother and Daughters: Jamaica Kincaid's Pre-Oedipal Narrative." In *Children's Literature: Annual of the Modern Language Association Seminar on Children's Literature and the Children's Literature Association.* New York: Modern Language Association, 1990.

Paravisini-Gebert, Lizabeth. *Jamaica Kincaid: A Critical Companion.* Westport, Conn.: Greenwood Press, 1999.

Perry, Donna. "Initiation in Jamaica Kincaid's *Annie John.*" In *Caribbean Women Writers: Essays from the First International Conference*, edited by Selwyn R. Cudjoe. Wellesley, Mass.: Calaloux, 1990.

Timothy, Helen Pyne. "Adolescent Rebellion and Gender Relations in *At the Bottom of the River* and *Annie John.*" In *Caribbean Women Writers: Essays from the First International Conference*, edited by Selwyn R. Cudjoe. Wellesley, Mass.: Calaloux, 1990.

Van Wyngarden, Bruce. "First Novel." *Saturday Review* 11 (May-June, 1985): 68.

Weather, Diane. "Jamaica Kincaid: Her Small Place." *Essence* 26 (March, 1996): 98-99.

—R. Baird Shuman/Rosemary M. Canfield Reisman

Martin Luther King, Jr.

BORN: Atlanta, Georgia; January 15, 1929
DIED: Memphis, Tennessee; April 4, 1968

King's speeches and essays united, motivated, and mobilized people of all colors during the civil rights struggles of the 1950's and 1960's.

TRADITIONS: African American

PRINCIPAL WORKS: *Stride Toward Freedom,* 1958; *Strength to Love,* 1963, "I Have a Dream," 1963; *Why We Can't Wait,* 1964; *Where Do We Go from Here: Chaos or Community?,* 1967; "I've Been to the Mountaintop," 1968; *A Testament of Hope: The Essential Writings and Speeches of Martin Luther King, Jr.,* 1986

Martin Luther King, Jr., was formally ordained at the age of nineteen, in the church over which his father presided, thus officially beginning his public-speaking career. Within ten years, he had secured a position as pastor of a Montgomery, Alabama, church and had established himself as a civil rights leader by leading a boycott against the Montgomery public transportation system. After the successful conclusion of the boycott, King founded the Southern Christian Leadership Conference, in the hope of harnessing the momentum of the movement to further the cause of racial equality.

Supported by a network of churches and civil rights organizations, King became the most vocal opponent to segregation, and thus became a lightning rod for criticism and accolades. On August 28, 1963, King led a march on Washington, D.C., at which he delivered his best-known speech, "I Have a Dream." The following year, he was awarded the Nobel Peace Prize. Also during 1963 and 1964, King was arrested four times on charges such as parading without a permit, trespassing, and contempt of court. One of King's most powerful works, "Letter from the Birmingham Jail," was composed while he was incarcerated during this time, and several other pieces were occasioned by the arrests and subsequent confinements.

The focus of most of King's writings was upon the necessity for all citizens to effect necessary social changes by using a system of passive resistance and economic empowerment. The tenets of his strategy were outlined in such speeches as "The Power of Nonviolence" (1957) and "Love, Law, and Civil Disobedience" (1961). In addresses such as "A Time to Break Silence" (1967), he spoke of the need for Americans to examine their beliefs about race and culture, with respect not only to conflicts within the United States but also in international relations, such as those with Vietnam.

King's later works, such as *Where Do We Go from Here: Chaos or Community?,* show King's reluctant recognition that the struggle for racial equality would

Martin Luther King, Jr. (©The Nobel Foundation)

be a long-term battle. Although he believed that civil rights would eventually be equally afforded to all Americans, he warned of the dangers of complacency and backsliding. In his final address ("I've Been to the Mountaintop"), given on April 3, 1968, he urged supporters of civil rights to continue the struggle in his absence. The next day, he was shot to death.

A Testament of Hope

TYPE OF WORK: Essays, interviews, speeches, and sermons
FIRST PUBLISHED: 1986

A Testament of Hope: The Essential Writings and Speeches of Martin Luther King, Jr. is a compendium of the writings of King and of transcripts of some of his better-known interviews, speeches, and sermons, all of which were compiled and published at the request of his widow, Coretta Scott King. The book is divided into subject matter sections and an appendix. The first section, "Religious: Nonviolence," explores the theological underpinnings of King's passive resistance philosophy. Because he was connected at an early age with the church, it is not surprising that many of the works in this section focus on the role of Christian love in the struggle for equal rights.

Most of the selections in the second section, "Social: Integration," are oriented toward the more practical aspects of the Civil Rights movement. Topics include the necessity of passive resistance, the need for eloquent speakers, and the difficulties caused by internal conflicts within the movement.

The third section, "Political: Wedged Between Democracy and Black Nationalism," addresses the difficulties King encountered while campaigning for immediate change; it was difficult to do so and not to lose the support of moderate and conservative sympathizers. This theme echoes through much of the next section, "Famous Sermons and Public Addresses," as well. The fourth section contains King's best-known speeches, including the "I Have a Dream" speech of 1963 and the "I've Been to the Mountaintop" speech, which was delivered shortly before King's death in 1968.

The fifth section of *A Testament of Hope* contains some of King's best-known essays, including the "Letter from the Birmingham Jail" (1963). In this and the title essay, King impugns not only the staunch conservatives who resist social change but also the apathetic moderates who, King charges, perpetuate social injustice.

The sixth section, "Interviews," contains transcripts of conversations King had with Kenneth B. Clark, *Playboy* magazine, *Meet the Press*, and *Face to Face*. The sixth and final section contains King's more formal written works, those that were written as, or developed into, books.

James M. Washington, editor of *A Testament of Hope*, admits that, as a public figure, King sometimes had help with the invention and composition of the works contained in this volume. This collection is valuable, he asserts, not only as a record of what King actually penned, but also of the principles he espoused and the ideals for which he stood. Because each section is arranged chronologically, it is possible to chart aspects of King's philosophical development. He changed in response to the changing political and social climate of America. His focus, however–the necessity of nonviolent civil disobedience in order to accomplish the greater good of racial equality–remains evident throughout.

SUGGESTED READINGS

Branch, Taylor. *Parting the Waters: America in the King Years, 1954-63.* New York: Simon & Schuster, 1988.

Fairclough, Adam. *Martin Luther King, Jr.* Athens: University of Georgia Press, 1995.

Miller, Keith D. *Voice of Deliverance: The Language of Martin Luther King, Jr., and Its Sources.* Rev. ed. Athens: University of Georgia Press, 1998.

Oates, Stephen B. *Let the Trumpet Sound: The Life of Martin Luther King, Jr.* New York: Harper & Row, 1982.

Phillips, Donald T. *Martin Luther King, Jr., on Leadership: Inspiration and Wisdom for Challenging Times.* New York: Warner Books, 1999.

Stull, Bradford T. *Amid the Fall, Dreaming of Eden: Du Bois, King, Malcolm X, and Emancipation.* Carbondale: Southern Illinois University Press, 1999.

—T. A. Fishman

Maxine Hong Kingston

BORN: Stockton, California; October 27, 1940

Kingston's autobiographical books and her novel, brilliantly interweaving imagination and fact, convey Chinese American immigrant experience to a wide readership.

TRADITIONS: Chinese American
PRINCIPAL WORKS: *The Woman Warrior: Memoirs of a Girlhood Among Ghosts*, 1976; *China Men*, 1980; *Tripmaster Monkey: His Fake Book*, 1989

Born Maxine Ting Ting Hong, Kingston's first language was Say Up, a Cantonese dialect spoken by her immigrant parents, who made their living in California by running a laundry. They struggled to retain their Chinese identity and values in a new world peopled by ominous aliens: immigration officials, teachers, non-Chinese. Kingston's mother admonished and inspired her six children, particularly her daughters, with talks of the disasters that befell women who broke men's rules and of legendary heroines who dared battle for justice.

Silent and wordless among "white ghosts," Kingston was also threatened in childhood and adolescence by the specter of traditional Chinese prejudices against women. "Better to raise geese than girls," was a family motto. Kingston nevertheless became an A student and entered the University of California at Berkeley, where she drank in all the idealism of the Civil Rights and anti-Vietnam War movements of the 1960's.

Kingston married classmate and actor, Earll Kingston, and for many years pursued a career as a teacher, first in California and then in Hawaii. Meanwhile, finding her voice and experimenting with the linguistic means by which she could express the rich imagery and rhythms of Chinese American speech in her writing, she began working on two autobiographical books simultaneously. Enthusiastic critical acclaim accompanied the publication of the best-selling *The Woman Warrior* and *China Men*. Often called novels, these autobiographies combine imaginative flights and her memories of Chinese myths with the facts of Chinese immigrant history. In these works, Kingston claims full citizenship for Chinese Americans. "We Chinese belong here. This is our country, this is our history, we are a part of America. If it weren't for us, America would be a different place." Kingston says that, in telling the story of the Chinese in America, a major influence was William Carlos Williams's *In the American Grain* (1925).

Besides asserting the justice of the struggle against racism, Kingston also affirms the right of women of all races to full equality. Her writings make important contributions to feminist literature and women's studies. She stands as the most widely read and influential interpreter of the Chinese American experience.

Maxine Hong Kingston (Franco Salmoiraghi)

China Men
TYPE OF WORK: Memoir
FIRST PUBLISHED: 1980

In *China Men,* Kingston tells the stories of her male relatives who came to America. The opening chapter, "Our Fathers," signals her intention to embrace the community of Chinese immigrants. She challenges readers to reconsider the Eurocentric version of American history by bringing to their attention the contributions of Chinese to the building of America.

Kingston weaves her narrative from a poetic association of folklore, fantasy, and fact. In "On Discovery," she relates a Chinese legend: the arrival in North America of Tang Ao during the reign of the Empress Wu (694-705). Captured and forced to become a transvestite, feet bound, face powdered and rouged, ears studded with jade and gold, Tang Ao was forced to serve meals to the court. The bewildering experience of this precursor is a metaphor for the emasculation of Chinese men in America as racism disempowered them, forcing them to perform women's tasks: laundering and cooking.

In America, Kingston's forefathers find themselves off center as they are marginalized by U.S. laws. A chapter on laws, in the middle of *China Men*, documents the legislation and court decisions that, beginning in 1868, systematically excluded Chinese immigrants from normal treatment until 1958. Particularly dehumanizing was the law prohibiting the immigration of the wives and children of Chinese men working in America.

Through the portraits of her many forefathers, Kingston describes a multitude of immigration experiences. Great-grandfather Bak Goong sails to Hawaii in the hold of a ship and works for endless years under the whip on a sugar plantation. His dream of saving enough money to reach Gold Mountain is a mirage. The story of grandfather Ah Goong details the courage and skills of the Chinese who built the most difficult and dangerous section of the transcontinental railroad. They worked for lower wages and endured longer hours than white laborers but were denied the right to own property and become citizens. Nevertheless, Ah Goong prophesies: "We're marking the land now. The tracks are numbered."

Kingston's father, Baba, a man of scholarly accomplishment in China, enters America full of hope, only to be reduced to washing other people's clothes. Then, demonstrating the changing status of the Chinese in America after World War II, his son, drafted into the U.S. Navy to serve in the Vietnam War, receives the highest level of security clearance. "The government was certifying that the family was really American, not precariously American but super-American." Kingston's brother declines the invitation to attend language school, however, because he fears his improved Chinese will be used by intelligence to "gouge Viet Cong eyes, cattleprod their genitals."

Kingston thus ends her chronicle of Chinese American history on a questioning note. The Chinese American is now a full citizen but must share in all that is questionable in American culture.

The Woman Warrior

TYPE OF WORK: Memoir
FIRST PUBLISHED: 1976

The Woman Warrior: Memoirs of a Girlhood Among Ghosts is an autobiographical novel of Kingston's life, illuminated by references to the women whose histories influenced her. In the United States, the meager opportunities available to Chinese immigrants force her parents to earn a living by running a small laundry. Kingston's mother, Brave Orchid, a midwife in China, is a forceful character who admonishes her daughter with ever-changing renditions of Chinese legends and myths as well as tales about women who have been driven to madness or death by a culture that has traditionally viewed girls and women as subordinate to boys and men.

In "No Name Woman," Kingston recalls the haunting story of her aunt, who gave birth to a child years after her husband had gone to America. Driven to madness by the persecution of vengeful neighbors, a disgrace to her kin, she drowns herself and the baby in the family well. "Now that you have started to menstruate what happened to her could happen to you," Brave Orchid cautions. It is one of many frightening lessons for the young Kingston as she becomes increasingly aware of the different expectations placed upon women by the Chinese traditions that continue to dominate the attitudes of immigrants.

The book takes its title, however, from Fa Mu Lan, the legendary woman warrior who, disguised as a man, sword in hand, goes forth to fight for justice. Kingston takes inspiration from this story and imagines herself an avenger of the hurts she experiences as a woman and an Asian American. As she acquires a nontraditional consciousness, her listing of grievances transcends personal and family hurts to embrace broader struggles against racism and war. Kingston loses her job at a real estate firm when she refuses to type invitations to a banquet at a restaurant that discriminates against African Americans. She also struggles to evade the expectations that she sees American girls facing: wearing makeup, becoming cheerleaders, learning to be typists, marrying rich men.

In the final chapter, "A Song for a Barbarian Reed Pipe," Kingston testifies to her passage out of the confinements and prejudices that obsess her parents. She discovers that she can speak her mind. She alludes to the story of the Chinese princess, Ts'ai Yen, who, carried off by barbarians, finds her voice and sings high and clear like a flute, a song that blends the sounds of China and of the world beyond.

The Woman Warrior is distinguished by its rich, poetic language. Chinese oral tradition and classical literature blend with the myriad impressions crowding into the mind of a Chinese American girl striving to make sense of the competing mores of California's diverse populations.

SUGGESTED READINGS

Cheung, King-Kok. *Articulate Silences: Hisaye Yamamoto, Maxine Hong Kingston, Joy Kogawa.* Ithaca, N.Y.: Cornell University Press, 1993.

Ho, Wendy. *In Her Mother's House: The Politics of Asian American Mother-Daughter Writing.* Walnut Creek, Calif.: AltaMira Press, 1999.

Islas, Arturo. "Maxine Hong Kingston." In *Women Writers of the West Coast: Speaking of Their Lives and Careers,* edited by Marilyn Yalom. Santa Barbara, Calif.: Capra Press, 1983.

Juhasz, Suzanne. "Maxine Hong Kingston." In *Contemporary American Women Writers: Narrative Strategies,* edited by Catharine Rainwater and William J. Scheick. Lexington: University Press of Kentucky, 1985.

Kim, Elaine H. "Such Opposite Creatures: Men and Women in Asian American Literature." *Michigan Quarterly Review* 29, no. 1 (1990): 77-83.

Kingston, Maxine Hong. "Talk with Mrs. Kingston." Interview by Timothy Pfaff. *The New York Times Book Review,* June 18, 1980, 1, 26-27.

Li, David Leiwei. "China Men: Maxine Hong Kingston and the American Canon." *American Literary History* 2 (Fall, 1990): 482-502.

Ling, Amy. "Focus on America: Seeking a Self and a Place." In *Between Worlds: Women Writers of Chinese Ancestry.* Elmsford, N.Y.: Pergamon Press, 1990.

Simmons, Diane. *Maxine Hong Kingston.* New York: Twayne, 1999.

Skandera-Trombley, Laura E., ed. *Critical Essays on Maxine Hong Kingston.* New York: G. K. Hall, 1998.

–Joseleyne Ashford Slade

Joy Kogawa
(Joy Nozomi Goichi)

BORN: Vancouver, British Columbia, Canada; June 6, 1935

Kogawa's novel Obasan *brings literature of the World War II internment camp experience to a new level of psychological depth and lyrical brilliance.*

TRADITIONS: Japanese American

PRINCIPAL WORKS: *A Choice of Dreams,* 1974; *Jericho Road,* 1977; *Obasan,* 1981; *Woman in the Woods,* 1985; *Itsuka,* 1992; *The Rain Ascends,* 1995

Joy Kogawa grew up in the relatively sheltered environment provided by her minister father in Vancouver. That security was shattered with World War II relocation policies, which sent Japanese Canadians to internment camps in the inhospitable interior lands of Canada. The atomic bombs dropped on Hiroshima and Nagasaki by the United States also profoundly affected her.

As a young woman Kogawa attended the University of Alberta, the Anglican Women's Training College, and the Conservatory of Music. She married David Kogawa on May 2, 1957; they had two children, Gordon and Deirdre. The years 1967 to 1968 seem to have been a transitional period in Kogawa's life, since her first book of poems (*The Splintered Moon,* 1968) was published, she divorced David Kogawa, and she returned to college, attending the University of Saskatchewan, in those two years.

Joy Kogawa

The next ten years of Kogawa's life were increasingly productive. Her second collection of poems, *A Choice of Dreams,* was published in 1974. Kogawa worked in the Office of the Prime Minister in Ottawa, Ontario, as a staff writer from 1974 to 1976. A third collection of poetry, *Jericho Road,* was published in

1977. During this time Kogawa worked primarily as a freelance writer. Kogawa contributed poems to magazines and journals in Canada and the United States.

In 1981, *Obasan* was published. Widely acclaimed as one of the most psychologically complex and lyrically beautiful novels on the topic of Japanese Canadians' wartime experiences, *Obasan* continues to intrigue readers and critics alike with its powerful story of a silent, reserved woman, Megumi Naomi Nakane, learning of the fate of her family in Japan many years after the fact. Naomi's experience of dispossession, relocation, and internment, as well as the loss of her parents, has made her ethnicity, her self-image, and her relationships with others deeply problematic. Published in 1986, *Naomi's Road* retells the tale of *Obasan* in a manner intended for child readers.

Itsuka is Kogawa's sequel to *Obasan*. *Itsuka* follows Naomi's political awakening and the healing of her wounds from the past.

Obasan
TYPE OF WORK: Novel
FIRST PUBLISHED: 1981

Kogawa's *Obasan* has forced critics to include Asian Canadians in their study of ethnic literature; it is such a fine work no critic can ignore it. Kogawa has defined political and cultural connections between the Japanese immigrants of Canada and America. Both groups were held in internment camps during World War II. Their property was seized, and their families were often separated. In Canada and the United States the men of the families fought for their new countries while their wives, children, and siblings remained interned. Arguably one of the finest literary renderings of this experience, *Obasan* investigates what happened as a result of these practices.

Naomi Nakane, the protagonist of *Obasan*, appears emotionally paralyzed at the beginning of the novel. Unable to move beyond her own past in the camps and unable to reconcile the loss of her parents, Naomi has retreated into silence and isolation. Canada has essentially told Japanese Canadians that they are untrustworthy, second-class citizens at best, so Naomi retreats from her ethnic identity as well. Her Aunt Emily, however, is articulate, learned, professional, and politically active. Aunt Emily encourages Naomi to learn about the terrible things done to Japanese Canadians and to act on her anger. Naomi gains the impetus for change.

Shortly before the family's relocation to the internment camps (when Naomi is a child), Mrs. Nakane leaves to visit family in Japan. She never returns and the family carefully guards the secret of her fate. It is only as a thirty-six-year-old adult that Naomi is given the letters that reveal her mother's story of disfigurement and subsequent death as a result of the atomic bombing. The mother, herself, has imposed silence on the other family members. Naomi tries to engage her mother's presence, to heal the rift between them, although her mother is not physically there. In writing the novel Kogawa has constructed an elaborate attempt to embrace the absent voice, to contain the mother in some manner useful to Naomi's own construction of identity.

Poetic passages describe this imagined reunion. Dream sequences also punctuate the narrative, providing the touching lyricism that moves the novel beyond most of the literature written around the internment camp experience. Bound with the sociopolitical analysis provided by Aunt Emily and Naomi's personal history, the novel sets high standards for literature on ethnic identity.

SUGGESTED READINGS

Cheung, King-Kok. *Articulate Silences: Hisaye Yamamoto, Maxine Hong Kingston, Joy Kogawa.* Ithaca, N.Y.: Cornell University Press, 1993.

Darias-Beautell, Eva. *Division, Language, and Doubleness in the Writings of Joy Kogawa.* La Laguna, Canary Islands: Universidad de La Laguna, 1998.

Davidson, Arnold E. *Writing Against the Silence: Joy Kogawa's "Obasan."* Toronto: ECW Press, 1993.

Lim, Shirley Geok-Lin. "Japanese American Women's Life Stories: Maternality in Monica Sone's *Nisei Daughter* and Joy Kogawa's *Obasan.*" *Feminist Studies* 16, no. 2 (Summer, 1990): 289-312.

Wong, Sau-ling Cynthia. *Reading Asian American Literature: From Necessity to Extravagance.* Princeton, N.J.: Princeton University Press, 1993.

—Julie Tharp

Jerzy Kosinski

BORN: Lodz, Poland; June 14, 1933
DIED: Manhattan, New York; May 3, 1991

Kosinski is best known for his depiction of the Holocaust in The Painted
Bird *and for his creation of characters who grapple with the absurdity and
cruelty of contemporary life.*

TRADITIONS: Jewish

PRINCIPAL WORKS: *The Painted Bird,* 1965; *Steps,* 1968; *Being There,* 1971; *The
Devil Tree,* 1973; *Cockpit,* 1975; *Blind Date,* 1977; *Passion Play,* 1979; *Pinball,*
1982; *The Hermit of Sixty-ninth Street: The Working Papers of Norbert Kosky,*
1988

Jerzy Kosinski achieved immediate success with his first novel, *The Painted
Bird,* which Kosinski claimed was an autobiographical account of his childhood experiences during the German occupation of Poland. The author spent
the rest of his life defending those experiences, and the autobiographical
content of his other books, against his critics and supporters.

There are two central questions raised by Kosinski's work. First, were his
novels merely records of his extraordinary life—and his life was without
question extraordinary—as many have claimed, or are the novels a creative
refashioning of his experience? Kosinski experienced enormous popularity
as a novelist; his books sold in the tens of millions of copies. As one critic has
noted: Can a writer who pandered to the crassest commercial standards of
popular fiction by employing graphic sex and violence, conventional fictional
types, and sensational contemporary events really have anything seriously
significant to say to his readers? The search for answers to such questions has
dominated the writing about Kosinski's life and art.

There is no question that Kosinski's life had a profound effect on his
writing. The search for identity, with all that implies, is the primary focus of
his fiction and began with his own quest occasioned by his profoundly
unsettling experiences as a child. Most of his protagonists try on a series of
personas, creating roles with which to attempt to cope with the perplexity of
contemporary life. The most obvious of these is Chance, the central character
in *Being There,* whose whole life is formed by his television watching. Chance
is not unique in reflecting Kosinski's fascination with popular culture and its
effect in determining identity.

The implications Kosinski pursued regarding personality-shaping events
make him, along with Albert Camus, one of the primary writers to deal with
important postwar existentialist questions. His search for personal definition

in a hostile and alienating world earned for him a prominent place among writers of the late twentieth century.

The Painted Bird

TYPE OF WORK: Novel
FIRST PUBLISHED: 1965

The Painted Bird is one of the most powerful novels about World War II and the Holocaust. Since it only obliquely deals with both events, the novel is a kind of allegory for the senseless cruelty and brutality of any war. Kosinski claimed, falsely, that the novel was based on his own experiences. He was not averse to creating fiction in more than one realm; he was candid about this practice. The point of Kosinski's claim, it may be argued, is that the book's unspeakable brutalities are realistic—indeed, they are much less than what happened.

Characterization is notably thin in *The Painted Bird*, and even the narrator is two-dimensional. The scenes that he narrates are, however, often over-whelming, and the power of the novel comes in large part from its simple language and imagery.

At one level, this short, episodic novel is an allegory. Kosinski has written that the novel is a fairy tale experienced by a child rather than told to him, and this is an apt description. Each incident in *The Painted Bird* can be considered as a stepping stone in an allegorical *Bildungsroman*, or novel of education. In each encounter, the boy learns another lesson, only to discard it for a new lesson in the following chapter or incident—religion from the priest, politics from Gavrila, vengeance from Mitka and the Silent One, and so on. The final answer with which Kosinski leaves readers is ambiguous. At the end, the boy is losing the muteness into which the horror of the world forced him. There is evil in the world, surely, and, as the boy has seen, neither the religious nor the political solution cancels it—in fact, they often exacerbate it. The only thing that is certain is the individual.

At another level the novel is about not merely an individual boy but also the Holocaust of World War II. *The Painted Bird* can be read as one of the most powerful indictments of the madness and terror of the Holocaust in literature. Although the horrors depicted in *The Painted Bird* are much less brutal than the actuality—no death camps or gas ovens are in the novel—they are horrible for their starkness and immediacy; they are the concrete and individual horrors of one alien child in a world gone mad.

The major thematic question the novel raises is the one at the center of the Book of Job and other classic pieces of literature: What is one to make of the evil of the world? Kosinski has no clear answer—except that the novel, with all its horror, is its own answer. The boy begins to speak again; the novel is testimony to what he has witnessed—the powerful communication is that *The Painted Bird* exists.

For all of its realistic detail, the novel also has a symbolic meaning. There are a number of incidents that have this symbolic quality–the story to which the title makes reference, for example. The painted bird is an apt symbol for the boy himself. Lekh captures a bird, paints it, and releases it. The bird's own flock, not recognizing it, pecks the bird to death. This bird also represents all those who are marked as aliens and who thus are destroyed–including the millions in the death camps of World War II. Kosinski's novel, in language and theme, forces readers to confront the potential horror of human behavior, without recourse to easy answers.

Steps
TYPE OF WORK: Novel
FIRST PUBLISHED: 1968

Winner of the National Book Award in 1969, *Steps* is experimental fiction belonging to the "new wave" school led by the French author Alain Robbe-Grillet. Events dominate, and readers must participate in the action if they are to find meaning. Its unusual, brilliant tone and technique sets the work apart from other fiction of its time.

In 1967, Kosinski received a Guggenheim Fellowship to write the novel. His purpose, as he explained it, was to discover the self through incidents that were symbolic of the world. He said that the book's characters and their relationships existed in a fissure of time between past and present.

The significance of the title is elusive. Steps should go somewhere, but these steps seem only to travel between experiences. Some readers see the steps as a moral descent into hell, but it is certain that the author hoped that the steps would be his narrator's progression toward self-discovery.

Place names are not given. Poland may be the setting for some of the incidents, America that for others. The author lived in both places. There is no unifying plot, no order to time. Characters are like stick figures, stripped to their bare bones. They have no personality and are nameless. Only women are allowed admirable traits.

The narrator is a man trying to discover who he is in a world he considers hostile. Having come from a Communist country where human beings are externally controlled, he is surprised to find that there are collective forces in the new country that prevent the self from being free. Both society and religion exert control over people.

Much of Kosinski's writing is autobiographical. He spews the horrors he encountered in Poland out onto his pages in graphic form, colored dramatically by his vivid imagination. The jobs held by his narrator are jobs that Kosinski, too, held at various times.

An outgrowth of his first novel, *The Painted Bird* (1965), in which he was a child, *Steps* shows the author as a young man. The incidents seem disconnected, like a mirror that has been broken and the fragments scattered. If the protagonist could only find the pieces and put them together again, perhaps he could look into the reflective surface and see himself clearly. His self is shattered like the narrative, and the chaotic society in which he lives seems shattered as well. A former photographer, Kosinski records each event in visual detail as a camera would see it. He uses sight to achieve neutrality. The book is almost totally without emotion.

The theme of the book may be that brutality and violence are so destructive that they make life meaningless. Dispassionate acceptance of crude, degrading acts in an uncaring world gives tremendous power to the narrative. Distinguished by a commanding structure, poetic prose, and, despite its portrayal of depravity, an underlying morality, the work has been called existential. Its epigraph from the *Bhagavad Gita* (c. fifth century B.C.E.) indicates that the author hoped for peace and happiness to be restored to human life. That cannot occur if manipulative sex and brutal violence are the sum total of an individual's experience. The stark reality of this powerful novel is an admonition to modern society that bizarre relationships and fragmented experiences are capable of destroying the self.

SUGGESTED READINGS

Cahill, David. "Jerzy Kosinski: Retreat from Violence." *Twentieth Century Literature* 18, no. 2 (April, 1972): 121-132.

Coale, Samuel. "The Quest for the Elusive Self: The Fiction of Jerzy Kosinski." *Critique: Studies in Modern Fiction* 14, no. 3 (1973): 25-37.

Everman, Welch D. *Jerzy Kosinski: The Literature of Violation.* San Bernardino, Calif.: Borgo Press, 1991.

Lavers, Norman. *Jerzy Kosinski.* Boston: Twayne, 1982.

Lilly, Paul R., Jr. *Words in Search of a Victim: The Achievement of Jerzy Kosinski.* Kent, Ohio: Kent State University Press, 1988.

Lupack, Barbara Tepa, ed. *Critical Essays on Jerzy Kosinski.* New York: G. K. Hall, 1998.

_____. *Plays of Passion, Games of Chance: Jerzy Kosinski and His Fiction.* Bristol, Ind.: Wyndham Hall Press, 1988.

Sherwin, Byron L. *Jerzy Kosinski: Literary Alarmclock.* Chicago: Cabala Press, 1981.

Sloan, James Park. *Jerzy Kosinski.* New York: E. P. Dutton, 1996.

—Charles L. P. Silet/David Peck/Josephine Raburn

Stanley Kunitz

BORN: Worcester, Massachusetts; July 29, 1905

Kunitz achieves a complexity and coherence unique in lyric poetry.

TRADITIONS: Jewish

PRINCIPAL WORKS: *Intellectual Things*, 1930; *Passport to the War: A Selection of Poems*, 1944; *Selected Poems, 1928-1958*, 1958; *The Testing-Tree: Poems*, 1971; *The Terrible Threshold: Selected Poems, 1940-1970*, 1974; *Next-to-Last Things: New Poems and Essays*, 1985; *Passing Through: The Later Poems, New and Selected*, 1997

While a scholarship student at Harvard University, Stanley Kunitz won a prize for a poem anticipating his acknowledged themes of time and mutability. Critics speculate that Kunitz's thematic preoccupations stem from an event that occurred weeks before his birth: his father's suicide. Kunitz suffered a further blow at the age of fourteen when his beloved stepfather died.

Significantly, the dramatized "I"–the protagonist throughout Kunitz's poetry–is the ever-questing self, determined to survive against the odds, "the hurt/ Which is unanswerable [and] fill[s] the brow/ with early death." The basis of Kunitz's work is personal, but he is not a poet of the confessional school. He intends his poetry to be a vehicle that transforms private themes and events into legend. That is, the poetry is meant to give the particular and the personal a universal dimension. "All the essential details of the poem are true as dreams are," Kunitz explains in his commentary on "Father and Son."

The "I" in "Father and Son" pursues his ghostly father across a dreamscape. His face a "white ignorant hollow," the figure remains to the end wordless, incapable of imparting knowledge. Kunitz characteristically sounds the note of bitterness against family and tradition in his early poetry. "Let sons learn from their lipless fathers how/ Man enters hell," he declares in "For the World Is Flesh."

With World War II, during which, as a conscientious objector, he took a noncombatant role, Kunitz appears to have reforged links with his Jewish immigrant heritage. In "Reflection by a Mailbox," then-current horrors in Adolf Hitler's Europe precipitate an imaginative journey backward through time to the pogroms that brought his parents from Russia to America. The discovery of Russian poetry, which he began to translate, also revived ancestral ties. "Journal for My Daughter," occasioned by Kunitz's divorce in 1958, marks a major development toward reconciliation in his work, as he confronts his own parental responsibility for a child's suffering.

Kunitz's love of the natural world, traced to his boyhood solace in exploring the woods and fields surrounding his home, has remained a source of renewal, evident particularly in the expansive perspective of his later poetry. Recognition has included the Pulitzer Prize in poetry in 1959 for *Selected Poems, 1928-1958*, designations as Library of Congress consultant on poetry from 1974 to 1976 and, in 1987, State Poet of New York.

"Father and Son"
TYPE OF WORK: Poetry
FIRST PUBLISHED: 1944, in *Passport to War: A Selection of Poems*

"Father and Son" is about the desire for a source of psychological and spiritual certitude. It is also about the acute frustration in the individual prematurely deprived of one who could have provided it. Yet the poem is not for the fatherless or orphaned alone. In the ordinary course of life, everyone loses his or her parents. Later, one may yearn, consciously or not, for a bygone security that they represent. Such feeling does not require that security to have existed in fact. It is fueled by loss and by the alienation and dissolution which often follow from it. Moreover, the one lost may or may not have possessed the love requisite to this need.

The two-line stanza that concludes the poem reveals the fruit of the son's entreaties—a vision of the father's skull. Nothing remains to be conveyed. The brevity of this climax and denouement is arresting. The son's yearning and his belief in his father's love make "the white ignorant hollow of his face" an unexpected and shocking final image. Does the concluding couplet, then, cynically denigrate this yearning? Probably not, because this desire and its gratification are imagined as in a dream, suggesting their unconscious nature. The voice of the poem is not engaged in a realistic social exchange. What the son finally realizes is not the sort of rebuff one gets from an impatient realist. It is more like the half-conscious, desultory insight that follows a dream embodying some personal unhappiness. Such an insight could be as salutary in the long run as it is disquieting for the moment.

Maturity finally requires one to acknowledge that a dead source of surety cannot be otherwise. In addition, an absolute and dead guarantor of one's well-being, by its magical, unconscious empowerment, enslaves one. (The dead father's "indomitable love" has kept the son in "chains.") One may esteem that love, real or not, but one wishes the person who seeks it free of bondage as well. Thus, the terrible experience of the "white ignorant hollow" is ultimately liberating. Learning to live independently of perfect guidance is often a painful experience, but it vitalizes one's autonomy and self-reliance. The son is finally free to be a real moral agent, to act through his own judgment, even ignorance, there being no morally omniscient guide anyway, as the innocently "ignorant . . . face" makes clear.

"Three Floors"

Type of work: Poetry
First published: 1971, in *The Testing-Tree*

"Three Floors" is a short formal poem; divided into four rhyming stanzas, it resembles a ballad or hymn. The title suggests the interior of a house and raises the question of what is happening on each floor. The reader is thus led to expect some contrast or tension.

"Three Floors" is one of several poems in which Kunitz mentions his father—or rather the felt absence of his father. In the final stanza, the poem itself becomes a vehicle for the imagination, creating a father for the son. The child adds the possessive pronoun and the lowercase ("my father"—he cannot call him "Father") as he wills him into being. The father is "flying," though. Even as he is apprehended, he seems to be leaving. In a frenzy, the child perceives an elemental loss where the external world reflects his own amorphous grief.

Loss is at the heart of this poem. The mother is hardly real as she hovers on the other side of the door. The sister is soon to be lost, and the child is all too aware of her impending marriage. The father has never been there at all; he becomes a mystery to be solved. The child picks at the metaphorical lock of the family, hoping to discover his own identity. In the trunk, he finds only a hat that suggests a secret adult male society and a walking stick, with its implications of freedom and mobility. These powerful absences add up to a very real (if imagined) presence.

The sister has a fiancé—a "doughboy," or soldier—who has recently asked her to marry him. The boy listens as she plays the piano, one sound over and over, *Warum.* The word means "why" in German. The sister plays the song, almost absentmindedly, thinking of her soldier and the war. Behind loss is the question "why?" The question, along with its rhythm, pervades the poem, establishing a fatal sense that some things have no reason. The father's death, the mother's anger, the child's internalized conflict—nothing makes sense. Without an answer, the child is fated to ask this question throughout his life. The imaginative act, then, is seen as a way of discovering meaning—of making a divided house, however briefly, whole.

In sixteen lines, "Three Floors" has peopled the house with ghosts: The mother is sensed but not seen, the sister is remembered as a scrap of song, and the few vestiges of the father are locked in a trunk. The small boy is literally caught in the middle between the past (his father's loss) and the future (his sister's marriage, his own manhood). The poet re-creates the various claims on his affections as he presents the immediate moment of the poem—the darkness and the visionary sight of his father flying. His private thoughts are depicted as turbulent, guilty, and psychologically necessary. The reader is drawn into the poem's emotional complex in such a way that childhood itself, with all of its confusions, is awakened in memory.

SUGGESTED READINGS

Gaffke, Carol T., ed. *Poetry Criticism: Excerpts from Criticism of the Works of the Most Significant and Widely Studied Poets of World Literature.* Vol. 19. Detroit: Gale Research, 1997.

Hagstrum, Jean H. "The Poetry of Stanley Kunitz: An Introductory Essay." In *Poets in Progress,* edited by Edward Hungerford. Evanston, Ill.: Northwestern University Press, 1962.

Hénault, Marie. *Stanley Kunitz.* Boston: Twayne, 1980.

Orr, Gregory. *Stanley Kunitz: An Introduction to the Poetry.* New York: Columbia University Press, 1985.

Rodman, Selden. *Tongues of Fallen Angels.* New York: New Directions, 1974.

—Amy Allison/David M. Heaton/Judith Kitchen

Tony Kushner

BORN: New York, New York; July 16, 1956
Kushner's work brings together issues of national politics, sexuality, and community.

TRADITIONS: Jewish

PRINCIPAL WORKS: *A Bright Room Called Day*, pr. 1985, pb. 1991; *Angels in America: A Gay Fantasia on National Themes*, part 1, *Millennium Approaches*, pr. 1990, pb. 1993, part 2, *Perestroika*, pr. 1991, pb. 1994; *Thinking About the Longstanding Problems of Virtue and Happiness*, 1995 (including the play *Slavs!*, pr. 1994); *Death and Taxes: Hydrioptaphia, and Other Plays*, 1998

Tony Kushner grew up in Lake Charles, Louisiana. His parents, musicians, immersed him in culture, leftist politics, and the arts. He returned to New York City, his birthplace, to attend Columbia University, where he studied medieval history, developed an interest in Marxist thought, and began to come to terms with his homosexuality. He underwent psychoanalysis during his early years in New York, attempting to "cure" himself of being gay. After being graduated from Columbia in 1978, Kushner earned a Master in Fine Arts degree in directing from New York University in 1984.

Kushner is best known for *Angels in America: A Gay Fantasia on National Themes*, a play about life in Ronald Reagan's America and the pandemic of acquired immunodeficiency syndrome (AIDS). Much of *Angels in America*–and of Kushner's other work–focuses on political thought, especially the connections between world history and contemporary politics. Kushner's first major play, *A Bright Room Called Day*, uses an artistic character to draw explicit links between the rise of Nazism in Germany in the 1930's and what Kushner saw as the smothering conservatism of the 1980's. *Slavs!*, Kushner's sequel to *Angels in America*, opens with a character from *Perestroika*, Aleksii Antedilluvianovich Perlapsarianov, the world's oldest Bolshevik. The play focuses on a postsocialist world in which leftist politics has lost out to its more conservative counterparts. Kushner sees the loss of the left to be a loss of hope and a foreboding of a dangerous, heartless future. These themes are also developed in *Angels in America*, but in *Slavs!* Kushner does not use sexuality as a major symbol, although two main characters of *Slavs!* are a lesbian couple.

Kushner writes what he has referred to as Theater of the Fabulous. His plots examine the close relationship between the public, political world and the private lives of people. An activist who has been arrested more than once at demonstrations against government inaction in the face of the AIDS crisis, Kushner sees himself as an inheritor of Bertolt Brecht's explicitly political theater. In order for theater to be socially relevant, moving, and artistically successful, Kushner believes that theater must be confrontational, that it must not leave its audience comfortable or satisfied with the status quo. Theater, for Kushner, is an art of engagement, with politics, with issues, and with audiences—and theater is always political.

Angels in America
TYPE OF WORK: Drama
FIRST PUBLISHED: *Millennium Approaches*, pr. 1990, pb. 1993 (part 1); *Perestroika*, pr. 1991, pb. 1994 (part 2)

A two-part, seven-hour play, *Angels in America: A Gay Fantasia on National Themes* is an epic of life in America in the mid-1980's. In the play, self-interest has overtaken love and compassion, acquired immunodeficiency syndrome (AIDS) is decimating the gay male population, and victory in the ideological battle between liberals and conservatives seems to be going to the conservatives. Kushner's leftist politics are unmistakably present in his play, but *Angels in America* is not a polemic. Instead, it is a fantastic journey through the lives of two couples. One couple is Louis, a Jewish word processor, and Prior Walter, a former drag queen who has AIDS. The other is Joe Pitt, a Mormon republican and lawyer, and his wife, Harper. Another key player is the ethically questionable lawyer Roy Cohn, a dramatized version of the real person. (Cohn was counsel to Senator Joseph McCarthy during the "Communist witch-hunts" of the 1950's.) Cohn is dying of AIDS and is in the process of being disbarred.

Angels in America uses AIDS as a metaphor for an investigation of life in the 1980's. Kushner views the greed of that era as having frightening implications for personal relations. Louis spouts grand ideas in bombastic speeches but flees when faced with a lover who has AIDS. Louis is unable to face the responsibilities associated with caring for a person with AIDS. Joe, who becomes Louis's lover, abandons his wife, deciding that he can no longer repress his homosexuality. Cohn tries to enlist Joe's help in stopping the disbarment process by getting Joe a job in the Reagan Administration, but Joe refuses.

Prior, the protagonist, is the character who suffers most. As AIDS-related complications jeopardize his health, he becomes more panicked. He also becomes a prophet after being visited by an angel at the end of part 1, *Millennium Approaches*. With the help of Hannah Pitt, Joe's mother, he learns how to resist the Angel and how to make the Angel bless him. In spite of his failing health, Prior tells the Angel: "We live past hope. If I can find hope anywhere, that's it, that's the best I can do. It's so much not enough, so inadequate. . . . Bless me anyway. I want more life."

This message of hope, near the end of part 2, *Perestroika*, affirms the movement of the play toward the interconnectedness of people across boundaries of race, religion, sexuality, or ideology. Julius Rosenberg and Ethel Rosenberg say kaddish over the dead body of Cohn. Hannah, a devout Mormon, nurses Prior, a stranger to her. Belize, a black, gay nurse, advises Cohn on his medical treatment. Louis and Prior get back together, as the epilogue reveals.

SUGGESTED READINGS

Clum, John. *Acting Gay: Male Homosexuality in Modern Drama.* New York: Columbia University Press, 1994.

Felman, Jyl Lynn. "Lost Jewish (Male) Souls: A Midrash on *Angels in America.*" *Tikkun* 10, no. 3 (May, 1995): 27-30.

Kushner, Tony. Interview by David Savran. In *Speaking on Stage: Interviews with Contemporary American Playwrights*, edited by Philip C. Kolin and Colby H. Kullman. Tuscaloosa: University of Alabama Press, 1995.

Savran, David. "Ambivalence, Utopia, and a Queer Sort of Materialism: How *Angels in America* Reconstructs the Nation." *Theater Journal* 47 (1995): 207-227.

Vorlicky, Robert, ed. *Tony Kushner in Conversation.* Ann Arbor: University of Michigan Press, 1998.

—*Chris Freeman*

Nella Larsen

BORN: Chicago, Illinois; April 13, 1891
DIED: New York, New York; March 30, 1964

*Larsen's novels are among the first to portray realistically the dilemma
of identity for biracial women.*

TRADITIONS: African American
PRINCIPAL WORKS: *Quicksand*, 1928; *Passing*, 1929

In common with her protagonists–Helga Crane in *Quicksand* and Clare
Kendry in *Passing*–Nella Larsen, throughout her life, never thoroughly re-
solved the crisis of her identity. Larsen often invented details about her life
to suit her audience and the effect she wanted to have on it; it may be said
that she learned this habit of invention from her parents. Mystery surrounds
her identity because she wanted it that way.

Even in such matters as her birth certificate, school records, and early
childhood whereabouts, it is possible that no absolutely definitive history will
arise. Thadious M. Davis, in the biography *Nella Larsen, Novelist of the Harlem
Renaissance: A Woman's Life Unveiled*, makes a thorough summary of the
information available on the basics of Larsen's identity. Nella Larsen was
born Nellie Walker, child of a Danish woman and a cook designated as
"colored." The baby was designated, therefore, as "colored." When the girl
entered school, she did so under the name Nellie Larson. It is possible that
her supposed stepfather, Peter Larson, was in fact the same person as her
"colored" father, Peter Walker, and that Peter Walker had begun to pass for
white. Nellie Larson also attended school as Nelleye Larson. In 1907, she
began to use the surname Larsen. The 1910 census of her household does not
include her (her officially white sister, Anna, is mentioned), perhaps because
her birth certificate, with the word "colored," was being disassociated from
the family. Later, she adopted the first name Nella; with marriage, she became
Nella Larsen Imes. Larsen thus had considerable experience in her life with
such issues as passing and identity.

After completing a nursing degree at Lincoln Hospital, Larsen worked as
a nurse at Tuskegee Institute in Alabama. As does her character Helga, Larsen
quickly tired of the uplifting philosophy at Tuskegee and headed north.
Larsen worked for the New York City Department of Health and married
Elmer S. Imes.

Between 1921 and 1926, Larsen worked for the New York City Public
Library in Harlem. There, Larsen became involved with Harlem Renaissance
writers, capturing her own following with the publication of several critically

acclaimed short stories. Shortly afterward, Larsen wrote *Quicksand*, a novel for which she was awarded a Harmon Award in literature. Following the success of this book and her next novel, *Passing*, Larsen became the first African American woman to receive the prestigious Guggenheim Fellowship.

Her popularity ended, however, with the public embarrassment of being accused in 1930 of plagiarizing one of her short stories, "Sanctuary," and a messy divorce from her husband, whose unfaithfulness was the talk of the town. Larsen's readership abandoned her, and she retreated to nursing at New York City's Gouverneur Hospital, transferring to Metropolitan Hospital in 1961. In 1963, she endured a period of depression that may have been because her white sister (or perhaps half-sister) had shunned Larsen for the last of many times. In 1964, her absence from work being noted, Larsen was found dead in her apartment.

Nella Larsen

Larsen enjoyed literary success only briefly during her lifetime. Her literary talents and achievements went largely unrecognized until reappraisal of women's literature elevated her works as contributing a distinctive voice to American literature.

Quicksand

TYPE OF WORK: Novel
FIRST PUBLISHED: 1928

Quicksand, Larsen's masterpiece, is the story of Helga Crane's quest, through a series of excursions in black and white society, for racial identity and acceptance. Her rejection by her black father and by her white stepfather and her mother's early death leave Helga an orphan subject to the charity of white relatives, who pay for her education.

Helga's search begins with her brief tenure at Naxos, a Southern black college, where she fails to assimilate the racial attitudes of middle-class educated blacks there who expound the philosophy of racial uplift. She escapes to Chicago and then New York. Despite associations with middle-class blacks there, she still feels detached from the culture. A monetary gift from her uncle and his advice to visit her mother's sister in Denmark take Helga abroad. In Denmark, Helga rejects becoming her relatives' social showpiece of primitivism and a marriage proposal from an artist who sees in Helga "the warm, impulsive nature of the women of Africa" and "the soul of a prostitute."

Hearing a Negro spiritual at a symphony concert, Helga can no longer resist returning to America. When she returns, she finds that Robert Anderson, her only love interest, has married her mentor. Anderson underscores Helga's alienation when, despite his clandestine sexual advances, he rejects her. Devastated, Helga finds herself at a storefront revival, where she experiences a spiritual conversion. The intensity of emotion and her weak health occasion her meeting the Reverend Mr. Pleasant Green, a scurrilous "jack-leg" preacher who takes advantage of this opportunity to gain a wife and sexual partner. Transplanted to the South and drowning in the domestic hell of babies and marriage, Helga bids an angry and bitter farewell to her dreams and resigns herself to "the quagmire in which she had engulfed herself." She resolves to get out of her predicament, but she understands "that this wasn't new. . . . something like it she had experienced before." Life offers no healing balm for Helga, as her journey ends in the squalor of a filthy house, the revulsion she feels for her slovenly, lecherous husband, and her ultimate failure to find any redeeming purpose or value for her life.

Larsen's character is more than the archetypal tragic mulatto. Helga's restlessness and predictable flights from her cultural surroundings portray a woman uncomfortable with and deeply confused about her identity. Larsen was among the first to render depth and dimension to the emotional and physical motivations for her mixed-race characters' actions.

SUGGESTED READINGS

Bone, Robert A. *The Negro Novel in America.* Rev. ed. New Haven, Conn.: Yale University Press, 1965.

Davis, Thadious M. *Nella Larsen, Novelist of the Harlem Renaissance: A Woman's Life Unveiled.* Baton Rouge: Louisiana State University Press, 1994.

Gayle, Addison, Jr. *The Way of the World: The Black Novel in America.* Garden City, N.J.: Anchor Press, 1975.

Larson, Charles, ed. *An Intimation of Things Distant: The Collected Fiction of Nella Larsen.* Garden City, N.J.: Anchor Books, 1992.

Miller, Ericka M. *The Other Construction: Where Violence and Womanhood Meet in the Writings of Wells-Barnett, Grimke, and Larsen.* New York: Garland, 2000.

Thorton, Hortense. "Sexism as Quagmire: Nella Larsen's *Quicksand.*" *CLA Journal* 16, no. 3 (1973): 285-301.

—Betty L. Hart

Evelyn Lau

BORN: Vancouver, Canada; July 2, 1971

Lau's writing features young women, often entangled in prostitution, drug abuse, and bizarre sexual subcultures, who are in search of love and acceptance.

TRADITIONS: Chinese American

Principal works: *Runaway: Diary of a Street Kid,* 1989, 1995; *You Are Not Who You Claim,* 1990; *Oedipal Dreams,* 1992; *Fresh Girls,* 1993; *In the House of Slaves,* 1994; *Other Women,* 1996; *Choose Me,* 1999

Evelyn Lau started to write when she was six years old in 1977; at fourteen, her self-described obsession with writing led her to run away from her Chinese Canadian family, who did not permit her to pursue this passion. Keeping journals and penning poetry kept Lau's spirit alive while she descended into a nightmare world of juvenile prostitution, rampant drug abuse, and homelessness.

Lau left the streets at sixteen, and wrote *Runaway: Diary of a Street Kid* (1989, 1995) about her experience. She also published her first collection of poetry, *You Are Not Who You Claim,* in which her harrowing ordeals find artistic expression. The persona of Lau's poetry is often a woman who resembles Lau, and her voice hauntingly evokes the mostly futile search for human warmth and genuine affection in a nightmare adult world.

In Lau's poetry and fiction, lovemaking can end sadly. Thus, "Two Smokers" ends on a note of complete alienation: While the sleeping lover of the persona "gropes at the wall" and "finds flesh in his dreams," the woman "watches the trail of smoke" from her cigarette "drift towards the ceiling,/ hesitate, fall apart."

The haunting lucidity, freshness of imagination, and stunning power of Lau's writings have earned for her important literary prizes. Her first poetry collection won the Milton Acorn People's Poetry award, and her second collection, *Oedipal Dreams,* which contains many interrelated poems reflecting on a young woman's relationship with her married psychiatrist and lover, was nominated for the Governor-General's Award, Canada's highest literary honor. Perhaps most important, Lau's youth has given her writing a sharp awareness of the startling coexistence of mainstream and alternative lifestyles. Her poems and stories feature many a professional man who shows pictures of his children to the teenage sex worker whom he has hired to be his dominatrix. Similarly, the persona of *In the House of Slaves* watches a squirrel as a customer drips hot wax on her body. As has the author, the main character of *In the House of Slaves* has lived simultaneously in the world of pop culture adolescence and in hell.

Fresh Girls, and Other Stories

TYPE OF WORK: Short fiction
FIRST PUBLISHED: 1993

Fresh Girls, and Other Stories, Lau's collection of short stories, centers around young women who seek love and human affection in a netherworld of prostitution and bizarre, alternative sexual lifestyles. Many of the stories' protagonists live on two or more levels. They often wear a mask during the sex work they perform, but have retained a different identity in which they long for a more conventional life and for loving acceptance.

Lau's stories are told from the perspective of the young women, who chase after a dream which continues to elude them. The reader is made to share, for example, the sadness of the drug-addicted teenage narrator of the title story. Looking around the massage parlor where she works, she suddenly recognizes that, although many of her friends still look nice in regular clothes and outside their work, they have lost that special youthful freshness after which their clients lust with such depravity.

The astonishing ease with which men and women cross from an arcane subculture of sadomasochism to a mainstream life that is officially unaware and innocent of the other world is described with brilliant sharpness in "The Session" and "Fetish Night." Alternate identities are taken on quickly, and discarded just as easily, as young women agree to perform strange sexual acts on men who want to live out their secret fantasies and change from a position of power into that of helpless submission.

A core of stories explores the unhappy relationships of young women in love with older, married men who refuse to commit to their new lovers. In these stories, a man's wedding band takes on the identity of a weapon "branding" the narrator's skin. Fiercely subjective in her view, the protagonist of "Mercy" feels that "we are victims of each other," as she sexually tortures her lover on his wife's birthday.

The pain of the experience sometimes proves too much for the young women to bear. Out of a feeling of self-hatred and despair, "Glass" implies, a dejected girl cuts her wrists while she smashes her window, ready to follow the falling glass onto the street below. What gives artistic shape to Lau's collection is her unflinching, sympathetic look at a world that is alien to most readers. Her young, often nameless narrators are allowed to speak for themselves and scrutinize their tortured identities. In Lau's stories, the literary perspective is not that of a prurient voyeur who looks in but that of young souls who look out. Lau's stories challenge readers to examine the abyss of their own lives.

Runaway

TYPE OF WORK: Autobiography
FIRST PUBLISHED: 1989; 1995 (with a new epilogue)

Based on the journals that Lau kept, *Runaway: Diary of a Street Kid* chronicles her two-year experience as a young Chinese Canadian woman who left home because she could no longer stand her parents' oppression of her desires to write poetry. She sought to be anything but an obsessively studious, meekly obedient model pupil. *Runaway* became Lau's start in a successful career as a young writer.

After telling of her terrible life at home in a prologue, Lau's autobiography opens on the first day after she ran away from home: March 22, 1988. Staying with friends at first, she attempts suicide on the day she is turned in to the authorities. Recovering at a mental hospital, Lau falls into Canada's well-developed social safety net designed to rescue troubled teenagers.

For months, Lau tries to put distance between her old and new selves as she self-destructively experiments with drugs and sex. Twice she goes to the United States only to turn herself in to be shipped back home to Vancouver. She frustrates social workers and her two psychiatrists, who are unable to prevent her descent into teenage prostitution and drug abuse.

Throughout the chronicle of Lau's ordeal, the reader becomes aware of her extremely low self-esteem and her self-loathing, which her parents' perfectionist behavior has instilled in her. The reader almost cries out in despair at Lau's inability to value herself, even as her budding career as a writer begins with awards and letters of acceptance for her poetry.

Despite her ability to keep up with her writing and her occasionally seeing her position with lucidity, Lau refuses to stop hurting herself. She becomes attached to unsuitable men such as Larry, a drug addict on a government-sponsored recovery program, which he abuses with cunning. To keep Lau, Larry provides her the potent pharmaceuticals without which she could not abide his presence.

In the end, Lau frees herself of Larry, lives on her own in a state-provided apartment, and readies herself for college. Her writing has sustained her through dark hours, and, at sixteen, she is only a short time away from turning the journals into a manuscript. *Runaway* does not have a real closure. The reader leaves Lau as she seems to have overcome the worst of her self-abusive behavior, yet her life is still a puzzle waiting to be sorted out completely. In the epilogue added in 1995, Lau provides a firm sense that she has found a way out of the crisis of her adolescent life.

SUGGESTED READINGS

Books in Canada. Review of *Runaway: Diary of a Street Kid*, by Evelyn Lau. January, 1990, 23.

Canadian Literature. Review of *Fresh Girls*, by Evelyn Lau. Summer, 1995, 147.

Dieckmann, Katherina. Review of *In the House of Slaves*, by Evelyn Lau. *Village Voice Literary Supplement*, April, 1994, 32.

Halim, Nadia. Review of *In the House of Slaves*, by Evelyn Lau. *The Canadian Forum* 73 (October, 1994): 41.

Hungry Mind Review. Review of *Fresh Girls*, by Evelyn Lau. Summer, 1995, 25.

James, Darlene. Review of *Runaway: Diary of a Street Kid*, by Evelyn Lau. *Maclean's*, November 13, 1989, 81.

Kirkus Review. Review of *Fresh Girls*, by Evelyn Lau. 63 (January 1, 1995): 13.

Los Angeles Times Book Review. Review of *Fresh Girls*, by Evelyn Lau. September 3, 1995, 6.

−R. C. Lutz

Wendy Law-Yone

BORN: Mandalay, Burma (now Myanmar); April 1, 1947

Law-Yone's novels describe the alienation caused by harsh upbringings, political turmoil, and immigration.

TRADITIONS: Asian American
PRINCIPAL WORKS: *The Coffin Tree*, 1983; *Irrawaddy Tango*, 1993

Wendy Law-Yone's novels reflect the events in her turbulent life. In 1962, while a teenager in Burma, she watched her country become a military dictatorship and imprison her father, a newspaper publisher and political activist. In 1967, attempting to leave the country, she was captured and held for two weeks before being released. After living in Southeast Asia, she immigrated to America in 1973. She was graduated from college two years later and worked as a writer, publishing in the *Washington Post Magazine* and researching and writing *Company Information: A Model Investigation* (1983).

Her first novel, *The Coffin Tree*, portrays an Asian American immigrant in a different situation than that of many other novels. In many books, protagonists need to choose between, or reconcile, their native culture and American culture. Law-Yone's heroine, however, lacks connections to both cultures. Growing up with no mother and a distant father, she develops no attachment to Burma and is never nostalgic. When she and her brother immigrate, however, she remains detached from and unenthusiastic about America. Unable to express or follow her own desires, she obeys her tyrannical father and grandmother in Burma and her deranged brother in America. When brother and father die, twisted logic leads her to attempt suicide to fulfill her newly "uncovered . . . identity." Although she survives, institutional treatment engenders only a mild affirmation of life: "Living things prefer to go on living."

Irrawaddy Tango also describes a woman living more for others than herself: In a fictionalized Burma, a friend inspires her to love dancing. She marries an officer who becomes the country's dictator; when kidnapped by rebels, she agrees to be their spokeswoman. After her rescue, she helps other refugees before drifting into homelessness in America; she then returns to publicly reconcile with the dictator. Despite her political activities, she evidences no commitment to any cause and also can express herself only by violence, finally murdering her husband.

Law-Yone does not fully account for her heroines' alienation and lack of self-esteem, though possible factors include unhappy childhoods—with cold fathers and absent mothers. Politics is also corrosive in Law-Yone's fiction, leading parents and spouses to neglect personal relationships. Finally, fate forces some to lead unrewarding lives. The absence of easy answers in her fiction demonstrates her maturity as a writer.

The Coffin Tree

TYPE OF WORK: Novel
FIRST PUBLISHED: 1983

The Coffin Tree explores a young woman's growth into adulthood from the perspective of two cultures: Burma and the United States. Against the back-drop of large-scale political instability and threat of war in Burma, Law-Yone depicts a subtle kind of brutality at work beneath the veneer of prosperity and efficiency in the United States. The narrator's matter-of-fact description of the rebuffs and humiliation that she experiences in her attempt to adapt to a foreign culture is a powerful indictment of the United States' insensitivity to its immigrant population. The narrator and her half brother Shan are edu-cated and speak English, but this does not prevent them from being misun-derstood and maligned by Americans who show no understanding that people from other cultures operate according to different codes of behavior. *The Coffin Tree* suggests that cruelty caused by a failure to empathize with one's fellow human beings can take many guises. For example, the narrator's employer in New York does not give her a chance to explain her absence from work because his thinking is controlled by negative stereotypes. He thought-lessly fires her just when she has spent her last money on a doctor's house call to the mentally ill Shan, who has malaria.

Ultimately, however, the main focus of the novel is not on the narrator's eventual cultural assimilation, which is glossed over in a few paragraphs, but on her inner emotional state. Her dreams are as important to her as waking reality. While not always as overtly symbolic as in her dream of the threaten-ing half-man, half-horse whose energy, impatience, and violence is suggestive of her father, most of the dreams nevertheless disclose her anxieties and her longings. Yet, though the narrator's explanation of her feelings and motives constitutes the novel's reason for being, she never indulges in self-pity or self-justification. As she records events, memories, and emotions, the rapid pace and alternating settings drive the narrative forward without sentimental-ity. Incorporated stories and legends add a touch of the mythic to the realism of the novel. Law-Yone portrays a broad range of human experience in *The Coffin Tree* without straying from her central focus on the narrator's search for meaning.

The process of a young person's developing individuality and the forma-tion of gender roles are pervasive concerns in contemporary American society. Law-Yone shows that the narrator has the same basic psychological needs as young American women, even though Burmese culture dictates different practices and standards regarding communication, social interaction, and family ties. Law-Yone also reveals through her depiction of patients in a mental hospital that psychological disorders are not restricted to any one social or ethnic group but tend to be rooted in personal history and family relationships.

SUGGESTED READINGS

Forbes, Nancy. Review of *The Coffin Tree*, by Wendy Law-Yone. *The Nation* 236 (April 30, 1983): 551.

Kim, Elaine H. "Asian American Writers: A Bibliographical Review." *American Studies International* 22, no. 2 (1984): 41-78.

Law-Yone, Wendy. "Life in the Hills." *The Atlantic Monthly* 264, no. 6 (December, 1989): 24-36.

Lee, Rachel, C. "The Erasure of Places and the Re-siting of Empire in Wendy Law-Yone's *The Coffin Tree*." *Cultural Critique* 35 (Winter, 1996-1997): 149-178.

Ling, Amy. "Wendy Law-Yone." In *The Oxford Companion to Women's Writing in the United States*, edited by Cathy N. Davidson and Linda Wagner-Martin. New York: Oxford University Press, 1995.

—Gary Westfahl/Patricia L. Watson

Gus Lee
(Augustus Samuel Jian-Sun Lee)

BORN: San Francisco, California; August 8, 1946

Lee's novels capture the dilemma of an Asian American youth who tries to please the demands of two opposing cultures.

TRADITIONS: Chinese American
PRINCIPAL WORKS: *China Boy*, 1991; *Honor and Duty*, 1994; *No Physical Evidence*, 1998

Gus Lee came to writing late in life, at age forty-five, after careers in the military and as a lawyer. In 1989, his daughter asked him a question about his mother, and that simple question led to his first book, *China Boy*, in 1991. Born in San Francisco in a tough black neighborhood, the Panhandle, Lee found his childhood full of danger on the streets. At home he felt divided. His father and mother had come from mainland China in the early 1940's and

were wealthy and edu-
cated. His father had a military background and had
fought for the Nationalist
army. His mother had been
educated by Christian mis-
sionaries. Lee's mother died
when he was five years old,
and his new stepmother
had new ideas about the
traditional Chinese ways.
Lee had to fight in the
streets, with the help of
boxing courses he took at
the Young Men's Christian
Association (YMCA). He
also had to battle at home
with his stepmother, who
wanted him to become
more American.

His first novel, *China
Boy*, uses many autobio-

Gus Lee (Asian Week)

graphical events to tell the story of a young boy, Kai Ting, who is growing up in San Francisco. Skinny, weak, and timid, Kai Ting finds a friend at the neighborhood YMCA, learns self-defense, and returns to the streets with more confidence.

Lee describes the early days as being very stifled by rules at home. Lee rebelled against his controlling stepmother, reading his homework but refusing to concentrate. He got good grades but was not involved. Lee's father also attempted to direct him, objecting to the Christianity that the stepmother taught her stepson and projecting an atheistic approach that Lee felt was not right. Lee kept his mind focused on one goal: He wanted to become a West Point cadet. When he was appointed, he felt great relief, even though his life away from home as a plebe would be hellish. Lee actually found the harassment as a plebe at West Point to be easier than living at home.

His second novel, *Honor and Duty*, also uses Kai Ting as his fictional hero and takes this character through many tough days at West Point. Kai Ting must obey the older cadets, he must study mathematics, and he must obey the West Point honor code. Coming upon a group of cadets who are cheating, Kai Ting agonizes about reporting them to the authorities, knowing that they will be removed from West Point if he informs on them.

In Lee's life, after a long tenure as an Army Command Judge Advocate and later as senior Deputy District Attorney in Sacramento, Lee found himself unfulfilled. Then his daughter's question provoked Lee to write about an Asian American adjusting to life in the United States.

China Boy
TYPE OF WORK: Novel
FIRST PUBLISHED: 1991

China Boy is the story of Kai Ting, the American-born son of a Shanghai refugee family. Ending an odyssey across both friendly and unfriendly terrain, the Ting family finally settles in San Francisco.

China Boy is a *Bildungsroman*, or rite-of-passage story. Although the novel covers only approximately one year and a half of Kai's life, it depicts a pivotal point in his growth, a time of great change and uncertainty out of which he will gather strength and survive or to which he will succumb. With the death of his mother, the physical and emotional distance of his father, the cruelty of his stepmother, and the everyday violence that he faces on his neighborhood streets, Kai is plunged into a seemingly inescapable dungeon. To escape, Kai has to draw on the very last dregs of a personal integrity—the somehow unquenchable resilience of a seven-year-old—in order to salvage a childhood gone awry. Facing violence both within and without his home, Kai nevertheless soldiers along, and despite incredible odds neutralizes a neighborhood bully in the defining battle of his short life. This culminating act signals a breakthrough for Kai, and the novel leaves the reader with the hope that with one battle won, Kai is set to win others and, ultimately, to win the long war of his childhood.

The novel is also about displacement, about the suspension between two clearly defined, seemingly irreconcilable cultures. The culture represented by Kai's mother (Mah-mee) and Uncle Shim seems, with Mah-mee's death, to slip away with each day. Kai, speaking a five-year-old's broken "Songhai," is the flotsam from that culture. The reality of a relentlessly alien culture is all around him, but without its language, without recognizable points of reference to help him in his transition, Kai is in danger of becoming both a refugee from one culture and an unwanted stranger in another.

Ultimately, though, the novel is about the possibility of reconciliations: between past and present, between ethnicity and nationality, between passivity and action. There is time for Kai to recollect the lost pieces of his past in order to give direction and purpose to his present. Confronted by racism both at home and on the streets, Kai is befriended and aided by individuals who recognize the inherent stranger in themselves and who see in Kai only the human quality of need. Physically and emotionally brutalized by both his stepmother and the neighborhood boys, Kai is unable to retaliate. His understanding of *yuing chi*, or karma, seems to feed his childish fatalism. With the bodybuilding and mind-building at the YMCA, however, Kai seems finally to be able both to assert himself and to preserve his integrity. In the novel's epilogue, Kai confronts his stepmother at their doorway. He has just survived his fight with the bully, and his clothes are drenched with blood. Edna is concerned only that he has rung the doorbell too early and that she will once again have to bleach the blood—the Asiatic blood—out of his clothes. As a recognition of his past and present, of his ethnicity, of his action, of his new self, Kai tells her, "You are not my Mah-mee! . . . I ain't fo' yo' pickin-on, no mo'!"

SUGGESTED READINGS

Olson, K. Review of *China Boy*, by Gus Lee. *The New York Times Book Review*, July 21, 1991.

Simpson, Janice C., and Pico Iyer. "Fresh Voices Above the Noisy Din." *Time* 137 (June 3, 1991): 66-67.

———. "From Ghetto to West Point: Gus Lee's *China Boy* Becomes a Man of Honor." *Time* 143 (March 28, 1994): 66.

So, Christine. "Delivering the Punch Line: Racial Combat as Comedy in Gus Lee's *China Boy*." *MELUS* 21 (Winter, 1996): 141-155.

Stone, Judy. "Gus Lee: A China Boy's Rites of Passage." *Publishers Weekly* 243 (March 18, 1996): 47-48.

—Larry Rochelle/Pat M Wong

Li-Young Lee

BORN: Jakarta, Indonesia; 1957

Lee's writing is inspired by his relation to his father and his family.

TRADITIONS: Chinese American
PRINCIPAL WORKS: *Rose*, 1986; *The City in Which I Love You*, 1990; *The Winged Seed: A Remembrance*, 1995

When Li-Young Lee's first collection of poetry, *Rose*, was published, its Chinese American author had lived in America for twenty-two of his twenty-nine years. The poet's immigrant experience, his strong sense of family life, and his recollections of a boyhood spent in Asia have provided a background to his writing.

Lee was born in Jakarta; his Chinese parents were exiles from Communist China. They traveled until their arrival in Pittsburgh in 1964. The sense of being an alien, not a native to the place where one lives, strongly permeates Lee's poetry and gives an edge to his carefully crafted lines. There is also a touch of sadness to his poetry: The abyss lurks everywhere, and his personae have to be circumspect in their words and actions, since they, unlike a native, can take nothing for granted in their host culture. Looking at his sister, the speaker in "My Sleeping Loved Ones" warns "And don't mistake my stillness/ for awe./ It's just that I don't want to waken her."

Faced with a new language after his arrival in America, Lee became fascinated with the sound of words, an experience related in "Persimmons." Here, a teacher slaps the boy "for not knowing the difference/ between persimmon and precision." After college work at three American universities, Lee focused on his writing. Before the publication of his second collection, *The City in Which I Love You*, he received numerous awards.

Lee has always insisted that his writing searches for universal themes, and the close connection of his work to his life cannot be discounted. His father, for example, appears in many poems. Lee offers, in *The Winged Seed*, a factual yet poetic account of his young life. Lee's poetry and his prose reveal a writer who appreciates his close family and strives to put into words the grief and the joy of a life always lived in an alien place.

The Winged Seed

TYPE OF WORK: Memoir
FIRST PUBLISHED: 1995

To a large extent, *The Winged Seed: A Remembrance* is a lyrical and sometimes surrealistic memorializing of Lee's father and the author's relationship with him. This memoir is also, as its title indicates, the saga of the Lee family's participation in the twentieth century diaspora of Asians fleeing from the political upheavals of Asia and seeking to take root in the promise of America. Thus the book is a complex fabric made up, on the one hand, of a highly subjective psychological history about the formation of dominant themes and images in a poetic imagination that is woven, on the other hand, with factual history of world events.

By the time Lee was born, his father, Kuo Yuan, had already left China, which had been taken over by the Communist regime. He had migrated to Jakarta, Indonesia, and become a vice president at Gamaliel University in the late 1950's, a time when President Sukarno was blaming his country's economic woes on its Chinese inhabitants. Swept into the undertow of ethnic cleansing, Kuo Yuan was imprisoned in 1959. Physically abused, he bribed his way into less harsh incarceration in an insane asylum. There Kuo Yuan preached the gospel powerfully, first to inmates and then to their jailers.

By bribery and luck, the Lee family escaped to Hong Kong, where Kuo Yuan preached to throngs numbering in the thousands. Thence they migrated in 1964 to the United States, where, at the age of forty, he attended theological school. A changed and subdued man, he was appointed a minister in a Pennsylvania town whose congregation called him their "heathen minister." Kuo Yuan emerges as an intelligent, gifted, tenacious survivor with traits of integrity and spiritual power that did not flourish on American soil.

Although Lee's father is the dominant presence in the book, Lee also provides fascinating glimpses of his mother, Jiaying. There are brilliantly recollected vignettes of her life growing up in the privileged class of China. Jiaying was living in the French quarter of Tientsin when Lee's father joined her destiny with his. In Lee's memoir, Jiaying emerges as a capable mother and fiercely loyal wife.

One gathers that Lee's early childhood experiences in Indonesia played a formative role in shaping his imagination, even though there are few overt references to those experiences in his poetry. In Indonesia, Lee was largely cared for by his Javanese nanny, Lammi. Through her, he became aware of family conflicts and love affairs; more important, Lammi took Lee to her village home, where he watched performances of *wayang* (Indonesian folk theater) and imbibed the mythological tales they dramatized. Through Lammi and her friends, Lee was exposed to stories of spellbinding *bomohs*, medicine men and women whose power was confirmed by the Lee family's experience of hailstorms bombarding their house until their mother agreed to sell it. Lee's early childhood exposure to the folk art and shamanistic tradition of Southeast Asia may have contributed to the qualities of mythic resonance and paraordinary sensation that mark some of his writing.

The Winged Seed is a finely wrought memoir affording fascinating insights into the formation of a literary imagination and the origins of the most powerful images and themes that stir it. The book also provides revealing glimpses of some decisive political moments in twentieth century China and Indonesia.

SUGGESTED READINGS

Berk, L. Review of *The City in Which I Love You*, by Li-Young Lee. *Choice* 28 (June, 1991): 1640.

Chicago Tribune. Review of *The Winged Seed*, by Li-Young Lee. 14 (April 23, 1995): 6.

Greenbaum, Jessica. Review of *Rose*, by Li-Young Lee. *The Nation*, October 7, 1991, 416.

Kirkus Reviews. Review of *The Winged Seed*, by Li-Young Lee. 62 (December 1, 1994): 1592.

Los Angeles Times. Review of *The Winged Seed*, by Li-Young Lee. July 3, 1995, E6.

Muske, Carol. Review of *The City in Which I Love You*, by Li-Young Lee. *The New York Times Book Review*, January 27, 1991, 20.

Waniek, Marylin. Review of *The City in Which I Love You*, by Li-Young Lee. *Kenyon Review* 13 (Fall, 1991): 214.

Wisner-Broyles, Laura A., ed. *Poetry Criticism: Excerpts from Criticism of the Works of the Most Significant and Widely Studied Poets of World Literature*. Vol. 24. Detroit: Gale Research, 1999.

—R. C. Lutz/C. L. Chua

Audre Lorde

BORN: Harlem, New York; February 18, 1934
DIED: Christiansted, St. Croix, U.S. Virgin Islands; November 17, 1992

*Lorde's poetry, essays, and autobiographical fiction are among the best
American black lesbian feminist writings.*

TRADITIONS: African American
PRINCIPAL WORKS: *Cables to Rage*, 1970; *New York Head Shop and Museum*, 1974;
Coal, 1976; *The Black Unicorn*, 1978; *The Cancer Journals*, 1980; *Chosen Poems,
Old and New*, 1982 (revised edition, *Undersong: Chosen Poems, Old and New*,
1992); *Zami: A New Spelling of My Name*, 1982; *Sister Outsider: Essays and
Speeches*, 1984; *The Marvelous Arithmetics of Distance: Poems 1987-1992*, 1993;
The Collected Poems of Audre Lorde, 1997

Audre Lorde began writing poems at an early age, as a child of West Indian
heritage growing up in New York City's Harlem. Her early work progressed
from personal consciousness to encompass a radical critique of her society.
Lorde was graduated from Hunter College in New York, then went on to
study for a year at the National University of Mexico. She obtained a library
science degree from Columbia University in 1961.

Lorde married attorney Edwin Ashley Rollins in 1962, had two children
with him, and was divorced in 1970. From 1970 onward, there was a lesbian
focus in her life as well as in her work. In *Zami*, Lorde examines the powerful
erotic journey of a young black woman who comes to terms with her lesbian
sexual orientation. Powerful, deeply erotic scenes based in New York City's
gay-girl milieu of the 1950's reflect Lorde's efforts to grapple with her own
personal, sexual, and racial identity.

A teacher of writing at New York City area colleges, Lorde was keenly
aware of racism—a condition she experienced as a child in New York City.
This awareness was reflected in a radicalism in her work, including *Coal* and
Sister Outsider: Essays and Speeches.

The Cancer Journals
TYPE OF WORK: Memoir
FIRST PUBLISHED: 1980

The Cancer Journals, Lorde's documentation and critique of her experience
with breast cancer, is a painstaking examination of the journey Lorde takes

Audre Lorde (Inmar Schullz/W. W. Norton)

to integrate this crisis into her identity. The book chronicles Lorde's anger, pain, and fear about cancer and is as frank in its themes of "the travesty of prosthesis, the pain of amputation, and the function of cancer in a profit society," as it is unflinching in its treatment of Lorde's confrontation with mortality.

Lorde speaks on her identity as a black, lesbian, feminist mother and poet with breast cancer. She illuminates the implications the disease has for her, recording the process of waking up in the recovery room after the biopsy that confirms her cancer, colder than she has ever been in her life. The following days, she prepares for the radical mastectomy through consultation with women friends, family, her lover, and her children. In the days that follow, Lorde attributes part of her healing process to "a ring of women like warm bubbles keeping me afloat" as she recovers from her mastectomy. She realizes that after facing death and having lived, she must accept the reality of dying as "a life process"; this hard-won realization baptizes Lorde into a new life.

The journal entries for 1979 and 1980, written while Lorde recovered from the radical mastectomy she chose to forestall spread of the disease, show Lorde's integration of this emergency into her life. She realizes that she must give the process a voice; she wants to be more than one of the "socially sanctioned prosthesis" women with breast cancer, who remain quiet and isolated. Instead, Lorde vows to teach, speak, and fight.

At the journal's end, Lorde chooses to turn down the prosthesis offered her, which she equates with an empty way to forestall a woman's acceptance of her new body, and thus, her new identity. If, Lorde realizes, a woman claims her full identity as a cancer survivor and then opts to use a prosthesis, she has made the journey toward claiming her altered body, and life. Postmastectomy women, however, have to find their own internal sense of power. *The Cancer Journals* demonstrates a black, feminist, lesbian poet's integration of cancer into her identity.

Coal

TYPE OF WORK: Poetry
FIRST PUBLISHED: 1976

Coal explores Audre Lorde's identities as a black woman, mother, wife, and lover of women. Several of her life issues are examined and refracted in the poems. Lorde's lifelong journey toward claiming her West Indian, African American heritage is given voice in "Coal"; her motherhood is the subject of "Now That I Am Forever with Child"; and her women-centered existence is described in "On a Night of the Full Moon."

As a black woman of West Indian heritage, Audre Lorde knew the struggles of black Americans to claim their place and voice in American society. Raised in Harlem during the 1930's and 1940's, Lorde became aware of racism at an early age. The poem "Coal" claims a positive, strong voice for Lorde–a voice deeply embedded in her black heritage.

In "Coal," Lorde effectively transforms black speech into poetry: "I/ is the total black, being spoken/ from the earth's inside." Lorde defines poetic speech as a force that embraces blackness; then, she goes on to question how much a black woman can speak, and in what tone. Yet "Coal" defines Lorde as a black female poet who breaks the boundaries of silence and proclaims the sturdiness of power of her own words: "I am Black because I come from the earth's inside/ now take my word for jewel in the open light."

Fire imagery suffuses the book. The fire that marks the edges of many poems defines the anger and hostility engendered by a patriarchal and racist society. Lorde learns to empower herself by using the fire of anger and despair to create her own vision of spiritual and sexual identity. Embarked on her own journey toward truth, Lorde proclaims in the poem "Summer Oracle" that fire–which she equates with a warming agent in a country "barren of symbols of love"–can also be a cleansing agent. Fire burns away falsehoods and lets truth arise.

Lorde was widely praised by her contemporaries for her determination to see truth in everyday life. *Coal* could be called an uneven book, but her portraits of city life, love, anger, and sorrow make *Coal* a book of poetic transition from which Lorde would emerge into a life of more radical feminism and richer fulfillment.

Zami

TYPE OF WORK: Novel
FIRST PUBLISHED: 1982

Zami: A New Spelling of My Name, Lorde's prose masterpiece, examines a young black woman's coming to terms with her lesbian sexual orientation. An autobiographical novel, *Zami* has earned a reputation as much for its compelling writing as for its presentation of a coming-of-age story of a black lesbian feminist intent on claiming her identity.

At the age of nineteen, Zami flees New York City, where she was raised by her West Indian parents, for Mexico. There, she falls in love with an older expatriate woman named Eudora, who opens up her sensual life to the younger woman. Through her relationship with Eudora, Zami realizes the paralyzing consequences of the "racist, patriarchal and anti-erotic society" that Eudora fled when she left the United States. Zami returns to live in the "gay girl" milieu of Greenwich Village in the 1950's. She commits herself to a long-term relationship with Muriel, a white woman with whom she builds a home. Muriel completes the sexual awakening that Eudora began. Muriel is threatened, however, when Zami enters therapy and enrolls in college. As Zami forges an identity that integrates her sensual, intellectual, and artistic sides, Muriel moves out of the Greenwich Village apartment. Zami moves forward, even in grief, toward her new-found life.

Erotic language and scenes pepper the story. Zami learns to accept her own erotic impulses toward women, and her acceptance leads her into a larger life where love for women is central. Her eroticism is about the acceptance of the stages of a woman's physical life. Eros is also language that she uses to infuse her poems with life. As Zami goes to college, begins to send out her own poetry, and opens to life while Muriel declines, she meets a female erotic figure of mythic proportions: Afrekete.

Years earlier, Zami met a black gay woman whom she named Kitty: a woman of pretty clothes and dainty style. The two women meet again at the novel's end. Kitty has become a fully erotic woman, who has assumed the mythic name Afrekete. After her liaison with Afrekete, Zami finds that her own life has become a bendable, pliable entity that challenges myths and, in the end, makes a new myth of its own.

SUGGESTED READINGS

Bloom, Harold, ed. *Black American Women Poets and Dramatists.* New York: Chelsea House, 1996.

Brown, Catherine M. "Reflections on a 'Black, Militant, Lesbian Poet.'" *Essence* 29 (March, 1999): 68.

Christian, Barbara, ed. *Black Feminist Criticism: Perspectives on Black Women Writers.* Elmsford, N.Y.: Pergamon Press, 1985.

Evans, Mari, ed. *Black Women Writers (1950-1980): A Critical Evaluation.* Garden City, N.Y.: Doubleday, 1984.

Keating, AnaLouise. *Women Reading Women Writing: Self-Invention in Paula Gunn Allen, Gloria Anzaldúa, and Audre Lorde.* Philadelphia: Temple University Press, 1996.

Lorde, Audre. *Sister Outsider.* Freedom, Calif.: The Crossing Press, 1984.

Martin, Joan. "The Unicorn Is Black: Audre Lorde in Retrospect." In *Black*

Women Writers (1950-1980): A Critical Evaluation, edited by Mari Evans. Garden City, N.Y.: Doubleday, 1984.
Tate, Claudia. *Black Women Writers at Work.* New York: Continuum Press, 1983.

–R. C. S.

Claude McKay

BORN: Sunny Ville, Jamaica; September 15, 1889
DIED: Chicago, Illinois; May 22, 1948

McKay's writings capture the dialect of his native Jamaica, ushered in the Harlem Renaissance, and added a black voice to the early years of Soviet Communism.

TRADITIONS: African American, Caribbean

PRINCIPAL WORKS: *Constab Ballads*, 1912; *Songs of Jamaica*, 1912; *Spring in New Hampshire and Other Poems*, 1920; *Harlem Shadows*, 1922; *Home to Harlem*, 1928; *Banjo*, 1929; *Gingertown*, 1932; *Banana Bottom*, 1933; *A Long Way from Home*, 1937; *Harlem: Negro Metropolis*, 1940; *Selected Poems of Claude McKay*, 1953

Claude McKay was the youngest of eleven children in a rural Jamaican family. His parents instilled pride in an African heritage in their children. McKay's brother Uriah Theophilus and the English folklorist and linguist Walter Jekyll introduced McKay to philosophy and literature, notably to English poetry.

When he was nineteen McKay moved to Kingston and worked as a constable for almost a year. Encouraged by Jekyll, McKay published two volumes of poetry in Jamaican dialect in 1912, *Songs of Jamaica* and *Constab Ballads*. The first collection echoes McKay's love for the natural beauty of Jamaica while the second reflects his disenchantment with urban life in Kingston.

In 1912 McKay left Jamaica for the United States and studied at Tuskegee Institute in Alabama and at Kansas State College before moving to Harlem in 1914. His most famous poem, "If We Must Die," was published in 1919 and proved to be a harbinger of the Harlem Renaissance. The poem depicts violence as a dignified response to racial oppression.

Soon thereafter McKay published two other volumes of poetry, *Spring in New Hampshire and Other Poems* and *Harlem Shadows*, which portray the homesickness and racism that troubled McKay in the United States. Some of McKay's poems were anthologized in Alain Locke's *The New Negro* (1925), the bible of the Harlem Renaissance.

McKay also spent time in Europe and North Africa. In the Soviet Union in 1922 and 1923, he was lauded as a champion of the Communist movement and published a poem in *Pravda*. While in France in the 1920's, McKay preferred Marseilles over the white expatriate community in Paris.

McKay wrote three sociological novels about the attempts of black people to assimilate as outsiders in various places around the world: *Home to Harlem* is set in Harlem, *Banjo* in Marseilles, and *Banana Bottom* in Britain and Jamaica. The seamy realism of black urban life depicted in the first novel did not appeal to African American thinkers such as W. E. B. Du Bois, who preferred more uplifting and optimistic black art.

McKay continued to examine the place of black people in Western culture in his autobiography, *A Long Way from Home*, and in some of his posthumously published *Selected Poems of Claude McKay*. His conversion to Catholicism in his final years was the last step in his search for aesthetic, racial, and spiritual identity.

Banana Bottom
TYPE OF WORK: Novel
FIRST PUBLISHED: 1933

Banana Bottom is the story of a young Jamaican woman's discovery of her country, her people, and herself. The novel begins with the return to Jamaica of twenty-two-year-old Tabitha "Bita" Plant, who has been abroad for seven years. After a flashback in which he explains the reasons for her absence, McKay tells the story of Bita's life from her homecoming to her marriage, concluding with a brief epilogue that shows her as a contented wife and mother.

Banana Bottom is based on a less simplistic view of the black experience than some critics have assumed. A close look at the novel shows how far McKay's underlying meaning is from the easy dichotomy between a white society of repression, which is evil, and a black culture of expression, which is good, with all the characters lined up on one side or the other.

One of McKay's major themes has little to do with that kind of dichotomy. His Jamaica is almost entirely black, and the social hierarchy that he finds so stultifying is maintained by blacks, not by whites. The reason that the highly educated, intelligent, charming Bita can aspire no higher than her seminarian is that, in the view of her own society, no one so dark in skin color can marry a professional man or a government official. Granted, the Jamaican system is based on the old white colonial belief in black inferiority; however, it is not whites who enforce this social stratification. By showing how this system traps people of unquestionable ability at an arbitrary level in society, McKay is arguing for a change of mind within the black community itself.

An even more important theme of *Banana Bottom* is the issue of what lifestyle is most fulfilling for a black person, specifically for an intelligent, well-educated individual such as Bita. Again, it has been easy for critics to see the prudish and repressed Priscilla Craig as the representative of white society and Herald Newton Day as an example of a black man destroyed when he attempts, like his white sponsor, to repress his black sexual vitality. McKay, however, does not make arbitrary classifications of either his whites or his blacks. In Malcolm Craig's dedication to black freedom and autonomy and in Squire Gensir's passion for black culture, McKay shows that some whites are capable not only of kindness but also of selflessness.

Similarly, he uses two of Bita's suitors to show that black people are not necessarily noble. Certainly both Hopping Dick Delgado and Tack Tally are unworthy of McKay's heroine. Unlike both Herald and Tack, the man whom Bita chooses is a truly free one who finds the meaning of life not in the supernatural but in nature itself, in his wife, in his family, in his own sexual vitality, and in the land to which he is devoting his life. Instead of denying Bita the expression of her own identity, Jubban encourages her even in those interests that are not his own. The life that Bita and Jubban build together, then, is not a rejection of one culture or another but a fusion of the best of two worlds.

Banjo
TYPE OF WORK: Novel
FIRST PUBLISHED: 1929

Banjo: A Story Without a Plot is an episodic narrative involving a small group of relatively permanent residents of the Vieux Port section of Marseilles, France, and a larger cast of incidental characters who are encountered briefly in the varied but fundamentally routine activities of unemployed black seamen trying to maintain a sense of camaraderie and well-being. It is, therefore, basically a picaresque fiction that offers a measure of social criticism.

The novel reiterates McKay's constant themes: that the folk rather than the black intelligentsia represent the best in the race; that blacks should have a high regard for their heritage and hence a racial self-esteem; that the ideal life is one of vagabondage, of natural gusto and emotional response, allowing one to "laugh and love and jazz and fight." The breakup of the beachboys at the end of parts 2 and 3 suggests that cohesiveness is less powerful among McKay's favorite people than individualism—the very characteristic of the materialistic, commercial class that Ray inveighs against in his numerous diatribes and asides. Ironically, this assertion of individuality plays into the arms of those classes and attitudes that Ray sees as inimical to racial betterment.

Ray is the mouthpiece for an unrelenting indictment of white civilization. In his eyes, its chief shortcomings are crass commercialism; an unwarranted sense of racial superiority; hypocrisy (white Europeans assert that they make the best pornographic films, yet they condemn the uninhibited—even justifiable—sexuality of the blacks); nauseating patriotism, rather than internationalism; standardization; and Calvinist attitudes toward sex, alcohol, music, and entertainment.

Yet the behavior of Banjo and the others is far from admirable–if one excepts Ray, who is moderate, literate, and emotional. When he arrives in port, Banjo has 12,525 francs–a considerable sum–but quickly spends it on a girl who leaves him as soon as he is broke. He is wholly improvident and far from admirable. Accordingly, it is difficult to maintain any sympathy for him and to feel that he is anything more than a wastrel, a womanizer, a loafer, and an impractical dreamer.

If McKay means *Banjo* to be a paean to the free life, the life of the spirit and the emotions untrammeled by responsibilites, he seems to be suggesting that his motley sybarites are enviable models. They most certainly are not: They are irresponsible and without any admirable ambition. Their parallels are the Europeans who attend the "blue" cinema, who are rootless, affected, and suffering from ennui. (Their Satanism and sexual aberrations have cut them off from their cultural bearings.) It is hard to believe that the beach-boys–and Banjo in particular–are to be admired for their instinctive, spontaneous, sensual behavior. Moreover, at the end most of them express their dissatisfaction with pointless drifting, with unemployment, with poverty, and with temporary liaisons dependent on money alone. It is little wonder, then, that *Banjo* has been criticized for not having a clearly defined and defensible theme. Similarly, one can see a weakness in Banjo's saying that his instrument is his "buddy," that it is more than a "gal, moh than a pal; it's mahself." The Jazz Age had not ended, but the banjo was a symbol of a past era, and its owner, who places a thing above persons, seems to be disoriented. Banjo has become an anachronism.

Home to Harlem
TYPE OF WORK: Novel
FIRST PUBLISHED: 1928

This novel is an account of life in Harlem as seen through the experiences of Jake, who has come to regard Harlem as his hometown and is constantly comparing it with other places in his experience. Though the brief sojourn of Jake gives a linear development to the plot, *Home to Harlem* is actually a cyclical novel, for it is apparent that Jake has opened and closed one episode of his life in Petersburg, Virginia, another in Europe (with the Army), and a third in Harlem, before entering on yet another in Chicago with Felice.

Home to Harlem is essentially a story without a plot. Felice is lost for a time and then found by chance. Everything else in the novel is introduced to let the reader know what life is like in Harlem. Life in the Black Belt is depicted as serendipitous, often unfair, and dangerous. The participation of the Haitian immigrant Ray in the life of Jake is short-lived and fundamentally ineffective. In this way, McKay seems to suggest that there is no possibility of amelioration from the outside and from would-be saviors who are transient and not from within the social structure.

On the other hand, Jake, who is part of Harlem and who has become accustomed to its harshness and brutality, can see the possibility of finding love, affection, and even self-satisfaction and self-improvement by leaving it all behind. Prostitution, he seems to suggest, is nothing to hold against a woman if society has forced her into it for survival.

McKay, a longtime resident of Harlem after migrating from Jamaica, thought of Harlem as dehumanizing in the extreme. His attitude is reflected in Ray's comment that if he married Agatha he soon "would become one of the contented hogs in the pigpen of Harlem, getting ready to litter little black piggies." It is this image that McKay presents throughout the novel: Where people are overcrowded and treated like animals, they become animals.

It is the pervasive contrast between Jake and Ray that gives *Home to Harlem* its principal thematic development. Jake is forthright, versatile, optimistic, and persevering; he comes in contact with Ray, who is deliberate, cynical, pessimistic, and unpredictable. Jake is impressed by the intellect and interests of Ray, yet he discerns that a person made "impotent by thought" is irrelevant to the lives of Harlem's masses. Jake is principled: He will be unemployed rather than be a strikebreaker; he will live with a woman, but he will not be a kept man; he sees that the white world is one of materialism and opportunism, but he does not want to participate in it; he sees that the lives of the black folk are difficult, but he does not succumb to the blandishments of purported prophets and saviors. Nevertheless, he feels that he can survive and perhaps even succeed in life. The dialectic permeates the novel.

Only occasionally does McKay allow his own political and social views to intrude explicitly. The black-white issue that absorbed him in his journalism is never directly introduced, though it can be discerned by implication. The authorial voice is to be seen in Jake and Ray, for they represent the two sides of McKay himself: the body and the mind.

Poetry

FIRST PUBLISHED: *Songs of Jamaica*, 1912; *Constab Ballads*, 1912; *Spring in New Hampshire and Other Poems*, 1920; *Harlem Shadows*, 1922; *Selected Poems of Claude McKay*, 1953

McKay has been posthumously proclaimed Jamaica's national poet, and he has been the subject of an international conference of literary scholars. Paul Laurence Dunbar, Countée Cullen, and Langston Hughes also helped in the development of modern African American poetry, but only Hughes could legitimately be proposed as a better and more important poet than McKay.

Although there are some true gems of both concept and expression in McKay's initial two volumes of poetry, it is unlikely that any except Jamaicans and scholars will take any real pleasure in reading them. Even in 1912, McKay's mentor Walter Jekyll thought it necessary to add extensive footnotes to *Songs of Jamaica* to explain the poems' contractions, allusions, and pronunciation, and both a glossary and footnotes were added to *Constab Ballads*. There is no doubt that McKay's use of dialect in his poems was an advance on the use of dialect by such predecessors as Dunbar, who used it largely for either comic or role-establishing purposes; McKay used dialect for social verisimilitude, to attempt to capture the Jamaican inflections and idiom, to differentiate the speech of the folk from that of the colonial classes. Upon quitting Jamaica for the United States, however, McKay discontinued his use of dialect, even when, in some of his American "protest" poems that make use of African American diction, dialect would be appropriate and even effective.

Spring in New Hampshire and Other Poems, McKay's first volume of poetry in Standard English, which was published in London, and *Harlem Shadows*, which appeared two years later in New York, established him as a major poet in the black community and as a potentially important one in English literature. *Harlem Shadows*, with its brilliant evocation of life in the black ghetto of New York City, more than any other book heralded the beginning of the Harlem Renaissance, from which developed the great florescence of African American culture in subsequent years.

In his post-Jamaican poetry, McKay became attached almost exclusively to the sonnet form, eschewed dialect, and showed no strong inclination to experiment with rhyme, rhythm, and the other components of the sonnet. Further, he displayed the influence of his early reading of the English Romantics and in the words of Wayne Cooper, McKay's biographer, "his forthright expression of the black man's anger, alienation, and rebellion against white racism introduced into modern American Negro poetry an articulate militancy of theme and tone which grew increasingly important with time."

The sense of being a black man in a white man's world pervades McKay's poetry, as does the sense of being a visionary in the land of the sightless–if not also the sense of being an alien (an islander) in the heart of the metropolis. As John Dewey noted, "I feel it decidedly out of place to refer to him as the voice of the Negro people; he is that, but he is so much more than that." McKay is the voice of the dispossessed, the oppressed, the discriminated against; he is one of the major poetic voices of the Harlem Renaissance; he is one of a select group of poets who have represented the colonized peoples of the world; and he is one of the voices for universal self-respect and brotherhood.

SUGGESTED READINGS

Cooper, Wayne F. *Claude McKay: Rebel Sojourner in the Harlem Renaissance, a Biography*. Baton Rouge: Louisiana State University Press, 1987.

Gayle, Addison, Jr. *Claude McKay: The Black Poet at War.* Detroit: Broadside Press, 1972.

Giles, James R. *Claude McKay.* Boston: Twayne, 1976.

Hathaway, Heather. *Caribbean Waves: Relocating Claude McKay and Paule Marshall.* Bloomington: Indiana University Press, 1999.

McLeod, A. L., ed. *Claude McKay: Centennial Studies.* New Delhi, India: Sterling, 1992.

Rahming, Melvin B. *The Evolution of the West Indian's Image in the Afro-American Novel.* Millwood, N.Y.: Associated Faculty Press, 1986.

Stoff, Michael B. "Claude McKay and the Cult of Primitivism." In *The Harlem Renaissance Remembered,* edited by Arna Bontemps. New York: Dodd, Mead, 1972.

Tillery, Tyrone. *Claude McKay: A Black Poet's Struggle for Identity.* Amherst: University of Massachusetts Press, 1992.

—Douglas Edward LaPrade/Rosemary M. Canfield Reisman/A. L. McLeod

Terry McMillan

BORN: Port Huron, Michigan; October 18, 1951

McMillan's novels and short stories explore the complex relationships among urban black women of the late twentieth century, their families, and the men in their lives.

TRADITIONS: African American

PRINCIPAL WORKS: *Mama*, 1987; *Disappearing Acts*, 1989; *Breaking Ice: An Anthology of Contemporary African-American Fiction*, 1990 (editor); *Waiting to Exhale*, 1992; *How Stella Got Her Groove Back*, 1996

Terry McMillan was reared near Detroit by working-class parents and later moved to Los Angeles, where she attended community college and read widely in the canon of African American literature. In 1979, at the age of twenty-eight, she received her bachelor of science degree from the University of California, Berkeley. In 1987, she began a three-year instructorship at the University of Wyoming, Laramie, and in 1988 received a coveted fellowship from the National Endowment for the Arts. After teaching in Tucson at the University of Arizona from 1990 to 1992, McMillan pursued writing as her full-time career.

The environment in which McMillan's views were formed prepared her for early marriage and a family, not the life of an intellectual and an artist. Her failure as an adult to meet the expectations of her culture and family created pressures that her work has consistently sought to address. Not surprisingly, her own struggle to adapt to cultural expectations resulted in an emphasis in her work on the tension in relationships between professional and blue-collar blacks, between women and men, and between members of the nuclear family. *Mama* depicts an acceptance by an intellectual daughter of her flawed mother. *Disappearing Acts* follows a love affair between a professional, responsible woman and an uneducated tradesman. *Waiting to Exhale* builds an ambitious collage of images from all three types of relationships.

McMillan's fiction addresses the archetypal dilemma of the disadvantaged—escaping the limitations imposed by one's culture and family while trying to preserve the advantages they inevitably offer. This dilemma leads her characters into conflicts of ideology; their struggle is the struggle for truth, their quest the search for meaning.

While some reviewers have attacked McMillan for her use of vulgar language, others have defended its realism and immediacy. The same is true of the explicit sexual references throughout her work, and indeed for her character portrayals themselves. Critics observe that MacMillan's characters all seem at times to have been exaggerated to achieve a calculated effect. McMillan's popularity, however, suggests that she understands her craft and that her audience approves her purpose.

Waiting to Exhale
TYPE OF WORK: Novel
FIRST PUBLISHED: 1992

Waiting to Exhale, McMillan's third novel, was an instant popular success when it was first published in 1992. The book found wide acceptance, both critical and public, largely because of the honesty of its character portrayals and the timeliness of its themes. All four main characters in *Waiting To Exhale* are seeking the acceptance of culture and family but are also determined to escape their limiting influences. The conflicts that arise in the lives of the characters reflect the concerns of black feminist writers in general, and critics generally regard McMillan as having a finger on the pulse of 1990's educated black women. The novel's popularity is a reflection of the growing number of middle-class African Americans who wish to participate in black cultural life and preserve its heritage.

Terry McMillan (Marion Ettlinger)

The title of *Waiting To Exhale* is a metaphor for the tension in each of the novel's four protagonists's lives. All are waiting to find the right man, and each is figuratively holding her breath until he comes along. Each protagonist's story delineates a different type of coping strategy for the alienation and anxiety each suffers. In the face of criticism from their families, their culture, and themselves, the four women develop a friendship that enables them to stand fast against the many temptations to "settle" for an unhealthy relationship. The novel's setting, Phoenix, implies the possibility of glorious rebirth, but the symbolic implications are muted and ultimately unfulfilled; still, the characters achieve integration and a new sense of identity through their relationships with one another.

Savannah takes a cut in pay to move to Phoenix, where her old roommate from college, Bernadine, is living the perfect life. By the time Savannah completes the move, Bernadine's marriage is in shambles, her husband and the father of their two children having deserted her with his young blonde bookkeeper. Robin, a mutual friend, is frustrated, self-conscious, and anxious, looking for self-esteem through the eyes of the men she meets. Gloria, their hairdresser, is the single mother of a sixteen-year-old son, whose emerging sexuality creates fear in her and hostility in him. Savannah moves, Bernadine spends, Robin casts horoscopes, and Gloria eats; ultimately all their defense mechanisms crumble under one anothers' affectionate but witheringly, relentlessly honest scrutiny.

SUGGESTED READINGS

Gates, Henry Louis, Jr. Introduction to *Reading Black, Reading Feminist: A Critical Anthology*, edited by Gates. New York: Meridian, 1990.

Golden, Marita. "Walking in My Mother's Footsteps to Love." In *Wild Women Don't Wear No Blues: Black Women Writers on Love, Men, and Sex*, edited by Marita Golden. New York: Doubleday, 1993.

Henderson, Mae Gwendolyn. "Speaking in Tongues: Dialogics, Dialectics, and the Black Woman Writer's Literary Tradition." In *Reading Black, Reading Feminist: A Critical Anthology*, edited by Henry Louis Gates, Jr. New York: Meridian, 1990.

Hernton, Calvin C. *The Sexual Mountain and Black Women Writers*. New York: Doubleday, 1987.

Richards, Paulette. *Terry McMillan: A Critical Companion*. Westport, Conn.: Greenwood Press, 1999.

Seller, Frances Stead. Review of *Waiting To Exhale*, by Terry McMillan. *Times Literary Supplement*, November 6, 1992, 20.

—Andrew B. Preslar

D'Arcy McNickle

BORN: St. Ignatius, Montana; January 18, 1904
DIED: Albuquerque, New Mexico; October 18, 1977

In novels, short stories, children's books, and scholarly works, McNickle focuses on communication problems between Native Americans and the dominant culture.

TRADITIONS: American Indian

PRINCIPAL WORKS: *The Surrounded*, 1936; *La Política de los Estados Unidos sobre los gobiernos tribales y las empresas comunales de los Indios*, 1942 (with Joseph C. McCaskill); *They Came Here First: The Epic of the American Indian*, 1949, rev. 1975; *Runner in the Sun: A Story of Indian Maize*, 1954; *Indians and Other Americans: Two Ways of Life Meet*, 1959, rev. ed. 1970 (with Harold E. Fey); *Indian Man: A Life of Oliver La Farge*, 1971; *Native American Tribalism: Indian Survivals and Renewals*, 1973; *Wind from an Enemy Sky*, 1978; *The Hawk Is Hungry and Other Stories*, 1992

Born to a Scotch-Irish father and a French Canadian mother of Cree heritage, D'Arcy McNickle knew from an early age the problems of mixed identity that many Native Americans experience. Reared on a northwestern Montana ranch, McNickle, along with his family, was adopted into the Salish-Kootanai Indian tribe. Attending Oxford University and the University of Grenoble in France after completing his undergraduate education at the University of Montana, McNickle was as firmly grounded in Native American culture as he was in the white world.

Completing his formal education when the United States was gripped by the Depression, McNickle was among the writers who joined the Federal Writer's Project, with which he was associated from 1935 to 1936. His first novel, *The Surrounded*, was an outgrowth of this association. This book focuses on how an Indian tribe disintegrates as the United States government encroaches upon and ultimately grabs tribal lands and then sets out to educate the Native American children in such a way as to denigrate their culture and integrate them into the dominant society. Like McNickle, the protagonist of this novel, Archilde, has a mixed identity, being the offspring of a Spanish father and a Native American mother.

In his children's book, *Runner in the Sun*, McNickle deals with similar questions of identity centering on the inevitable conflicts between whites and Native Americans. The Native Americans strive in vain to preserve their culture and retain their grazing lands.

Such also is the focus of McNickle's posthumous novel, *Wind from an Enemy*

Sky, in which tribal lands are condemned for the building of a dam and the sacred medicine bundle is given to a museum for display. McNickle also produced several works of nonfiction that grew out of his tenure with the Bureau of Indian Affairs and his directorship of the Bureau's division of American Indian development.

The Surrounded

TYPE OF WORK: Novel
FIRST PUBLISHED: 1936

The Surrounded has strong autobiographical overtones. The novel focuses on Archilde, through whom the readers see the identity conflicts that trouble the racially mixed hero. Archilde is caught between the white and the Indian cultures, neither of which is unambiguously good or bad, making his position even more difficult.

One of the ways that the novel emphasizes this cultural conflict is by describing many characters and events as opposing pairs. Catharine LaLoup Leon and Max Leon, for example, each present to Archilde some of the positive aspects of Indian and white culture, respectively. The Indian dancing on the Fourth of July, full of ancient meaning and beauty, is contrasted with the white people's meaningless dance in a dark, bare hall.

The novel expresses particular concern for the decline of Native American culture. McNickle describes in great detail the transformation of Mike and Narcisse as the older women prepare them for the dance, emphasizing the beauty of traditional culture. McNickle applies his expertise as an anthropologist to the detailed explanation of all the old dances, stressing each dance's particular meaning. This is contrasted with the scene at the Fourth of July dance, where white people come to laugh disrespectfully at the old men as they move slowly through the only dances that they are still allowed to do.

In addition, *The Surrounded* presents an interesting view of nature. Archilde goes into the wilderness to be alone, and nature is generally seen as an ally to the Indians, who can live in mountain caves and hunt for their food if they so choose. The scene in which Archilde sees the cloud-cross in the sky and ignores it because the bird ignores it, stresses the preeminence of nature. Archilde remembers this experience and teaches this same lesson to Mike and Narcisse: If the birds are not frightened by signs and demons, they should not be either. Nature is seen as a better source of encouragement and truth than are the priests.

An interesting aspect of the novel is the presence of two especially strong female characters. Elise is reckless and determined to get what she wants. She can ride and hunt as well as any man. She takes the initiative, not only in her relationship with Archilde but also in their escape into the mountains. She, like Catharine, is not afraid to kill when Archilde is threatened. Catharine is held in high regard, not only among the Indians but also among the whites (which is one reason that Max married her in the first place). Even in her advanced age, she hunts for herself. Her death is described as a triumphant moment. She dies unafraid, surrounded by her Indian family and friends.

The plot structure of *The Surrounded* demonstrates a certain circularity and reflects the work's thematic concern for Archilde's identity. Archilde left the reservation, trying to put some distance between himself and his people. When he returns, it is only for a short and final visit. Yet he continues to stay as he becomes increasingly entangled in events on the reservation. The apparent inaction—staying—is actually the action that helps him determine his identity as an Indian. He does not succeed in going to Portland to be a fiddler or even in running his father's farm. Archilde succeeds in finding his identity at those times when he feels most connected to his tribal heritage: at the dance and at his mother's death. His identity comes, not from breaking away and succeeding in isolation, but from living in his proper context, with his people and his land.

Wind from an Enemy Sky

TYPE OF WORK: Novel
FIRST PUBLISHED: 1978

In *Wind from an Enemy Sky*, McNickle writes of the difficult period in American history during which the United States government attempted to subdue Native Americans peacefully. McNickle, a government employee for most of his life, presents a balanced view of what occurred during this period in one small Native American enclave in the Flathead Lake-St. Ignatius area of Montana.

On the surface, McNickle presents the story of a Native American extended family that includes Pock Face, who, carrying his grandfather's rifle, steals furtively into a canyon where white developers have built a dam on tribal land. The Little Elk Indians equate the damming of their river with its murder. The dam has an immediate negative impact upon fishing and farming on their tribal lands. As Pock Face and Theobald, his cousin, approach the dam, they spy a white man walking across its surface. Pock Face fires one shot. Jim Cooke, ironically on his last day of work before going east to marry, dies instantly.

The remainder of the story revolves around the government's efforts to mete out justice to the murderer. This surface story, however, provides the justification for a compelling subtext that illustrates the difficulties involved when one well-established culture attempts to impose itself upon another. *Wind from an Enemy Sky*, maintaining throughout an objective view of two disparate cultures, proffers a poignant political and social statement about culture and values in multiethnic settings.

Wind from an Enemy Sky is concerned largely with the inability of the Native

American and dominant societies in the United States to communicate productively with each other. As McNickle presents it, Native American society is deeply suspicious of the dominant society that has, through the years, oppressed it. Promises made have seldom been promises kept. The suspicions that keep Indians from interacting productively with government agencies are spawned not by paranoia but rather by extensive bitter experience.

The dam the government built has diverted a river on which the Indians depend. The waters that the dam captures will nourish the fields of white homesteaders, to whom the government has sold Indian lands at $1.25 an acre. The Native Americans look upon these land sales as forms of robbery. Added to this justifiable charge is the charge that white officials have kidnapped Indian children and sent them to distant government schools against their will.

McNickle suggests the inevitability of tragedy in dealings between Native Americans and representatives of the dominant society. He also demonstrates how some Native Americans—Henry Jim and The Boy, for example—move into the white world or attempt to straddle the two worlds, placing them in impossible positions. For Henry Jim, it is impossible to shake the Native American heritage, which the dying man finally embraces again.

SUGGESTED READINGS

Bevis, William. "Native American Novels: Homing In." In *Recovering the Word: Essays on Native American Literature*, edited by Brian Swann and Arnold Krupat. Berkeley: University of California Press, 1982.

Oaks, Priscilla. "The First Generation of Native American Novelists." *MELUS* 5 (1978): 57-65.

Owens, Louis. "The 'Map of the Mind': D'Arcy McNickle and the American Indian Novel." *Western American Literature* 19 (Winter, 1985): 275-283.

_____. "The Red Road to Nowhere: D'Arcy McNickle's *The Surrounded* and 'The Hungry Generations.'" *American Indian Quarterly* 13 (Summer, 1989): 239-248.

Parker, Dorothy R. *Singing an Indian Song: A Biography of D'Arcy McNickle.* Lincoln: University of Nebraska Press, 1992.

Purdy, John Lloyd. *The Legacy of D'Arcy McNickle: Writer, Historian, Activist.* Norman: University of Oklahoma Press, 1996.

_____. *Word Ways: The Novels of D'Arcy McNickle.* Tucson: University of Arizona Press, 1990.

Ruppert, James. *D'Arcy McNickle.* Boise, Idaho: Boise State University Press, 1988.

_____. "Textual Perspectives and the Reader in *The Surrounded*." In *Narrative Chance: Postmodern Discourse on Native American Indian Literatures*, edited by Gerald Vizenor. Albuquerque: University of New Mexico Press, 1989.

Vest, Jay Hansford C. "Feather Boy's Promise: Sacred Geography and Environmental Ethics in D'Arcy McNickle's *Wind from an Enemy Sky.*" *American Indian Quarterly* 17 (Winter, 1993): 45-68.

—R. Baird Shuman/Kelly C. Walter

Bernard Malamud

BORN: Brooklyn, New York; April 26, 1914
DIED: New York, New York; March 18, 1986

Malamud's works present the outsider, usually a Jew, who epitomizes the individual who must make moral choices.

TRADITIONS: Jewish

PRINCIPAL WORKS: *The Natural,* 1952; *The Assistant,* 1957; *The Magic Barrel,* 1958; *A New Life,* 1961; *Idiots First,* 1963; *The Fixer,* 1966; *Pictures of Fidelman: An Exhibition,* 1969; *The Tenants,* 1971; *Rembrandt's Hat,* 1973; *Dubin's Lives,* 1979; *God's Grace,* 1982

Bernard Malamud's youth was spent in a setting much like that in *The Assistant.* His father was the owner of a small, struggling grocery store. His mother died when he was an adolescent. As a youth he had the freedom to wander around Brooklyn becoming intimately acquainted with the neighborhood. It was not a Jewish neighborhood, but Malamud came to understand the Jewish experience through his hardworking parents, immigrants from Russia.

Malamud began writing stories in high school, and his writing career reflects the discipline and determination of many of his characters. After graduating from Erasmus Hall High School, he earned a bachelor's degree from City College of New York. He then attended Columbia University and earned the master's degree that enabled him to teach. He taught immigrants in evening school in Brooklyn, then in Harlem, for eight years, while writing short stories, before getting a job at Oregon State College in Cascadia, Oregon. There he wrote four novels and a collection of short stories. Malamud received the National Book Award for the short-story collection, *The Magic Barrel,* in 1959. He also received the Pulitzer Prize in fiction and the National Book Award for *The Fixer* in 1967. He accepted a position at Bennington College in Vermont in 1961, where he spent the rest of his teaching career, except for two years as a visiting lecturer at Harvard.

Malamud's work has an allegorical quality like that of Nathaniel Hawthorne. His stories also reflect the Eastern European storytelling tradition. In this he is like such Yiddish writers as Sholom Aleichem and Isaac Leib Peretz. When Malamud describes, for example, a luckless character (called, in Jewish culture, a *schlemiel*) living in Brooklyn in the twentieth century, that person seems quite like someone living in the Jewish section of a Polish village. Malamud also captures in his works the sense of irony that pervades the folk stories of a people who recognize themselves as the chosen people and as the outcasts of society.

Malamud saw this paradoxical position as being the plight of all humanity, and he found in the Jew the ideal metaphor for the struggling human being. Acceptance of Jewish identity becomes, for his characters, acceptance of the human condition. Fusing this theme with a style that utilizes irony and parable, realism and symbolism, he presents the flourishing of the human spirit in an everyday reality of pressure and pain.

The Assistant
TYPE OF WORK: Novel
FIRST PUBLISHED: 1957

In *The Assistant,* Malamud carefully structures his realistic second novel so that the story of the intertwined fates of Frank Alpine and the Bobers grows to symbolize self-discipline and suffering. The hero, Frank Alpine, unlike the hero of Malamud's *The Natural* (1952), achieves self-integration and the subsequent identification with a group.

Frank enters the life of the Bobers when he comes with Ward Minoque, who represents his worst self, to the struggling neighborhood store of Morris Bober to steal. Unlike Ward, Frank immediately recognizes Morris as a suffering human being. Indeed, Morris is the suffering Jew, an Everyman. Now old, he has achieved none of his dreams and must deprive his daughter, Helen, of her dream of attending college.

To expiate his crime and to change his life, Frank returns to the store and, promising to work for nothing, persuades Morris to use him as an assistant. Unaware that Frank is the one who stole from him, Morris helps the hungry and homeless Frank with room and board and a small salary. Morris then becomes the moral guide Frank never had.

Frank begins to change, but his progress is fitful, and he steals small sums from the register. His moral growth is accelerated by his falling in love with Helen, an idealistic young woman who will give Frank her love if he earns it. Motivated by this hope and a

Bernard Malamud (Jerry Bauer)

memory of the beauty of the selfless life of Saint Francis of Assisi, Frank tries to discipline himself. When Frank has nearly won the love of Helen, his hopes slip away when Morris, who suspects that Frank has been stealing, catches him with his hand in the register. Sent away from the store on the day he expects Helen to proclaim her love, Frank gives in to despair and frustration. First saving her from rape by Ward, he then forces himself on her against her will.

Alienated from the Bobers, Frank's redemption comes when he moves beyond himself. The opportunity arises when Morris is hospitalized and then dies. Frank takes over the store when Helen and her mother are too over-whelmed by their misfortunes to protest. To support them all, he works two jobs. Though he sometimes questions the dreary life to which he has submit-ted himself, he patiently endures, replacing Morris, whose example he has internalized. After a year, Frank even sends Helen to college. He then reflects his new attitudes by having himself circumcised, a symbolic act of his transformation.

The Fixer
Type of work: Novel
First published: 1966

Based on the story of a Russian Jew, Mendel Beiless, who was tried and acquitted in czarist Russia for the ritual murder of a Christian child, *The Fixer* artistically re-creates that history. It also represents, in its theme, persecution in general. Malamud creates in this novel a story like a parable, similar in theme and style to his other works, that recounts the protagonist's spiritual growth and affirms personal dignity and moral integrity even in a world that seems incomprehensible. Yakov Bok, the hero, a Jew, comes to define him-self, value suffering, and feel most free when most confined.

Yakov, a fixer or handyman, has had bad luck. With little work in his Jewish village and a wife first disappointing him in being childless then deserting him, he feels himself a prisoner of his circumstances. He sets off for Kiev, a city known for its anti-Semitism, in hopes of changing his life. In Kiev, Yakov, finding no work in the Jewish sector, begins looking outside the ghetto, which is illegal. Coming upon a drunken man who is lying uncon-scious in the street, Yakov helps the drunk, although Yakov recognizes him as an anti-Semite. To reward Yakov, the man offers him a job, which Yakov accepts with misgivings because it is outside the ghetto. One day Yakov reads in the paper of the ritual murder of a Christian child. The next day he is accused of the murder and put in prison. He is held for thirty months before being brought to trial.

The next three-quarters of the novel describes Yakov's physical agonies and spiritual growth while imprisoned. This growth is presented in his actions, dreams, hallucinations, perceptions, and memories during the daily suffering he undergoes—from deprivation of basic necessities and the torture of poisoning and chaining to the humiliation of the daily physical searches. During this time, he learns.

He discovers the strength of hate, political power, and historical events and sees that an individual is, by force, a political being. Secretly reading the Old then the New Testament, he feels connected with his people, yet fully appreciates the story of Christ. He develops compassion for the suffering of others. He acknowledges the suffering of the guard, who tells his story. Yakov forgives his wife and acknowledges his own part in their failed relationship. He accepts fatherhood, symbol of adulthood and personal identity, by declaring paternity to her illegitimate child, enabling her to return to life in her village without shame. At the same time he refuses to sign any documents that will free him by blaming other Jews. He also refuses to admit guilt. He finds, in identifying with his group and in willingly suffering for them that, despite what may happen to him, he is free.

SUGGESTED READINGS

Astro, Richard, and Jackson J. Benson, eds. *The Fiction of Bernard Malamud.* Corvallis: Oregon State University Press, 1977.

Field, Leslie, and Joyce Field, eds. *Bernard Malamud: A Collection of Critical Essays.* Englewood Cliffs, N.J.: Prentice-Hall, 1975.

Hershinow, Sheldon J. *Bernard Malamud.* New York: Frederick Ungar, 1980.

Richman, Sydney. *Bernard Malamud.* New York: Twayne, 1966.

Sio-Castiñeira, Begoña. *The Short Stories of Bernard Malamud: In Search of Jewish Post-Immigrant Identity.* New York: Peter Lang, 1998.

Solotaroff, Robert. *Bernard Malamud: A Study of the Short Fiction.* Boston: Twayne, 1989.

Walden, Daniel, ed. *The Changing Mosaic: From Cahan to Malamud, Roth, and Ozick.* Albany: State University of New York Press, 1993.

—*Bernadette Flynn Low*

Malcolm X

BORN: Omaha, Nebraska; May 19, 1925
DIED: New York, New York; February 21, 1965

Malcolm X went from being a street hustler to being a black leader and a symbol of fearless resistance against oppression.

TRADITIONS: African American
PRINCIPAL WORKS: *The Autobiography of Malcolm X*, 1965 (with Alex Haley); *Malcolm X Speaks: Selected Speeches and Statements*, 1965; *By Any Means Necessary: Speeches, Interviews, and a Letter*, 1970

Malcolm X's (born Malcolm Little) early years were marked by unsettling events: His family, threatened by the Ku Klux Klan in Omaha, moved to Lansing, Michigan, only to have their house burned down by a white hate group. Malcolm's father died in 1931 under mysterious circumstances, leaving his mother with the task of raising eight children. Malcolm eventually moved to Boston in 1941 and to New York in 1943, where he first experienced the street life of the African American urban poor. After becoming a burglar, he received a six-year prison term for armed robbery. In prison, he converted to the Nation of Islam and read voraciously on philosophy, theology, and history. The Nation of Islam helped him to acquire self-respect and gave him a new worldview, one that celebrated African American history and culture and in which whites were seen as forces of evil. Two years after his release, Malcolm—who by then had changed his last name to "X" in order to shed any links to a past in which white slave masters gave African American slaves their last names— became minister of the New

Malcolm X (Library of Congress)

341

York Temple Number Seven and the national spokesperson for the Nation of Islam. He brought unprecedented attention to the Nation: At a time when much of the United States was still segregated, Malcolm X voiced fearlessly what others only thought and denounced white racist practices.

Advocating strong moral codes and behaviors, Malcolm X became disenchanted with the Nation, suspecting the covert immorality of some leaders. After leaving the Nation of Islam, Malcolm X went on a pilgrimage to Mecca, where his warm reception by white Muslims (and his earlier contact in America with white students and journalists) led him to reject his earlier declarations that all whites were evil, and he accepted Orthodox Islam as his faith. He adopted the name el-Hajj Malik el-Shabazz. Malcolm X traveled to Africa, meeting African leaders and recognizing the links between imperialist oppression of Africa and the situation of African Americans. Malcolm X was assassinated in New York after beginning to build Organization of Afro-American Unity, which featured cross-racial alliances and an international outlook.

The Autobiography of Malcolm X
TYPE OF WORK: Autobiography
FIRST PUBLISHED: 1965

The Autobiography of Malcolm X was hailed as a literary classic shortly after it appeared. Its description of Malcolm X's discovery of an African American identity continues to inspire its readers. The two most memorable phases of Malcolm X's life described in his autobiography, and quite possibly the two phases most formative of his identity, are his self-education and religious conversion while in prison and his last year of life, in which he set out to organize a multiracial coalition to end racism. The first of these phases followed a difficult childhood and life as a criminal. In prison, Malcolm X felt inspired by fellow inmates to improve his knowledge. He started on a rigorous program of reading books on history and philosophy. He also worked on his penmanship and vocabulary by copying an entire dictionary. His readings revealed to him that school had taught him nothing about African and African American history. School had also been silent on the crimes that Europeans and European Americans had committed against people of color. In prison, members of the Nation of Islam urged Malcolm X to reject the negative self-image he had unconsciously adopted and to replace it with black pride.

Malcolm X taught the Nation's doctrine of black self-reliance after his release from prison, and he married Betty Shabazz, eventually becoming the father of six children. Disappointed by the divergence between the practices of some of the leaders of the Nation of Islam and the rules of self-discipline and honor that the Nation taught, he left the Nation and, after traveling to

Mecca, became an orthodox Muslim. Islam and his experiences in the Middle East and Africa also changed his outlook on racial relations. Before, he had seen an unbridgeable gulf between African Americans and European Americans. His positive experiences with white Muslims, white students, and white reporters caused him to reevaluate that position. Deciding that cooperation between whites and blacks was possible, he remained devoted to the liberation of people of African descent to the end of his life.

The Autobiography of Malcolm X is important as an account of the life of a charismatic American intellectual. The book is also an important literary work in the African American tradition of the autobiographies of Frederick Douglass and W. E. B. Du Bois and in the American tradition of Benjamin Franklin. Like Douglass and Franklin, Malcolm X can be described as a self-made man.

SUGGESTED READINGS

Breitman, George. *The Last Year of Malcolm X: The Evolution of a Revolutionary.* New York: Pathfinder Press, 1984.

Carson, Clayborne. *Malcolm X: The FBI File.* New York: Carroll & Graf, 1991.

Clarke, John Henrik, ed. *Malcolm X: The Man and His Times.* New York: Collier Books, 1969.

Cone, James H. *Martin and Malcolm and America.* Maryknoll, N.Y.: Orbis Books, 1991.

Dudley, David L. *Intergenerational Conflict in African American Men's Autobiography.* Philadelphia: University of Pennsylvania Press, 1991.

Dyson, Michael Eric. *Making Malcolm: The Myth and Meaning of Malcolm X.* New York: Oxford University Press, 1995.

Myers, Walter Dean. *Malcolm X: By Any Means Necessary.* New York: Scholastic, 1993.

Stull, Bradford T. *Amid the Fall, Dreaming of Eden: Du Bois, King, Malcolm X, and Emancipation.* Carbondale: Southern Illinois University Press, 1999.

—Martin Japtok

Ved Mehta

BORN: Lahore, British India (now Pakistan); March 21, 1934

*Mehta vividly describes the cultures in which he has lived and the
experience of exile and blindness.*

TRADITIONS: South Asian
PRINCIPAL WORKS: *Face to Face*, 1957; *Fly and the Fly Bottle*, 1962; *The New
   Theologian*, 1966; *Daddyji*, 1972; *Mahatma Ghandi and His Apostles*, 1977;
   Mamaji, 1979; *Vedi*, 1982; *The Ledge Between the Streams*, 1984; *Sound-Shad-
   ows of the New World*, 1985; *The Stolen Light*, 1989; *Up at Oxford*, 1993;
   Remembering Mr. Shawn's "New Yorker": The Invisible Art of Editing, 1998

Ved Mehta has been telling the story of his own life for most of his career.
This story includes the cultures in which he has lived. Mehta was born into a
well-educated Hindu family in Lahore in 1934. At the age of three he lost his
eyesight as a result of meningitis. Mehta's education took him away from his
close-knit family and sent him to places that must have seemed like different
worlds: Arkansas in the era of segregation, a college campus in suburban
Southern California, and Oxford University. As a staff writer for *The New
Yorker* and in his many books, Mehta makes those different worlds, including
the world of blindness, come alive to the reader.

Mehta published his first book, *Face to Face*, when he was twenty-two. It is
a highly readable account of his childhood, of his family's sufferings during
the partition of India (they had to flee their native city when it became part
of the new Muslim nation of Pakistan), and of his experiences as a student in
America. The central subject, however, is Mehta's blindness and the ways in
which he learns to be independent and successful despite his disability.

For many years after the appearance of *Face to Face*, Mehta allowed no hint
of his disability to appear in his work, which he filled with visual descriptions.
He published a novel and became a master of nonfiction. He wrote books
introducing Indian culture and politics to Western readers; Mehta has also
written a series of books on the excitement of intellectual life. In books on
history and philosophy, theology, and linguistics, Mehta makes clashes of
ideas vivid by describing intellectuals not only as thinkers but as people.

When Mehta returned to autobiography, beginning with *Daddyji*, he
stopped suppressing the fact of his blindness. Instead, he tried to make the
things that had formed his identity—his family, his disability, his experiences
at schools for the blind, and the colleges and universities where he studied—as
vivid as his other subjects. Beginning with biographies of his mother and

father and working ahead through five more books to his graduation from Oxford, Mehta presents the story of his life, always as an exile seeking his place in the world, with eloquence and frankness.

Continents of Exile

TYPE OF WORK: Biography and autobiography
FIRST PUBLISHED: *Daddyji*, 1972; *Mamaji*, 1979; *Vedi*, 1982; *The Ledge Between the Streams*, 1984; *Sound-Shadows of the New World*, 1985; *The Stolen Light*, 1989; *Up at Oxford*, 1993

In the series *Continents of Exile*, Mehta has set himself the task of remembering and interpreting his life. In the seven volumes published before 1994, he examined his own development up to his graduation from the University of Oxford. Mehta's quest for self-understanding is also an introduction to the several different cultures through which Mehta has passed. From childhood Mehta has been an outsider seeking to understand worlds of which he is not fully a part. The loss of his eyesight at age three made him an exile in the world of the sighted, and his almost heroic struggle to secure an education sent him into exile—to Bombay from his native Punjab, to the United States, and to England. In describing his experiences, Mehta also gives the reader the flavor of different worlds, including India before and after its partition into India and Pakistan in 1947, Arkansas during segregation, suburban California in the tranquil 1950's, Oxford before the upheavals of the 1960's, and the world of blindness.

Continents of Exile is in some ways a sequel to Mehta's first book, *Face to Face* (1957). That book, written while Mehta was still an undergraduate, tells the story of his life up to almost the point reached in the seven later volumes. It lacks, however, the breadth, frankness, and detachment of the later volumes. In *Continents of Exile*, Mehta explores the power of memory. He has discovered that, with the aid of some research, memory yields much more than one might think. He also can analyze his experience with more detachment than his younger self could.

The series begins with biographies of Mehta's father and mother, *Daddyji* and *Mamaji*. Mehta's father's family embraced Western influences, the English language, and an "unsuperstitious" form of Hinduism. Mehta's mother's family was more resistant to Western influences, and Mehta's mother often sought cures through charms and native treatments. In telling the stories of his very different parents and their nevertheless successful marriage, Mehta recalls the world of a close-knit family. He left the family to seek an education. *Vedi* and *The Ledge Between the Streams* describe Mehta's childhood, including his first experience of exile at a boarding school for the blind in Bombay and his family's flight from their home during the chaos following partition. The next three volumes chronicle Mehta's education in America and

England. In *Sound-Shadows of the New World* (1985) Mehta recounts his years at the Arkansas School for the Blind. *The Stolen Light* takes Mehta to Pomona College in California, where he is a great success and an outsider. *Up at Oxford* describes Mehta's years at Balliol College and sketches portraits of some promising minds he met there.

SUGGESTED READINGS

Allen, Brooke. Review of *Remembering Mr. Shawn's "New Yorker": The Invisible Art of Editing*, by Ved Mehta. *New Criterion* 17 (September, 1998): 56.

Slatin, John M. "Blindness and Self-Perception: The Autobiographies of Ved Mehta." *Mosaic* 19, no. 4 (Fall, 1986): 173-193.

Sontag, Frederick. "The Self-Centered Author." *New Quest* 79 (July-August, 1989): 229-233.

—Brian Abel Ragen

Arthur Miller

BORN: New York, New York; October 17, 1915

Miller's plays are widely regarded to be among the best plays ever written by an American.

TRADITIONS: Jewish

PRINCIPAL WORKS: *All My Sons*, pr., pb. 1947; *Death of a Salesman*, pr., pb. 1949; *The Crucible*, pr., pb. 1953; *A View from the Bridge*, pr. 1956, pb. 1957; *The Misfits*, 1961; *After the Fall*, pr., pb. 1964; *The Theater Essays of Arthur Miller*, 1978; *Timebends: A Life*, 1987; *Broken Glass*, pr., pb. 1994

Arthur Miller first achieved success as a dramatist with *All My Sons. Death of a Salesman*, widely regarded as Miller's most important play, contains many of the themes of identity that give distinction to Miller's plays: the tension between father and son, the dangerous material lure of the American Dream, the influence of memory on the formation of personality, and the common man in a tragic situation.

Partly in response to the anticommunist hysteria that was led by Senator Joseph McCarthy and the House Committee on Un-American Activities that swept the nation in the early 1950's, Miller wrote *The Crucible*. In 1955, Miller was denied a passport by the State Department, and in June, 1956, he was accused of left-wing activities and called before the committee. Unlike the girls in *The Crucible*, Miller refused to name others, and he was convicted of contempt of Congress in 1956, only to be fully exonerated by the United States Court of Appeals in 1958. During the turbulent summer of 1956 Miller also divorced

Arthur Miller (Inge Morath/Magnum)

his college sweetheart Mary Slattery and quickly married the famous actress Marilyn Monroe. Reflections of those two events recur throughout Miller's works and give shape to the identity of many of his major characters.

After completing the screenplay for *The Misfits*, which starred Monroe, Miller divorced the actress and married Inge Morath, events which may be reflected in *After the Fall*. Miller's later years saw the publication of his influential *The Theater Essays of Arthur Miller*, numerous revivals of his major plays, and his illuminating autobiography *Timebends: A Life*.

Death of a Salesman

TYPE OF WORK: Drama
FIRST PRODUCED: 1949; first published, 1949

Death of a Salesman, widely regarded as Miller's best and most important play, chronicles the downfall and suicide of Willy Loman, a ceaselessly struggling New England salesman driven by dreams of success far greater than he can achieve. Almost a classical tragedy in its form, *Death of a Salesman* has provoked much controversy due to the unheroic nature of its protagonist. Although the play, like its Greek forebears, conveys a sense of the inevitability of fate, Willy himself possesses no greatness in either achievement or status. Willy's sheer commonness, rather, gives the play its power. In *Death of a Salesman*, Miller shows that tragedy comes not only to the great but also to the small.

On its most fundamental level, *Death of a Salesman* depicts the disintegration of Willy's personality as he desperately searches for the moment in his memory when his world began to unravel. The play's action is driven primarily by Willy's volcanic relationship with grown son Biff, who is every inch the failure that his father is. Willy's grandiose dreams of happiness and material success conflict with the reality of his failures as a salesman, as a husband to his wife Linda, and as a father to his two boys, Biff and Happy. The alternation between present action and presentations of Willy's delusional "memories" forms the play's thematic center. Willy's memory is populated by figures who idealize success, most notably his brother Ben, who became rich, Dave Singleman, a fabulously successful and well-liked salesman, and the woman in Boston with whom Willy has had an affair. Countering those empty fantasies are the realities of Howard, Willy's unsympathetic boss; Charley, Willy's best friend and neighbor (who gives Willy the money he needs to pay his bills); Charley's successful son Bernard; and of course Biff, who refuses to accept Willy's delusions. "We never told the truth for ten minutes in this house!" Biff says at one point. Willy cannot accept the piercing truth of Biff's description: "You were never anything but a hard-working drummer who landed in the ash can like all the rest of them!" Rather, Willy commits suicide by crashing his car. The play's final tragic irony comes out in the play's last scene: Although Willy strove all his life to be well-liked and remembered, his funeral is attended only by his close family and friends. Neither he nor they are finally free, but only alone.

SUGGESTED READINGS

Bloom, Harold. *Modern Critical Interpretations: Arthur Miller's "Death of a Salesman."* New York: Chelsea House, 1988.

_____. *Major Literary Characters: Willy Loman.* New York: Chelsea House, 1991.

Ferres, John H. *Arthur Miller: A Reference Guide.* Boston: G. K. Hall, 1979.

Murphy, Brenda. *Miller: "Death of a Salesman."* Cambridge, England: Cambridge University Press, 1995.

Nelson, Benjamin. *Arthur Miller: Portrait of a Playwright.* New York: David McKay, 1970.

Schlueter, June, and James K. Flanagan. *Arthur Miller.* New York: Frederick Ungar, 1987.

Siebold, Thomas, ed. *Readings on Arthur Miller.* San Diego, Calif.: Greenhaven Press, 1997.

−Gregory W. Lanier

Anchee Min

BORN: Shanghai, China; 1957

*Min's powerful story of the Cultural Revolution is about rebellion
against political and sexual repression.*

TRADITIONS: Chinese American
PRINCIPAL WORKS: *Red Azalea*, 1994; *Katherine*, 1995; *Becoming Madame Mao*,
2000

Born in Shanghai, Anchee Min experienced political turmoil from an early
age. During her childhood, Min's family was forced to move into a series of
shabby apartments while her parents were demoted from their teaching
positions to become factory workers. Min joined the Red Guards in elementary school and underwent a wrenching introduction to political survival
when she was forced to denounce her favorite teacher as a Western spy.

Min's major experience with the clash between personal and political
needs came at seventeen when she was assigned to an enormous collective
farm. Forced to become a peasant in order to become a "true" revolutionary,
Min witnessed the destruction of a friend whose relationship with a man led
to her madness and his death. Min therefore knew the danger she faced when
she fell in love with the leader of her workforce, the charismatic Yan. The two
eventually began a sexual relationship that violated the strictures against
premarital sex and committed the "counterrevolutionary crime" of lesbianism.

Fighting to maintain her relationship with Yan and to survive the brutal life
on the farm, Min received an unexpected respite when she was chosen to
audition for the lead in a propaganda film, by Jiang Qing, wife of Mao
Zedong, the Communist dictator of China. Min's return to Shanghai thrust
her into an even more ruthless environment than the collective farm–the
Shanghai film industry. Min was rescued finally through her relationship with
the enigmatic "Supervisor," the film's producer, who became Min's lover and
protector. Min's deliverance, however, was short-lived. Qing's fall from
power in 1976 brought about the political destruction of those associated with
her. The Supervisor was able to save Min from return to the collective farm,
but he was unable to keep her from being demoted to a menial position within
the film studio.

Faced with an uncertain future and continued repression, Min accepted an
offer from the actress Joan Chen, a fellow film student in Shanghai, to
emigrate to the United States, arriving in 1984. While learning English, she

worked at a variety of jobs and received a Master of Fine Arts degree from the Art Institute of Chicago in 1990.

The great strength of Min's autobiography, *Red Azalea*, is its combination of frank narrative and lyrical description. Linking the personal and the political, Min uses sexuality as a metaphor for the individual's hunger for connection; sexual freedom thus indicates political freedom, and sexual expression becomes a revolutionary act.

Red Azalea
TYPE OF WORK: Autobiography
FIRST PUBLISHED: 1994

In strikingly effective prose, Min reveals her determination to retain her individuality against the force of Mao's Cultural Revolution and its determination to submerge her into the role chosen by China's Communist Party.

Red Azalea is a coming-of-age story. Min writes of her struggles with issues of identity and sexuality within the repressive environment of Mao Zedong's Cultural Revolution (1966-1976). With this focus she differs from other Chinese men and women writing about their lives in the same period in two ways: in the intensely personal journey she relates and in the simple but powerful prose she writes.

Min is proud to be identified with the nation as a young Red Guard. Still, in her home life she is a Chinese daughter, until her name is blacked out in her family's official residence papers as she leaves for Red Fire Farm. At the farm, she and her comrades work in rows, sleep in crowded, sex-segregated dorms, and study and recite Mao's teachings. This new life is difficult, but in her commander, Yan Sheng Yan, Min finds a role model of heroic response to the Party and its decrees. At the same time Min is newly conscious of sexual yearnings, which she is supposed to repress until the Party allows them. Min and Yan listen to each other's stories and experience the intimacy of a close friendship. Their joy becomes dangerous when the two women move to sexual intimacy.

This great love falters when Min is selected to go to Shanghai and compete for the starring role in Madame Mao's film/opera *Red Azalea*. In Shanghai, Min struggles between her need for Yan and her ambition to be a star. Despite her efforts, she loses the competition and is shunted to the lowly job of set-clerk. Finally, when Yan takes a male lover, Min feels as if she does not exist anymore.

Min attracts the attention of the powerful Supervisor. He is a mysterious man, womanish in his demeanor and dress, a Party loyalist but attracted to Min's individuality. She is excited by his attention, not because of any sexual attraction but because he is the key to fulfilling her heretofore thwarted ambitions to be a star. They become lovers, risking their lives by doing so.

He arranges for a screen test, ousts Min's competitor, and gives Min a new chance for the starring role. She cannot say the words as he wants, and in a powerful scene he convinces Min not to play the role of Red Azalea, the ultimate Chinese heroine, but to *be* Red Azalea.

At this point, however, China changes: Mao dies, and Madam Mao and her cohorts, including the Supervisor, fall out of favor. Min is once again told to return to Red Fire Farm, but in a final act of generous love, the Supervisor arranges for her to be reassigned to her post as set-clerk–probably for the rest of her life. Thus Min's story ends. She seems a Party-controlled menial laborer, luckily escaping punishment for her antirevolutionary actions.

In the epilogue, Min states that after six years, in 1984, she left China for America. In *Red Azalea* she tells her story, her personal story of love affairs, of romance, the story that in the years of the Cultural Revolution was not to be told, not to be lived. She is Red Azalea, a Chinese heroine, because she narrates in her own voice the intimately human story she lived in China's recent history. The true revolutionary, one concludes, was Min.

SUGGESTED READINGS

Chang, Jung. *Wild Swans: Three Daughters of China*. Garden City, N.J.: Anchor Press, 1992.

Huntley, Kristine. Review of *Becoming Madame Mao*, by Anchee Min. *Booklist* 96 (March 15, 2000): 1293.

Liang, Heng, and Judith Shapiro. *After the Nightmare*. New York: Alfred A. Knopf, 1986.

_____. *Son of the Revolution*. New York: Alfred A. Knopf, 1983.

The New York Times Book Review. Review of *Red Azalea*, by Anchee Min. 99 (February 27, 1994): 11.

The New Yorker. Review of *Red Azalea*, by Anchee Min. 52 (February 21, 1994): 119.

Viviano, Frank. *Dispatches from the Pacific Century*. Reading, Mass.: Addison-Wesley, 1992.

—Margaret W. Batschelet/Francine Dempsey

Nicholasa Mohr

BORN: New York, New York; November 1, 1935

Mohr writes of Puerto Ricans in New York, and her work features feminist characters.

TRADITIONS: Puerto Rican
PRINCIPAL WORKS: *Nilda*, 1973; *El Bronx Remembered: A Novella and Stories*, 1975; *In Nueva York*, 1977; *A Matter of Pride and Other Stories*, 1997

The daughter of Puerto Rican immigrants, Nicholasa Mohr documents life in New York City's barrios. Mohr examines the Puerto Rican experience from the perspective of girls and young women. Her female characters face multiple social problems associated with the restrictions imposed upon women by Latino culture. The struggle for sexual equality makes Mohr's literature central to Latina feminism.

Mohr's characters are an integral part of her realistic portrayal of life in a barrio. The parallels between her characters and her experience are evident. Nilda Ramírez, for example, is a nine-year-old Puerto Rican girl who comes of age during World War II. She also becomes an orphan and is separated from her immediate family. There are close parallels between these events and those of Mohr's life. In other stories as well girls must face, alone, social adversity, racism, and chauvinistic attitudes. Gays also frequently appear in her work. Gays and girls or young women (especially those who have little or no family) have often been subjected to mistreatment in the male-dominated Puerto Rican culture.

Mohr, a graphic artist and painter, studied at the Brooklyn Museum Art School from 1955 to 1959. Her advocacy to the social underclass is visible in her visual art, which includes elements of graffiti. Her use of graffiti in her art attracted the attention of a publisher who had acquired several of her paintings. Believing that Mohr had a story to tell, the publisher convinced her to write a short autobiographical piece on growing up Puerto Rican in New York. Many changes later, that piece became *Nilda*, her first novel, which has earned several prizes. Mohr has also drawn pictures for some of her literary work.

New York City is as important to Mohr's writing as her Puerto Rican characters. The city, with its many barrios, provides a lively background to her stories. Her short-story collections *El Bronx Remembered* and *In Nueva York* stress the characters' relationship to New York. Mohr's work can be described as cross-cultural, being a careful and artistic portrait of Puerto Rican culture in New York City.

El Bronx Remembered

TYPE OF WORK: Short fiction
FIRST PUBLISHED: 1975

Mohr's *El Bronx Remembered* is a collection of short stories depicting life in a Puerto Rican barrio in New York City during the 1960's and 1970's. Well known for her treatment of child, adolescent, and young adult characters, Mohr's depiction of Puerto Rican urban life concentrates on subjects of particular importance to those age groups. Mohr's narratives do not offer a denunciation of the troubled lives of these immigrants and children of immigrants. Instead, her stories bring forward voices that were often, in literature, considered unimportant. Female characters of several age groups and social backgrounds stand out for analysis.

Mohr writes from autobiographical memories; she grew up in a barrio much like the one in her stories. In her hands, the barrio is a strong presence that affects the lives of her characters in myriad ways. City life and traditional Puerto Rican family values are set against each other, producing the so-called Nuyorican culture, or Puerto-Rican-in-New-York culture. The clashes within that hybrid culture are the thematic center of Mohr's short stories.

The introduction to the collection sets a strong historical context for the stories. The 1940's saw an increase in Puerto Rican migration to New York. The arrival of thousands of immigrants changed the ethnic constitution of the city, especially of Manhattan's Lower East Side and the South Bronx. El Bronx, as it is called by the Puerto Ricans, became home to new generations of Puerto Rican immigrants. The center of Nuyorican culture, El Bronx challenges the Nuyorican characters in their struggle to survive in a world of rapid economic and technological changes.

The short stories in *El Bronx Remembered* speak openly about the struggles of the first immigrants with linguistic and other cultural barriers and with racist attitudes within institutions. Mohr's stories, however, attempt to go beyond social criticism. Puerto Rican characters challenge such obstacles. Some succeed in their attempts. Others are overwhelmed by city life, facing the barrio's multiple problems, including drug abuse and gang-related troubles. The message, however, is not pessimistic. Although some characters succumb to tragedy because they are ill prepared to face adversity, others around them survive by learning from the plight of the weak.

Mohr's contribution to ethnic American literature is significant. She has made an important contribution to Latino literature by describing Puerto Rican life in New York City. Her writing has a twofold significance. One, it links the Puerto Rican experience to that of other groups, emphasizing women's issues and those of other marginal characters, such as gays, within the Puerto Rican community. Two, Mohr's work provides a link between the literature written in English about Puerto Rican life in the United States and the literature in Spanish on Puerto Rican issues.

Suggested Reading

Barbato, Joseph. "Latino Writers in the American Market." *Publishers Weekly* 238, no. 6 (February 1, 1991): 17-21.

Marcus, Leonard S. "Talking with Authors." *Publishers Weekly* 247 (February 14, 2000): 98.

Mohr, Eugene V. *The Nuyorican Experience: Literature of the Puerto Rican Minority.* Westport, Conn.: Greenwood Press, 1982.

Mohr, Nicholasa. "An Interview with Author Nicholasa Mohr." Interview by Nyra Zarnowski. *The Reading Teacher* 45, no. 2 (October, 1991): 106.

Reed, Ishmael. *Hispanic American Literature.* New York: HarperCollins, 1995.

Zarnowski, Nyra. "An Interview with Author Nicholasa Mohr." *The Reading Teacher* 45, no. 2 (October, 1991): 106.

—Rafael Ocasio

N. Scott Momaday

BORN: Lawton, Oklahoma; February 27, 1934

Momaday's works are poetically brilliant accounts of the landscape, the sacredness of language, and self-knowledge.

TRADITIONS: American Indian

PRINCIPAL WORKS: *House Made of Dawn*, 1968; *The Way to Rainy Mountain*, 1969; *The Names*, 1976; *The Ancient Child*, 1989; *The Man Made of Words: Essays, Stories, Passages*, 1997

Among the most widely read and studied Native American authors, N. Scott Momaday manifests, in his writings, a keen awareness of the importance of self-definition in literature and life. From 1936 onward, his family moved from place to place in the Southwest, eventually settling in Albuquerque, where Momaday attended high school. He entered the University of New Mexico in 1954 and later studied poetry at Stanford University. In 1963, he received his doctorate in English and since then has held teaching jobs at various Southwestern universities.

In a semiautobiographical work, *The Way to Rainy Mountain*, Momaday writes that identity is "the history of an idea, man's idea of himself, and it has old and essential being in language." Momaday defines his characters in terms of their use or abuse of language; usually his characters find themselves relearning how to speak while they learn about themselves. Even the title of one of Momaday's essays, "The Man Made of Words," indicates his contention that identity is shaped by language. "Only when he is embodied in an idea," Momaday writes, "and the idea is realized in language, can man take possession of himself."

The forces that shape language—culture and landscape—are also crucial in Momaday's works. To Russell Martin, Western writing is concerned with the harsh realities of the frontier that "could carve lives that were as lean and straight as whittled sticks." This harsh landscape is present in Momaday's work also, but he has a heartfelt attachment to it. Having a spiritual investment in a place, in Momaday's writing, helps a person gain self-knowledge. To an extent, issues of identity were important to Momaday as well. Son of a Kiowa father and a Cherokee mother, Momaday belonged fully to neither culture. Furthermore, much of his early childhood was spent on a Navajo reservation, where his father worked, and he grew up consciously alienated from the surrounding culture.

To combat rootlessness, the imagination and its expression in language is essential. "What sustains" the artist, he writes in *The Ancient Child* "is the satisfaction . . . of having created a few incomparable things—landscapes, waters, birds, and beasts." Writing about the efforts of various people to maintain traditional culture in the face of the modern world, Momaday occupies a central place in the American literary landscape.

The Ancient Child
TYPE OF WORK: Novel
FIRST PUBLISHED: 1989

A complex and richly evocative work, Momaday's *The Ancient Child* is the story of two Native Americans—a middle-aged painter and a young woman—who come to a fuller understanding of themselves. Native American folklore and mythology are woven into their story, lending cultural and psychological depth to the two's quests for, essentially, rebirth.

Locke Setman, called "Set" throughout the novel, is in many ways a representative Momaday protagonist because he is cut off from his past and therefore lives an unexamined life. Brought up in an orphanage by an embittered academic, Set's connection to the Kiowa culture of his ancestors is tenuous. Because Set does not know his past "it was in Set's nature to wonder, until the wonder became pain, who he was." His quest to achieve a more profound sense of self begins when he receives a telegram begging him to attend the funeral of one Kope' mah. Mystified by a past he has never known, Set goes to the funeral and meets Grey, who is training to become a medicine woman because she "never had . . . to quest after visions."

Like Set, Grey has not achieved her true identity, largely because she rejects the modern world. After being raped by a white farmer, she goes to live in an abandoned sod house in a ghost town. She literally dwells in the past. She speaks Kiowan fluently, so she is befriended by Kope' mah, and becomes the link between Set's past and his future. When the two meet, Grey gives Set a medicine bag containing "the spirit of the bear." The bear, Set's unacknowledged totem animal, is as much a curse as a blessing, however, since the life that Set has lived must be stripped away before his true identity can be recognized. Set suffers a mental breakdown and his nightmares are dominated by "a dark, impending shape" that draws him into itself, into "the hot contamination of the beast."

Eventually, when he is completely stripped of illusions, Set is drawn back to Kiowan tribal lands, and back to Grey. Set is healed and the two forge a relationship, one tied to an awareness of themselves and their culture. Grey teaches Set to speak the language of her people, and by the novel's end, Set is profoundly aware of his place in their culture: "he knew . . . its definition in his mind's eye, its awful silence in the current of his blood." He belongs.

House Made of Dawn
TYPE OF WORK: Novel
FIRST PUBLISHED: 1968

House Made of Dawn, Momaday's first novel, is the story of an outcast who learns that his being is bound up in his culture. The novel, which relates the experiences of a mixed-race World War II veteran, was a signal achievement, winning the Pulitzer Prize in fiction for Momaday in 1969 and paving a way for other Native American novelists.

It begins with Abel's return to his ancestral village. Although he is so drunk that he does not recognize his grandfather, Abel's troubles run much deeper. He feels cut off from the Tanoan tribe yet unwilling to live in white America. Even more disturbing to Abel is his inability to "say the things he wanted" to anyone. His inability to express himself hampers his achieving a true identity. Wrapped up in his own problems, Abel is jealous and violent toward those who do participate in Tanoan culture. While at Walatowa, Abel loses a competition to an albino Indian and murders him.

After his release from prison, Abel tries to build a new life in California, where he comes in contact with a small community of Indians, who are also alienated from their cultures. The leader of this exile community is John Tosamah, a self-proclaimed priest of the sun, who sermonizes on the failure of white society to recognize the sacredness of the American landscape and of language. Tosamah victimizes Abel, however. Eventually, Abel is cast out of this group and is savagely beaten by a sadistic police officer, Martinez.

After the beating, Abel is physically what he was once only psychologically: an invalid. He returns to Walatowa, where his grandfather is dying. Aware that he must embrace his Tanoan heritage, if only to perform the burial rites for his grandfather, Abel begins to heal psychologically. At the novel's end, Abel participates in another ceremony, this time a race between the young men of the tribe, which his grandfather had won years before. Abel finds "a sort of peace of mind" through participation, but is certainly not healed by it. Unable to keep pace with the others, Abel keeps stumbling and falls behind. Abel's position in the tribe likewise remains unsettled. On the threshold between the world of his grandfather and that of modern America, on the threshold between spiritual values and lack of faith, Abel can do little but keep running, which becomes a gesture of hope and healing.

SUGGESTED READINGS
Coltelli, Laura. *Winged Words.* Lincoln: University of Nebraska Press, 1990.
Isernhagen, Hartwig. *Momaday, Vizenor, Armstrong: Conversations on American Indian Writing.* Norman: University of Oklahoma Press, 1999.
Martin, Russell, and Marc Barasch, eds. *Writers of the Purple Sage.* New York: Viking, 1984.

Momaday, N. Scott. "The Man Made of Words." In *The Remembered Earth: An Anthology of Contemporary Native American Literature*, edited by Geary Hobson. Albuquerque: University of New Mexico Press, 1980.

Ramsey, Jerold. *Reading the Fire.* Lincoln: University of Nebraska Press, 1982.

Trimble, Martha Scott. "N. Scott Momaday." *Fifty Western Writers: A Bio-Bibliographical Sourcebook*, edited by Fred Erisman and Richard W. Etulain. Westport, Conn.: Greenwood Press, 1982.

Velie, Alan R. *Four American Indian Literary Masters.* Norman: University of Oklahoma Press, 1982.

Vizenor, Gerald. *Manifest Manners.* Middletown, Conn.: Wesleyan University Press, 1994.

–Michael R. Meyers

Toni Morrison

BORN: Lorain, Ohio; February 18, 1931

Morrison is the first African American woman to receive the Nobel Prize in Literature.

TRADITIONS: African American

PRINCIPAL WORKS: *The Bluest Eye*, 1970; *Sula*, 1973; *Song of Solomon*, 1977; *Tar Baby*, 1981; *Beloved*, 1987; *Jazz*, 1992; *Playing in the Dark: Whiteness and the Literary Imagination*, 1992; *Paradise*, 1997

Toni Morrison was born Chloe Anthony Wofford; her family was blue-collar Midwestern. Her parents had migrated from the South in search of a better life. From her parents and grandparents, Morrison acquired a background in African American folklore; magic and the supernatural appear with frequency in her work.

At Howard University, where she earned a bachelor's degree, she changed her name to Toni. After receiving a master's degree in English from Cornell University, she taught at Texas Southern University and then at Howard, where she met Jamaican architect Harold Morrison. Their marriage ended after seven years. A single mother, Toni Morrison supported herself and two sons as a senior editor at Random House, where she encouraged the publication of African American literature. She has continued to teach at various universities, including Harvard, Yale, and Princeton.

Originally, Morrison did not intend to be a writer. She has said she began to write because she could not find herself, a black woman, represented in American fiction. In a conversation with novelist Gloria Naylor, published in *Southern Review*, Morrison speaks of reclaiming herself as a woman and validating her life through the writing of her first book, *The Bluest Eye*, in which a young black girl prays for the blue eyes that will bring her acceptance.

Morrison celebrates the culture of strong black women that she remembers from her childhood, especially in *Sula, Song of Solomon*, and *Beloved*. She believes that being able to recognize the contribution and legacy of one's ancestors is essential to self-knowledge. Her characters are forced to confront their personal and social histories and are often drawn back to their African heritage.

Some black male critics have challenged Morrison on the grounds that her male characters are too negative, but the literary world has honored her. In 1988, *Beloved* was awarded the Pulitzer Prize for fiction. In 1993, Morrison became the second American woman to receive the Nobel Prize in Literature.

Beloved

TYPE OF WORK: Novel
FIRST PUBLISHED: 1987

Beloved's dedication, "Sixty Million and more," commemorates the number of slaves who died in the middle passage–from Africa to the New World. Morrison's protagonist, Sethe, is modeled upon the historical figure of a fugitive Kentucky slave, who in 1851 murdered her baby rather than return it to slavery.

A pregnant Sethe flees on foot to Cincinnati, Ohio, sending her children ahead by way of the Underground Railroad. Her overwhelming concern is to join her baby daughter, who needs her milk. On the bank of the Ohio River she goes into labor, her delivery aided by a white girl who is herself fleeing mistreatment. The new baby is named Denver. Although Sethe reaches her destination, slave-catchers soon follow to return her to Kentucky. Frantic, she tries to kill her children rather than submit them to slavery, but she succeeds only with the older baby. "Beloved" is carved on the child's tombstone.

Sethe accepts her identity of black woman, escaped slave, wife, mother. Her antagonist is life, which has taken so much from her. She and Paul D, the man who becomes her lover, are the last survivors of Sweet Home, the Kentucky farm that was neither sweet nor home to them. Their charge is to endure memory and accept the unforgivable past.

A vengeful spirit, that of the dead baby, invades Sethe's house. After Paul D drives it away, a strange young woman appears in the yard, and they take her in. Her name is Beloved. She is the ghost of Sethe's dead child. She is also, less clearly, a ghost from the slave ships and an African river spirit. She alters relationships in the household, exerting control over the two adults and Denver. Denver hovers over Beloved; Beloved dotes on Sethe. Once Sethe recognizes Beloved as her daughter, she struggles to make amends while Beloved grows plump and cruel.

Denver develops a new identity. At eighteen, she is self-centered, jealous, and lonely.

Toni Morrison (Alfred A. Knopf)

Beloved becomes her dear companion. Gradually, Denver grows aware that Beloved's presence is destroying Sethe, who loses her job along with her meager income and begins to waste away. Denver, who has rarely ventured past her own yard because of the neighbors' hostility, realizes that only she can save her mother. Terrified, she walks down the road to seek work from strangers and, by accepting this responsibility, becomes a woman.

Morrison expected this painful, fiercely beautiful novel to be controversial. Instead, it was widely praised, receiving the Pulitzer Prize for fiction in 1988.

Song of Solomon
TYPE OF WORK: Novel
FIRST PUBLISHED: 1977

Song of Solomon, Morrison's third novel, received the 1978 National Book Critics Circle Award for fiction. In her first work to feature a male protagonist, she established the rich narrative voice for which she has become famous. Macon "Milkman" Dead, grandson of a slave, evolves from a self-centered youth to a man of compassion and understanding. He completes this transition as he searches for his family origins, thus exemplifying Morrison's belief in the importance of ancestors.

Originally, Milkman desires to know as little as possible about his family. Torn by the ongoing conflict between his parents, he sets out to find his inheritance, which he believes to be gold in the possession of his father's sister, Pilate. Instead, Milkman's quest leads him out of the Midwest to discover his true heritage, his ancestors. He gains pride in his family when he encounters old men who remember his father and grandfather. Before long he is more interested in locating his people than in the gold.

At the town of Shalimar, Virginia, after the symbolic initiation of a night hunt, Milkman recognizes his own selfishness. He learns that a child's game, the town itself, and many of the people bear some version of his Great-grandfather Solomon's name. The figure of Solomon is based upon a legend of the Flying African, who escaped slavery by leaping into the air and flying home to Africa. Milkman realizes that his great-grandfather has become a folk hero.

Heritage is symbolized by the importance of names. The powerful and eccentric Pilate wears her name, laboriously copied from the Bible by her father, in her mother's snuffbox, which has been made into an earring. She always carries her parents with her. Pilate, an imposing woman who has no navel, struggled with her identity in her teens, when she determined to live by her own rules. One of Morrison's strong, independent women, she cuts her hair short like a man's and becomes a bootlegger for practical reasons. She is also a mythic figure, birthing herself after the death of her mother. Pilate communicates comfortably with her father's ghost, a friendly presence that appears and tells her what she needs to know. She carries his bones around with her in a tarp. He is her guide to maturity; in turn, she becomes Milkman's. Through her, Milkman learns what she already accepts: "When you know your name, you should hang on to it."

SUGGESTED READINGS

Bakerman, Jane S. "Failures of Love: Female Initiation in the Novels of Toni Morrison." *American Literature* 52, no. 4 (January, 1981): 541-563.

Christian, Barbara T. "Layered Rhythms: Virginia Woolf and Toni Morrison." *Modern Fiction Studies* 39, nos. 3, 4 (Fall/Winter, 1993): 483-500.

Krumholz, Linda. "Dead Teachers: Rituals of Manhood and Rituals of Reading in *Song of Solomon*." *Modern Fiction Studies* 39, nos. 3-4 (Fall/Winter, 1993): 551-574.

Kubitschek, Missy Dean. *Toni Morrison: A Critical Companion.* Westport, Conn.: Greenwood Press, 1998.

Morrison, Toni. "An Interview with Toni Morrison." Interview by Nellie McKay. *Contemporary Literature* 24, no. 4 (Winter, 1983): 413-429.

Naylor, Gloria, and Toni Morrison. "A Conversation." *Southern Review* 21, no. 3 (July, 1985): 567-593.

Rand, Naomi R. *Silko, Morrison, and Roth: Studies in Survival.* New York: Peter Lang, 1999.

Rushdy, Ashraf H. A. "Daughters Signifyin(g) History: The Example of Toni Morrison's *Beloved*." *American Literature* 64, no. 3 (September, 1992): 567-597.

Samuels, Wilfred D., and Clenora Hudson-Weems. *Toni Morrison.* Boston: Twayne, 1990.

Schmudde, Carol E. "Knowing When to Stop: A Reading of Toni Morrison's *Beloved*." *College Language Association Journal* 37, no. 2 (December, 1993): 121-135.

–Joanne McCarthy

Bharati Mukherjee

BORN: Calcutta, India; July 27, 1940

*Mukherjee is perhaps the foremost fiction writer describing the
experience of Third World immigrants to North America.*

TRADITIONS: South Asian

PRINCIPAL WORKS: *The Tiger's Daughter*, 1972; *Wife*, 1975; *Darkness*, 1985; *The
Middleman and Other Stories*, 1988; *Jasmine*, 1989; *The Holder of the World*,
1993; *Leave It to Me*, 1997

Bharati Mukherjee was born to an upper-caste Bengali family and received
an English education. The most important event of her life occurred in her
early twenties, when she received a scholarship to attend the University of
Iowa's Writer's Workshop. Her fiction reflects the experimental techniques
fostered at such influential creative writing schools.

At the University of Iowa, Mukherjee met Clark Blaise, a Canadian citizen
and fellow student. When they moved to Canada she became painfully aware
of her status as a nonwhite immigrant in a nation less tolerant of newcomers
than the United States. The repeated humiliations she endured made her
hypersensitive to the plight of immigrants from the Third World. She realized
that immigrants may lose their old identities but not be able to find new
identities as often unwelcome strangers.

Mukherjee, relying on her experience growing up, sought her salvation in
education. She obtained a Ph.D. in English and Comparative Literature and
moved up the career ladder at various colleges and universities in the East
and Midwest until she became a professor at Berkeley in 1989. Her first novel,
The Tiger's Daughter, was published in 1971. In common with all her fiction, it
deals with the feelings of exile and identity confusion that are experienced by
immigrants. Being female as well as an immigrant, Mukherjee noted that
opportunities for women were so different in America that she was exhila-
rated and bewildered. Many of her best stories, dealing with women experiencing gender crises, have a strong autobiographical element.

Darkness, her first collection of stories, was well reviewed, but not until the
publication of *The Middleman and Other Stories* did she become internationally
prominent. She is dealing with perhaps the most important contemporary
phenomenon, the population explosion and flood of immigrants from have-
not nations. Mukherjee makes these newcomers understandable to themselves and to native citizens, while shedding light on the identity problems of
all the anonymous, inarticulate immigrants of America's past.

Bharati Mukherjee (Tom Victor)

Her protagonists are not the "huddled masses" of yesteryear; they are talented, multilingual, enterprising, often affluent men and women who are transforming American culture. Mukherjee's compassion for these newcomers has made her one of the most important writers of her time.

"The Management of Grief"

TYPE OF WORK: Short fiction
FIRST PUBLISHED: 1988, in *The Middleman and Other Stories*

Based on an actual event–the Sikh terrorist bombing of an Air India plane on June 23, 1985, which killed all 329 passengers and crew–"The Management of Grief" is Mukherjee's "tribute to all who forget enough of their roots to start over enthusiastically in a new land, but who also remember enough of their roots to survive fate's knockout punches." Mukherjee's story focuses on Shaila Bhave in the hours, days, and months following the deaths of her husband and two young sons. The story focuses on her forms of grief and guilt, which are specific to her culture. As an Indian wife, she never spoke her husband's name or told him she loved him–simple acts that Westerners take for granted. Her grief reveals who Shaila is, was, and will be. As do many of the characters in Mukherjee's stories and novels, she finds herself caught between cultures, countries, and existences. "At thirty-six," she considers, "I am too old to start over and too young to give up. Like my husband's spirit, I flutter between two worlds."

One of the worlds is Indian, including the highly supportive Hindu community in Toronto, from which she feels strangely detached. The Hindu community in Toronto is itself part of a larger Indian immigrant community that includes Muslims, Parsis, atheists, and even the Sikhs, tied by religion if not necessarily by politics to those responsible for the bombing, which is part of a struggle for autonomy being waged by Sikh extremists in India. Even within Toronto's Hindu community there are divided allegiances as parents "lose" their children to Western culture no less than to terrorist bombs. The other world, the "West," or more specifically Canada, is equally problematic, especially for Indian immigrants such as Mrs. Bhave, who are made to feel at best marginalized, at worst excluded altogether. She experiences the insensitivity of police investigators, the inadequacy of news coverage (the implicit message is that the victims and their families are not really Canadian), and finally the well-intentioned but ineffectual efforts of a government social worker's textbook approach to "grief management." The social worker enlists Mrs. Bhave's help in assisting those who have not been "coping so well."

The story's complex identity theme is reflected in its spatial diversity. It follows Mrs. Bhave from Toronto to Ireland (to identify remains) and then to India, where she believes she hears her husband's voice telling her: "You must finish alone what we started together." This seemingly irrational link to tradition, including her thinking that her husband and sons "surround her like creatures in epics," gives her the strength to leave India and return to Canada. Although she does not assume, as some of the older relatives do, that God will provide, she is provided for and in a way that precludes the reader's seeing her as entirely representative. Thanks to her husband's savings and the sale of their house, she is financially secure and so can afford to heed her dead husband's final admonition: "Go, be brave." Her future, including her future identity, may be uncertain, but in that uncertainty Shaila Bhave finds her freedom, one inextricably rooted in loss.

The Middleman and Other Stories
TYPE OF WORK: Short fiction
FIRST PUBLISHED: 1988

The Middleman and Other Stories deals with the clash between Western and Third World cultures as technology and overpopulation join diverse peoples in tragicomic relationships. "A Wife's Story" is a good example of Mukherjee's storytelling technique. It is told in the present tense, begins abruptly, and has an interest, characteristic of literary minimalism, in brand names and consumerism. The narrator sees her Indian husband through American eyes when he visits her in New York City, where she is attending college. He is captivated by the meretricious glamour and abundance of consumer goods. The narrator realizes how Americanized she has become and how comically provincial her husband appears.

Alfred Judah in "The Middleman" is a man without a country, a Jew living in Central America and hoping to make his way to the United States. Some think he is an Arab and others think he is an Indian; he is despised by everyone. In "Orbiting," an American woman is living with an Afghan lover who is another man without a country, unable to obtain legal entry into any of the developed countries being flooded with immigrants.

In "Buried Lives," an Indian who is prospering in Sri Lanka abandons his responsibilities for a new life in America. After leading a terrifying underground existence, he finds himself engaged to be married in Germany. "Danny's Girls" is about immigrants who come to the United States for a better life and who become prostitutes. "Jasmine" has a similar theme.

"The Management of Grief," dealing with the 1985 bombing of an Air India jetliner, focuses on a specific incident but reveals a macrocosm. Through the eyes of one bereaved woman, the reader glimpses the diaspora that has scattered Indians across five continents, creating alienation and countless minor tragedies.

Mukherjee's experience as an upper-caste woman losing her tradition-bound, privileged identity was the turning point in her life. As an immigrant she was sometimes mistaken for a prostitute, a shoplifter, or a domestic servant. Her stories reflect her sympathy for the psychological traumas suffered by the Third World immigrants who have lost their old identities and who are trying to create new ones. Mukherjee is an Old World intellectual who has adopted New World values. The blending of old and new is another striking characteristic of her fiction. She dramatizes the cataclysmic changes taking place in human consciousness as cultures collide.

SUGGESTED READINGS

Carter-Sanborn, Kristin. "'We Murder Who We Were': *Jasmine* and the Violence of Identity." *American Literature* 66, no. 3 (September, 1994): 573-593.

Chua, C. L. "Passages from India: Migrating to America in the Fiction of V. S. Naipaul and Bharati Mukherjee." In *Reworlding: The Literature of the Indian Diaspora*, edited by Emmanuel S. Nelson. Westport, Conn.: Greenwood Press, 1992.

Dlaska, Andrea. *Ways of Belonging: The Making of New Americans in the Fiction of Bharati Mukherjee.* Vienna, Austria: Braumüller, 1999.

Fakrul, Alam. *Bharati Mukherjee.* New York: Twayne, 1996.

Moyers, Bill. "An Interview with Bharati Mukherjee." In *Connections: A Multicultural Reader for Writers*, edited by Judith A. Stanford. Mountain View, Calif.: Mayfield, 1993.

Mukherjee, Bharati, and Clark Blaise. *The Sorrow and the Pity: The Haunting Legacy of the Air India Tragedy.* Markham, Ontario: Viking, 1987.

Nelson, Emmanuel S., ed. *Bharati Mukherjee: Critical Perspectives.* New York: Garland, 1993.

—Bill Delaney/Robert A. Morace

Gloria Naylor

BORN: New York, New York; January 25, 1950

Naylor's exploration of black communities stresses the relationship between identity and place.

TRADITIONS: African American
PRINCIPAL WORKS: *The Women of Brewster Place*, 1982; *Linden Hills*, 1985; *Mama Day*, 1988; *Bailey's Cafe*, 1992; *The Men of Brewster Place*, 1998

When she gave her introverted daughter a journal from Woolworth's, Gloria Naylor's mother opened the door to writing. In high school, two experiences shaped Naylor's emerging identity: Nineteenth century English literature taught her that language can be a powerful tool, and Martin Luther King, Jr.'s 1968 assassination turned her to missionary work. Instead of going to college, for the next seven years she traveled as a Jehovah's Witness, abandoning the work in 1975, when she began to feel constrained by the lifestyle.

At Brooklyn College, her introduction to black history and the discovery of such literary foremothers as Zora Neale Hurston and Toni Morrison gave her the inspiration to try writing herself. Completing her first novel, the best-seller *The Women of Brewster Place*, signified, she has indicated, her taking hold of herself and attempting to take her destiny into her own hands. After winning a scholarship to Yale University, Naylor discovered that, for her, graduate training was incompatible with writing fiction. She nevertheless completed a master's degree in 1983, when the Afro-American Studies department allowed her second novel, *Linden Hills*, to fulfill the thesis requirement. *Linden Hills* illustrates the effects of materialism on an elite all-black community that lacks a spiritual center.

The central feature of all of Naylor's novels is an enclosed black community where characters learn to embrace their identities in the context of place. Naylor's powerful settings combine elements of the ordinary with the otherworldly, allowing for magical events and mythic resolutions. For example, *Mama Day* takes place on the imaginary island of Willow Springs and weaves the history of the Day family from the point of view of the powerful matriarch Mama Day, a conjure woman. Naylor's own family history provides her with a rich sense of community, but she paradoxically treasures solitude. Married briefly, she refuses to remarry or have children and teaches writing to keep from being too much of a recluse. Naylor's strength is portraying convincing multigenerational characters in specific settings.

Bailey's Cafe

TYPE OF WORK: Novel
FIRST PUBLISHED: 1992

Set in 1948, *Bailey's Cafe*, Naylor's fourth novel, is her self-described "sexual novel." Similar to *The Women of Brewster Place*, it tells the tragic histories of female characters who suffer simply because they are sexual. The underlying structure of blues music recasts these feminist rewritings of biblical stories. The characters' own blues-influenced narrations provide the equivalent of melody, and the male narrator supplies the connecting texts linking one story to another.

The proprietor of Bailey's Cafe, who is the narrator, sets the pattern by telling how he was saved by Bailey's Cafe, a magical place. It is a cafe that does not serve customers, and its magic is not the redemptive kind. The cafe provides "some space, some place, to take a breather for a while" by suspending time. Not fixed in any one city, it is "real real mobile," so that anyone can get there. It features a back door that opens onto a void where patrons re-create scenes to help them sustain life, or, alternatively, to end it. The street on which Bailey's Cafe may be found contains three refuges that form a "relay for broken dreams": Bailey's Cafe, Gabe's Pawnshop, and Eve's Boardinghouse and Garden.

Eve transforms her suffering into a haven. She aids only those women who know what it means to "walk a thousand years." Her boarders include Esther, who hates men because of the sexual abuse she suffered as a child bride; Peaches, a woman so beautiful she disfigures herself; Jesse, a spunky heroin addict; and Mariam, a fourteen-year-old Ethiopian Jew who is pregnant but still a virgin. The community also includes men. The unforgettable Miss Maple is a man who forges a strong identity despite the racism that threatens his manhood. The novel explores positive models of masculinity and steadily subverts the idea that sexual women are whores. Such a characterization oppresses all women, who must transcend the personal consequences of this destructive label.

The arrival of the outcast and pregnant Mariam threatens to disrupt the characters' safety because the birth could destroy their world: "For all we knew, when that baby gave its first cry, this whole street could have just faded away." The women on the street fear they will find themselves back in "those same hopeless crossroads in our lives." Instead, the baby is born in Mariam's homeland, magically re-created in the void. All the characters gather to celebrate its arrival. Their participation in the Jewish birth ceremony brings hope for the future and shows the healing power of a diverse community.

The Women of Brewster Place

TYPE OF WORK: Novel
FIRST PUBLISHED: 1982

Naylor's first novel, *The Women of Brewster Place*, won the American Book Award for First Fiction in 1983 and was made into a film. Actually a novel in seven stories, it presents a series of interconnected tales about seven women who struggle to make peace with their pasts. The allegorical setting is Brewster Place, a dead-end ghetto street whose distinctive feature is the brick wall that bottles economic and racial frustration inside. Two interdependent themes bind the stories together: The violence that men enact on women is counteracted by the healing power of community. The novel's innovative structure is key to Naylor's purpose. Exploring the lives of different women on Brewster Place, Naylor attempts to create a microcosm of the black female experience in America.

The microcosm consists of seven African American women representing a range of ages, backgrounds, and sexualities. The first character introduced is Mattie Michael, whose fierce love for her son twice costs her the security and pride of a happy home. Her hard-won strength becomes the force that helps other women, such as Mattie's oldest friend, Etta Mae Johnson, and Lucielia Louise Turner (Ciel), whom Mattie helped raise. One of the most powerful scenes of the novel is the one in which Mattie saves Ciel, who loses her desire to live after the tragic deaths of her two children. Kiswana Browne is a would-be revolutionary who attempts to reclaim her African heritage and to improve Brewster Place by renouncing her parents' elite Linden Hills lifestyle. Cora Lee, her opposite, is a single mother of seven who wants babies but not children. Last are Lorraine and Theresa, the couple whom Brewster Place cruelly rejects when they seek a haven that will tolerate their love for each other. Women's dual identity as mother and daughter is a highlighted conflict throughout.

The symbolism of Brewster Place's brick wall contributes to the horrific climax when Lorraine is gang-raped in the alley formed by the wall, her blood spattering the bricks. Her effort to fight back, delayed by the trauma, causes her to attack Ben, the janitor who treats her like a daughter. She murders him with a brick. The novel appears to end triumphantly when the women tear down the wall, brick by brick, at a block party that celebrates the power of community. This is a deceptive resolution, however, because the block party has happened only in Mattie's dream. The ambiguity of the ending gives the story a mythic quality by stressing the continual possibility of dreams and the results of their deferral.

SUGGESTED READINGS

Gates, Henry Louis, and K. A. Appiah, eds. *Gloria Naylor: Critical Perspectives Past and Present.* New York: Amistad Press, 1993.

Montgomery, M. L. "Authority, Multivocality, and the New World Order in Gloria Naylor's *Bailey's Cafe.*" *African American Review* 29, no. 1 (1995): 27-33.

Naylor, Gloria. "Belles Lettres Interview: Gloria Naylor." Interview by Angels Carabi. *Belles Lettres: A Review of Books by Women* 7, no. 3 (1992): 36-42.

———. "Love and Sex in the Afro-American Novel." *The Yale Review* 78, no. 1 (1989): 19-31.

Puhr, Kathleen M. "Healers in Gloria Naylor's Fiction." *Twentieth Century Literature* 40, no. 4 (1994): 518-527.

Whitt, Margaret Earley. *Understanding Gloria Naylor.* Columbia: University of South Carolina Press, 1999.

Wilentz, Gay. "Healing the Wounds of Time." *The Women's Review of Books* 10, no. 5 (1993): 15-16.

—*Christine H. King*

Fae Myenne Ng

BORN: San Francisco, California; 1956

Ng brings the perspective of an Asian American to the American experience of immigration and assimilation.

TRADITIONS: Chinese American
PRINCIPAL WORK: *Bone*, 1993

Fae Myenne Ng's writing depicts a cultural divide between her assimilated generation and that of her Chinese parents. Reared in San Francisco's Chinatown by working-class parents who immigrated from China, Ng acquired an excellent education, receiving degrees from the University of California at Berkeley and an M.F.A. from Columbia University. *Bone*, her first novel, took her ten years to write, during which time she supported herself as a waitress and temporary worker, as well as by a grant from the National Foundation for the Arts. As does Leila, the narrator of the novel, Ng is an educated woman who understood her parents' working-class world. In the novel, the Chinese mother is a poorly paid, overworked garment worker. The father holds down a series of dead-end jobs that include janitor, dishwasher, houseboy, and laundry worker. The couple have worked their fingers to the bone to provide for their daughters. *Bone* is a tribute to the family's father, who represents a generation of Chinese men who sacrificed their personal happiness for the sake of their families. Ng's inspiration was the old Chinese men living alone and impoverished in single-room occupancy hotels in Chinatown. Chinese America's bachelor society came to America to work the gold mines, to build the railroads, and to develop California agriculturally. These immigrants became men without roots.

The novel also depicts the conflicts of the family's three daughters with their old-fashioned parents. There is the middle daughter Ona, whose suicide suggests she could not adjust to American society and maintain her identity as a dutiful Chinese daughter. Nina, the youngest daughter, affirms a modern identity and escapes to New York City. Leila, the eldest daughter, is a complicated combination of the old Chinese ways and new American cultural patterns. As does Nina, the rebellious daughter, Ng moved to New York City. Leila, with her ability to assimilate the new while keeping faith with the past, is the daughter who most mirrors Ng's identity as an Asian American. Ng's work adds to the tradition of the immigrant novel.

Bone

Type of work: Novel
First published: 1993

Ng's *Bone* continues in a tradition of Asian American novels by women that mediate between the demands of addressing issues of gender and of ethnicity. As a woman writing from a strongly patriarchal cultural heritage, Ng has had to create new strategies in order to express the paradox of resistance to and affirmation of her cultural heritage.

Bone relates the story of the Leong family, which has recently suffered the death by suicide of the Middle Girl, Ona. Ona committed suicide by jumping from one of Chinatown's housing projects. She left no note, and although the police reported she was "on downers," or depressants, there was no apparent cause for the suicide. The novel is narrated by the First Girl, Leila Fu Louie, Ona's half sister and the eldest daughter in the Leong family. Leila's attempts to come to terms with her sister's death, and thereby her own life, lead her to muse about incidents from their childhood and the everyday circumstances of the present. The novel unfolds in a series of stories that move from the present into the past.

The children of immigrants have often been called upon to translate for their parents. Their ability to switch from the language of their parents to the English of their birthplace makes them the bridge between the customs of the Old World and the expectations and demands of the New. This enormous responsibility can become an overwhelming burden. Although Leila must continually face the chasm between her parents' expectations and her own reality, her ability to build a bridge of translation is grounded in her strong need and appreciation for the family.

Her youngest sister, Nina, the End Girl, refuses to shoulder this burden of translation. Her rebellion has caused her to move to New York, far away from her parents in San Francisco's Chinatown. She declares her independence by refusing to lie about her life in order to appease her parents. It is the self-imposed silence of Ona, however, that is at the center of the novel. Ona, the middle child, is caught in the middle; she learned too well how to keep secrets.

Ng does not seek to solve the mystery of Ona's death in this novel. It is a mystery that is unsolvable; rather, through the narrative voice of Leila, Ng explores the languages and silences of love, grief, assimilation, avoidance, anger, guilt, and, finally, acceptance. Ng, who grew up in San Francisco, is the daughter of Chinese immigrants and in an interview explained the title of her novel: "Bone is what lasts. And I wanted to honor the quality of endurance in the immigrant spirit."

Bone is a journey into a territory that is the common heritage of all second-generation immigrant Americans and the particular traditions of Chinese immigrants. The path to assimilation into American society is fraught with contradictions and ambivalence. Ng provides few answers; she simply reveals one family's experience.

SUGGESTED READINGS

Ho, Wendy. *In Her Mother's House: The Politics of Asian American Mother-Daughter Writing.* Walnut Creek, Calif.: AltaMira Press, 1999.

Lim, Shirley Geok-Lin. "Feminist and Ethnic Literary Theories in Asian American Literature." *Feminist Studies* 19, no. 3 (Fall, 1993): 571-589.

Miller, Heather Ross. "America the Big Lie, the Quintessential." *Southern Review* 29, no. 2 (April, 1993): 420-430.

Ng, Fae Myenne. "False Gold: My Father's American Journey." *New Republic,* July 19-26, 1993, 12-13.

Stetson, Nancy. "Honoring Her Forebears." *Chicago Tribune,* April 4, 1993, C12.

Wong, Sau-Ling Cynthia. *Reading Asian-American Voices: From Necessity to Extravagance.* Princeton, N.J.: Princeton University Press, 1993.

—Margaret Boe Birns/Jane Anderson Jones

John Okada

BORN: Seattle, Washington; September, 1923
DIED: Seattle, Washington; February, 1971

Okada introduced Japanese American literature to the United States.

TRADITIONS: Japanese American
PRINCIPAL WORK: *No-No Boy*, 1957

John Okada was a Nisei, or second-generation Japanese American. He grew up in the Pacific Northwest and witnessed the internment of 120,000 Japanese Americans during World War II. Unlike the character Ichiro in *No-No Boy*, however, Okada was not a no-no boy (a person who answered no to two critical questions on the loyalty questionnaire—refusing to serve in the American armed forces and refusing to forswear allegiance to Japan and pledge loyalty to the United States). He volunteered for military service and was sent to Japanese-held islands to exhort Japanese soldiers to surrender. The experience helped him shape his perspective on the war.

After he was discharged from the military in 1946, Okada went to the University of Washington and Columbia University. He earned two B.A. degrees and an M.A. degree studying, in his own words, "narrative and dramatic writing, history, sociology." He started working on *No-No Boy* while he was an assistant in the Business Reference Department of the Seattle Public Library and at the Detroit Public Library. After a stint as a technical writer for Chrysler Missile Operations of Sterling Township, Michigan, he and his wife Dorothy moved back to Seattle. *No-No Boy* was completed in 1957. Okada had a hard time trying to find publishers who were interested in his work. *No-No Boy* was first published by Charles Tuttle of Tokyo. After Okada died, his wife offered all of his manuscripts, including the one of his second novel, to the Japanese American Research Project at the University of California at Los Angeles. They were rejected. Dorothy burned them shortly after, when she was preparing to move.

Okada was proud to be a Japanese American. He examined the double consciousness of the Japanese American community. *No-No Boy* portrays the psychological confusion and distress experienced by many Japanese Americans, especially second-generation Japanese Americans (U.S. citizens by birth, culturally Japanese) during and after World War II. *No-No Boy* portrays the struggle of those who are caught between two worlds at war.

No-No Boy
TYPE OF WORK: Novel
FIRST PUBLISHED: 1957

No-No Boy depicts a second-generation Japanese American's struggle to balance his loyalty to the Japanese culture, to his parents, and to his country, the United States. Ichiro Yamada is interned during World War II. He is put in jail for answering no to the two critical questions on the allegiance questionnaire. His two negative answers are his refusal to serve in the American armed forces and his refusal to forswear allegiance to Japan and pledge loyalty to the United States. After he is released from prison, Ichiro moves back to Seattle and is caught between two seemingly irreconcilable worlds. On one side, there are his parents, who are very proud of being Japanese. On the other side, there is the United States, a country to which he still feels he belongs.

During his search for his identity, Ichiro meets several people who help shape his perspective on himself and on his relationship with America. One of his close friends, Kenji, joins the military during the war. He loses a leg and has only two years to live. What Kenji physically goes through, Ichiro experiences emotionally. Being a no-no boy, Ichiro is looked down upon by his brother and other Japanese Americans who believe he has betrayed the country. During one of their conversations, Kenji and Ichiro jokingly discuss whether they want to trade places. The fact that both of them are willing to do it comments on the kind of social environment they have to deal with and on the choices they have made.

Kenji also introduces Ichiro to Emi, a person who can empathize with Ichiro's experience. Emi's husband has left her because he is ashamed of his brother Mike and of Emi's father, who elect to be repatriated back to Japan. Mike is a World War I veteran. He is incensed by how Japanese Americans are treated by their own government during World War II and eventually decides to go back to a country he does not know or love. Emi saves Ichiro from plunging into an emotional abyss. They find a friend and companion in each other. After witnessing the death of his friend, Freddie, who is also a no-no boy, Ichiro starts to think about his own future. In "the darkness of the alley of the community" that is "a tiny bit of America," he starts to chase that faint and elusive insinuation of promise as it continues "to take shape in mind and in heart."

SUGGESTED READINGS

Chin, Frank. Afterword to *No-No Boy*, by John Okada. Seattle: University of Washington Press, 1976.

_____. "Come All Ye Asian American Writers of the Real and the Fake." In *The Big Aiiieeeee! An Anthology of Chinese and Japanese American Literature*, edited by Frank Chin et al. New York: Meridian, 1991.

Kim, Elaine H. *Asian American Literature.* Philadelphia: Temple University Press, 1982.

Wong, Sau-ling C., and Jeffrey J. Santa Ana. "Gender and Sexuality in Asian American Literature." *Signs* 25, no. 1 (Autumn, 1999): 171-226.

−Qun Wang

Judith Ortiz Cofer

BORN: Hormigueros, Puerto Rico; February 24, 1952

Ortiz Cofer's fiction, poems, and essays describe the strengths and conflicts of Puerto Ricans, especially women, on the island and on the mainland.

TRADITIONS: Caribbean, Puerto Rican
PRINCIPAL WORKS: *Reaching for the Mainland*, 1987; *Terms of Survival*, 1987; *The Line of the Sun*, 1989; *Silent Dancing*, 1990; *The Latin Deli: Prose and Poetry*, 1993; *The Year of Our Revolution: New and Selected Stories and Poems*, 1998; *Woman in Front of the Sun: On Becoming a Writer*, 2000

Judith Ortiz Cofer did not begin writing for publication until after she had been in the United States for more than twenty years. During those years, however, she frequently returned to Puerto Rico to visit her extended family. Her writing is informed by her bicultural experiences: one in the urban apartment buildings in English-speaking New Jersey, where her father stressed the importance of learning American language and customs to succeed, and the other in the traditional island community where her mother and other Spanish-speaking relatives taught her not to forget her heritage.

Ortiz Cofer is bilingual, but she writes primarily but not exclusively in English. For example, her grandmother's home, filled with the community of women who nurtured the writer as a child, is warmly referred to as *la casa de Mamá* or simply her *casa*. Neither solely Puerto Rican nor simply American, Ortiz Cofer straddles both cultures and intermingles them in her writing. Although most of her life has been spent in New Jersey—where her father was stationed in the Navy—and later Florida

Judith Ortiz Cofer (John Cofer)

and Georgia, she considers herself a Puerto Rican woman. She identifies this connection to the island not merely through geographical association but also by invoking and reclaiming her family, their stories, and her memories through her writing.

As a Puerto Rican woman, Ortiz Cofer was expected to marry, bear children, and define herself through these relationships. She dreamed, however, of becoming a teacher and later a writer. Although she was married to Charles John Cofer in 1971 and later gave birth to a daughter, she did not follow the traditional Puerto Rican path of the married woman. After completing a bachelor's degree in 1974 from Augusta College, she earned a master's degree in English from Florida Atlantic University and received a fellowship to do graduate work at Oxford University in 1977. She taught English and creative writing at various schools in Florida before settling at the University of Georgia in 1984. In addition to her academic career, she also became a widely anthologized and acclaimed writer. Ortiz Cofer's writing pays homage to the strictly defined and highly ritualized lives of Puerto Rican women, but her life and her act of writing break that mold; she redefines what it means to be a Puerto Rican woman.

Silent Dancing

TYPE OF WORK: Autobiography (essays and poetry)
FIRST PUBLISHED: 1990

Silent Dancing: A Partial Remembrance of a Puerto Rican Childhood is Ortiz Cofer's collection of fourteen essays and accompanying poems looking back on her childhood and adolescence in Hormigueros, Puerto Rico, and Paterson, New Jersey. Her father joined the Navy before she was born, and two years later he moved them to Paterson, where he was stationed. When he went to sea for months at a time, he sent his wife and children back to Puerto Rico until he returned to New Jersey.

While her father urged the family to assimilate into the American melting pot and even moved them outside the Puerto Rican neighborhoods in New Jersey, her mother remained loyal to her own mother's home on the island. Her mother's quiet sadness emerges throughout the book, such as the voice of the poem "*El Olvido*" that warns that to forget one's heritage is to "die/ of loneliness and exposure."

The memoir chronicles significant moments, beginning with her birth ("They Say"). "*Quinceañera*" tells of the custom of a girl's coming-of-age party (at age fifteen). Her grandmother prepares her for Puerto Rican womanhood. The adult narrator also explores her and her mother's memories of the yearly trips to Puerto Rico in "Marina" and "The Last Word."

The central theme in the book is the traditional Puerto Rican "script of our lives," which circumscribes "everyone in their places." The narrator struggles with her family's expectations for her to become a traditional Puerto Rican woman: domestic, married, and fertile. This script allows little room for individual identity, so the maturing narrator focuses on those characters who rewrite the script and extemporize their own lives ("Some of the Characters").

The embodiment of Puerto Rican tradition is Mamá, the grandmother who ironically gives Ortiz Cofer the tools that enable her to redefine her own role. In "More Room," for instance, Ortiz Cofer tells the story about Mamá expelling her husband from her bedroom to avoid giving birth to even more children, thus liberating herself to enjoy her children, her grandchildren, and her own life. Similarly, "Tales Told Under the Mango Tree" portrays Mamá's queenly role as the matriarchal storyteller surrounded by the young women and girls of the family as she passes on *cuentos* (stories) about being a Puerto Rican woman, such as the legend of the wise and courageous María Sabida who is not controlled by love and is "never a victim."

Silent Dancing is ultimately a *Künstlerroman*, the story of an artist's apprenticeship. Ortiz Cofer has revised the script for her life as a Puerto Rican woman by inheriting Mamá's role as storyteller; she redefines what it means to be a Puerto Rican woman and tells her stories to a wider audience.

SUGGESTED READINGS

Acosta-Belén, Edna. "A MELUS Interview: Judith Ortiz Cofer." *MELUS* 18, no. 3 (Fall, 1993): 83-97.

Bruce-Novoa, Juan. "Judith Ortiz Cofer's Rituals of Movement." *The Americas Review* 19, nos. 3-4 (Winter, 1991): 88-99.

Ortiz Cofer, Judith. "The Infinite Variety of Puerto Rican Reality: An Interview with Judith Ortiz Cofer." Interview by Rafael Ocasio. *Callaloo* 17, no. 3 (Summer, 1994): 730-742.

_____. *Woman in Front of the Sun: On Becoming a Writer.* Athens: University of Georgia Press, 2000.

_____. "Puerto Rican Literature in Georgia? An Interview with Judith Ortiz Cofer." Interview by Rafael Ocasio. *The Kenyon Review* 14, no. 4 (Fall, 1992): 43-50.

—Nancy L. Chick

Cynthia Ozick

BORN: New York, New York; April 17, 1928

Ozick's fiction describes the difficulty of observing Jewish traditions in America's secular, assimilationist society.

TRADITIONS: Jewish
PRINCIPAL WORKS: *Trust*, 1966; *The Pagan Rabbi and Other Stories*, 1971; *Bloodshed and Three Novellas*, 1976; *Levitation: Five Fictions*, 1982; *The Cannibal Galaxy*, 1983; *The Messiah of Stockholm*, 1987; *The Shawl: A Story and a Novella*, 1989; *Portrait of the Artist as a Bad Character: And Other Essays on Writing*, 1996; *The Puttermesser Papers*, 1997; *Quarrel and Quandary: Essays*, 2000

Cynthia Ozick recalls her grandmother telling her stories, invariably conveying a lesson, about girlhood in a Russian Jewish village. From her drugstore-owning parents, she overhead "small but stirring adventures" confided by their Bronx neighbors. "Reading-lust" led her to fairy tales, to bachelor's and master's degrees in literature, and to a self-taught education in Judaism's textual tradition. From these various influences, Ozick creates fiction noted for its range and inventiveness. Her reputation is based largely on her short fiction. Ozick has more than once won the O. Henry Award.

Ozick's first book, however, was a novel, *Trust.* It concerns a young woman's search for identity. A predominant theme in Ozick's work has been the difficulty of sustaining one's Jewish identity in America's secular, assimilationist society. Assimilated, rootless Jews are frequently objects of satire in her fiction. What Ozick proposes, in terms of language, is a New Yiddish, understandable to English speakers yet preserving the tone and inflections of Yiddish, a language that is facing extinction as a result of the Holocaust and assimilation.

For Ozick, the Orthodox Jewish moral code remains the standard against which life and art are measured. America's materialistic culture, she maintains, is essentially pagan, and therefore hostile to Judaism. This conflict is clearly evident in "The Pagan Rabbi," a story in which attraction to nature drives the title character to suicide. The idea that the artist competes with God as creator also concerns Ozick. Particularly in "Usurpation (Other People's Stories)," Ozick intimates that writers are congenital plagiarizers and, more seriously, usurpers of God. The hubris of a person attempting godlike creation is approached humorously in "Puttermesser and Xanthippe," in which the female protagonist fashions a female golem, first to help with the housework, then to reform New York City. So convinced is Ozick of the pervasiveness of idolatrous ambition that her heroines display an arrogant singlemindedness that is more often associated with men. In the story "The Shawl" and its sequel, the novella "Rosa," Ozick, herself a mother, imagines a woman who idolizes the memory of a daughter murdered by the Nazis.

Ozick's vigilance against idolatry extends to her narrative style. Postmodernist, self-referential techniques–asides, interruptions, and explanations–alert readers to the illusions of fiction. Ironic in effect, they also deflate authorial claims to being like God.

Cynthia Ozick (Julius Ozick)

The Pagan Rabbi and Other Stories

TYPE OF WORK: Short fiction
FIRST PUBLISHED: 1971

The Pagan Rabbi and Other Stories, Ozick's first collection of short stories, was nominated for the National Book Award. Short fiction would subsequently form the basis of Ozick's literary reputation. The collection's seven stories–originally published in various periodicals–explore interrelated themes that mark Ozick's work: Jewish identity, the lure of secularism, and the vocation of the artist. In Ozick's view, Western civilization, rooted in Greek paganism, extols nature and physical existence and is therefore hostile to Judaism. The Western artistic tradition, moreover, dares usurp God's role as creator.

A prominent symbol in the title story, "The Pagan Rabbi," is the tree on which the protagonist eventually hangs himself with his prayer shawl. The tree's dryad and the heretical rabbi have coupled. In "The Dock-Witch," the protagonist's immersion in nature also leads to sexual union with a pagan goddess, yet because he is a Gentile, lacking Judaism's horror of idolatry, his seduction is guilt-free.

Lust for the world's beauty undoes these characters; lust for the world's acclaim corrupts others. In "Virility," an immigrant Jewish poet, who anglicizes his name to Edmond Gates, becomes a literary sensation, until he confesses that an elderly aunt wrote his verses. When poems are published under her name after her poverty-induced death, the same gift that when considered his was declared "seminal and hard" is dismissed as "a spinster's one-dimensional vision." Along with satirizing associations between sexuality and artistry, Ozick condemns Gates for rejecting kin and heritage. He lives out the rest of his life in penitential drag and dies a suicide.

The aging Yiddish poet Herschel Edelshtein of "Envy: Or, Yiddish in America" is in futile pursuit of a translator who would free him from the obscurity of writing in a dying language; meanwhile, he rails against popular American Jewish novelists, for whom history is a "vacuum." In "The Suitcase," a notable German architect and his son's Jewish mistress engage in a paradigmic struggle, as Jew cannot allow Gentile to forget history, particularly its production of an Adolf Hitler.

Some critics have questioned the accessibility of Ozick's work, with its self-consciously Jewish style and content. Others find that its imaginative reach transcends its specifics of cultural origin.

SUGGESTED READINGS

Bloom, Harold, ed. *Cynthia Ozick: Modern Critical Views*. New York: Chelsea House, 1986.

Cohen, Sarah Blacher. *Cynthia Ozick's Comic Art: From Levity to Liturgy*. Bloomington: Indiana University Press, 1994.

Finkelstein, Norman. *The Ritual of New Creation: Jewish Tradition and Contemporary Literature*. Albany: State University of New York Press, 1992.

Kauvar, Elaine M. *Cynthia Ozick's Fiction: Tradition and Invention*. Bloomington: Indiana University Press, 1993.

Lowin, Joseph. *Cynthia Ozick*. Boston: Twayne, 1988.

Pinsker, Sanford. *The Uncompromising Fiction of Cynthia Ozick*. Columbia: University of Missouri Press, 1987.

Rosenberg, Ruth. "The Ghost Story as Aggada: Cynthia Ozick's 'The Pagan Rabbi' and Sheindel's Scar." In *Haunting the House of Fiction: Feminist Perspectives on Ghost Stories by American Women*, edited by Lynette Carpenter and Wendy K. Kolmar. Knoxville: The University of Tennessee Press, 1991.

Walden, Daniel, ed. *The Changing Mosaic: From Cahan to Malamud, Roth, and Ozick*. Albany: State University of New York Press, 1993.

———. *The World of Cynthia Ozick*. Kent, Ohio: Kent State University Press, 1987.

—*Amy Allison*

Grace Paley

BORN: New York, New York; December 11, 1922

Paley's short stories and poems are among the finest contemporary Jewish American and feminist fiction.

TRADITIONS: Jewish

PRINCIPAL WORKS: *The Little Disturbances of Man: Stories of Men and Women in Love*, 1959; *Enormous Changes at the Last Minute*, 1974; *Later the Same Day*, 1985; *Leaning Forward*, 1985; *Long Walks and Intimate Talks*, 1991 (with paintings by Vera B. Williams); *New and Collected Poems*, 1992; *Just as I Thought*, 1998

Grace Paley began writing short stories in the mid-1950's, in her thirties, after having two children. She was born to Russian Jewish immigrants and was educated at Hunter College and New York University. She studied poetry with the famous British poet W. H. Auden. In 1942, she married Jess Paley, a veteran, freelance photographer, and cameraman.

After the war, the couple moved to lower Manhattan, where Paley has resided since. Her early interest in poetry and her ability as a storyteller and listener led her to write about her family experiences. Growing up as the Depression waned, Paley was optimistic, and her choice to marry and have children was made with the same liveliness and independence as was her decision to write. One of her first stories, "Goodbye and Good Luck," shows boldness in protagonist Rosie Lieber's decision to live with a lover and marry late in life, despite the disapproval of her family.

In the fifteen years after the publication of *The Little Disturbances of Man*, there was little separation between her identity as writer and her identities as mother, teacher at Sarah Lawrence College, and peace activist. Paley's writings typically have a distinctive personal voice. Published in *Enormous Changes at the Last Minute*, the stories that flowed from her experiences as a mother, family member, New Yorker, activist, and teacher include "A Subject of Childhood" and "Faith in a Tree," which focus on the attachment between mother and child and on the lives of women trying to end war and protect the future through peaceful protests.

Influenced by the sounds of New York neighborhoods, the identities of her characters also include many cultures and dialects—Yiddish, black, and Puerto Rican, for example. The themes of listening, voice, and telling one's story occur throughout much of her work. Stories such as "A Conversation with My Father," "The Story Hearer," and "Zagrowsky Tells" echo the conversations of her Jewish parents, and feature one or more characters–most often women or Jewish Americans–who must shape narratives as a way of shaping their history and the world.

In 1972, Paley and her husband were divorced, and Grace married her friend and co-activist Bob Nichols. Her reputation as a writer burgeoned after 1974, and her interest in women's lives and identities was widely recognized as feminist. In her latest works, Paley continues to explore identity as a function of vocal expression.

Grace Paley (Dorothy Marder)

Enormous Changes at the Last Minute

TYPE OF WORK: Short fiction
FIRST PUBLISHED: 1974

In Paley's *Enormous Changes at the Last Minute*, identity is a personal and a social issue in the struggle for a peaceful world. Most of the characters in this short-story collection are middle-aged women, such as Faith Darwin, who resembles, but is not intended to be, Paley's alter ego; others are simply those about whom stories are told—the children who have died or suffered from neglect, poverty, drug abuse, and the Vietnam War.

The main characters in these stories act with defiance and hope. In "Enormous Changes at the Last Minute," Alexandra is a middle-aged social worker who accidentally becomes pregnant through a liaison with Dennis, a cabdriver, poet, and commune member. Instead of joining the commune, Alexandra invites several of her pregnant clients to come live with her, a "precedent in social work which would not be followed or even mentioned in state journals for about five years." In the story "Wants," the woman narrator meets with her ex-husband, who criticizes her, telling her that she'll "always want nothing." In answer to herself and the reader, she recites the things she has wanted in her life, including ending the war before her children grew up. In "The Long-Distance Runner," Faith Darwin takes a long run through her old neighborhood and ends up living with the black family who now occupies her childhood apartment. All three of these women examine themselves midway, finding, as Faith does, that a "woman inside the steamy energy of middle age" may learn "as though she was still a child what in the world is coming next."

The collection's most acclaimed story, "A Conversation with My Father," features Faith, who, in dialogue with her father (modeled after Paley's father, I. Goodside, M.D.), invents the story of a middle-aged woman who becomes a junkie trying to identify with her son's generation. Faith's father laments the "end of a person," but is more upset when Faith adds her characteristic openness: In the "after-story life," the junkie becomes a "receptionist in a storefront community clinic." On one hand, Faith's response is emblematic of the way in which Paley's characters will not, as Faith's father exclaims, look tragedy "in the face." On the other hand, other stories in the collection—namely, "The Little Girl," "Gloomy Tune," and "Samuel"—do precisely that. These stories study the identities of the victimized—the teenage girl who is raped and strangled by a drug addict, the neglected boy branded in violence and delinquency, the black boy dying in a freak subway accident. "Never again will a boy exactly like Samuel be known," states the narrator.

With the publication of *Enormous Changes at the Last Minute*, Paley's reputation as a writer burgeoned. Her unique blend of poetic concision and concern for women's contributions to the future makes her an important feminist voice in contemporary literature.

Later the Same Day

TYPE OF WORK: Short fiction
FIRST PUBLISHED: 1985

Paley's *Later the Same Day* contains the stories of people speaking in the varied dialects of New York City. In these stories, identity is formed through people's acts and through their unique stories. As in Paley's earlier collection, *Enormous Changes at the Last Minute*, Faith Darwin is a recurring character, but here she is the mature woman, looking back at her life. In "The Story Hearer," for instance, Faith is asked to tell her lover, Jack, the story of her day. Despite her effort to "curb [her] cultivated individualism," she ends up sidetracking, watering her "brains with time spent in order to grow smart private thoughts." Jokingly, Faith comments on men's love of beginnings, and thus suggests that women move through stories and time quite differently, tempted by the private, rather than the "public accounting" of life. Similarly, in "Zagrowsky Tells," "Lavinia: An Old Story," and "In This Country, but in Another Language, My Aunt Refuses to Marry the Men Everyone Wants Her To," identity is a matter of individual stories told in first-person narratives and ethnic dialects.

In "The Story Hearer," Faith wants to rise above her time and name, but finds herself "always slipping and falling down into them, speaking their narrow language." In "The Expensive Moment," Faith's friends and families respond to the aftereffects of China's Cultural Revolution, relating their experiences to America's "revolutions" of the 1960's. A visiting Chinese woman quickly identifies herself as still a Communist, but later in the story, another Chinese woman asks about children and "how to raise them." Like Faith and other mothers in Paley's fiction, these women "don't know the best way." In a world and country divided by different voices, different genders, and different politics, there is still possibility for community and for common identities. "Friends" pays tribute to Faith's dying friend Selena, and the circle of women who go to visit her. Dying sets her apart from the others, but Selena is a mother, as are they, of a child in a generation "murdered by cars, lost to war, to drugs, to madness."

Later the Same Day was highly acclaimed by critics for its sensitivity to human and ethnic identity and for its experiments with storytelling. It continues to be significant in light of feminist concern with world peace, relationships among women, theories of women's language, and the importance of finding one's own voice.

SUGGESTED READINGS

Arcana, Judith. *Grace Paley's Life Stories: A Literary Biography*. Champaign: University of Illinois Press, 1993.

Baba, Minako. "Faith Darwin as Writer-Heroine: A Study of Grace Paley's

Short Stories." *Studies in American Jewish Literature* 7 (Spring, 1988): 40-54.

Bach, Gerhard, and Blaine H. Hall, eds. *Conversations with Grace Paley.* Jackson: University Press of Mississippi, 1997.

Gardiner, Judith Kegan. "On Female Identity and Writing by Women." In *Writing and Sexual Difference*, edited by Elizabeth Abel. Chicago: University of Chicago Press, 1982.

Isaacs, Neil. *Grace Paley: A Study of the Short Fiction.* Boston: Twayne, 1990.

Taylor, Jacqueline. *Grace Paley: Illuminating the Dark Lives.* Austin: University of Texas Press, 1990.

—Andrea J. Ivanov

Ann Petry

BORN: Old Saybrook, Connecticut; October 12, 1908
DIED: Old Saybrook, Connecticut; April 28, 1997

*Petry was the first African American woman to sell over a million
copies of a novel and the first African American woman to publish a
collection of short stories.*

TRADITIONS: African American

PRINCIPAL WORKS: *The Street*, 1946; *Country Place*, 1947; *The Drugstore Cat*,
1949; *The Narrows*, 1953; *Harriet Tubman, Conductor on the Underground
Railroad*, 1955; *Tituba of Salem Village*, 1964; *Legends of the Saints*, 1970; *Miss
Muriel and Other Stories*, 1971

Ann Lane Petry was born in Old Saybrook, Connecticut, to one of the town's
two African American families. Her father owned the village drugstore. A
1931 graduate of the University of Connecticut College of Pharmacy, for a
time Petry operated the pharmacy in Old Lyme, one of two family-owned
pharmacies. Petry grew up listening to stories of the African American
experience told by family, visiting friends, and relatives.

In 1938 Ann Lane was married to George Petry; they moved to New York
City. Petry left the pharmacy to follow a family tradition of storytelling. She
worked for two Harlem newspapers, the *Amsterdam News* and *People's Voice*.
Petry's first published work, "Marie of the Cabin Club," a tale of romance
and suspense, appeared under the pseudonym Arnold Petri in a Baltimore
weekly newspaper.

In 1943, "On Saturday the Siren Sounds at Noon," appeared in *Crisis*, a
magazine founded by W. E. B. Du Bois. This story brought her to the attention
of a book editor, who encouraged Petry to apply for the Houghton Mifflin
Literary Fellowship. In 1945, Petry entered and won the award. Her entry
would become the first chapters of the novel *The Street*.

Petry returned to Old Saybrook in 1947, the debut year of her second
novel, *Country Place*. In 1949, Petry launched a career as a children's and
young adults' writer with *The Drugstore Cat*. Other works for children and
young adults include *Harriet Tubman, Conductor on the Underground Railroad*,
Tituba of Salem Village, and *Legends of the Saints*.

Petry continued to write short stories while she published novels and
juvenile literature. Most of these stories were first published in African
American journals. With one previously unpublished story, "Mother Africa,"
these stories were collected in *Miss Muriel and Other Stories*.

The core of Petry's writing is racial identity, racism in America, and the experience of the African American woman. She is lauded by scholars and writers such as Toni Morrison, Alice Walker, Calvin Hernton, and Maya Angelou as a great storyteller in the African American literary canon.

The Street

TYPE OF WORK: Novel
FIRST PUBLISHED: 1946

The Street portrays the economic plight of African Americans in Northern cities. Themes of the novel include the problem of latchkey children, single parenting, and sexual oppression. This novel is perhaps the first written by an African American woman that probes the triple threat to African American women of race, gender, and class.

Much of the action of *The Street* takes place on 116th Street in Harlem in 1944. The central character, Lutie Johnson, leaves an unemployed womanizing husband and a nice frame house in Jamaica, New York. She moves to Harlem with her eight-year-old son, Bub. Lutie moves to the city to realize a comfortable life. Instead of an independent and prosperous life in New York City, Lutie finds herself living in a tenement. The janitor, William Jones, is a sociopath who lusts after Lutie. A major presence on the street is Mrs. Hedges, who runs a whorehouse. Qualified for clerical or secretarial employment, Lutie can find only menial work in a laundry. Instead of ownership of a piece of the American Dream, Lutie finds herself trapped in a nightmare.

Lutie becomes fair game for males. William makes advances and tries to molest Lutie. Junto, the white business partner of Mrs. Hedges, tries to seduce Lutie. Boots Smith, a musician in a bar that Junto owns, charms Lutie with visions of a better life with him. Boots lures her to his apartment, where he attempts to rape her. In an effort to ward off Boots's rape, Lutie kills him. Vowing revenge on Lutie, William tricks Bub into stealing and gets him in trouble with the law. Disillusioned and defeated, Lutie abandons Bub and runs away to Chicago.

Sexual politics drive the novel and rest on a concept that African American women are sexual prey. Negative sexual imagery of Lutie and by extension of all African American women is held by black and white males and by white females. A mixture of race and gender politics pushes Lutie over the edge. Lutie represents all the walking wounded of 116th Street and all of Harlem's downtrodden residents. *The Street* is not merely a graphic portrayal of what it means to be female and to be poor; it is also a story of protest and defeat. *The Street* presents the African American woman as the center of the family and the community. She shoulders the moral responsibilities of the race.

"The Witness"

TYPE OF WORK: Short fiction
FIRST PUBLISHED: 1971, in *Miss Muriel and Other Stories*

"The Witness" is a short story about a man who is a victim of and witness to a crime. He must flee and the crime must go unreported. This story is of one person and one incident but is also the story of American race relations. Wheeling, New York, is seeking an English teacher and needs an African American to demonstrate that the schools are integrated. Charles Woodruff, a retired English professor from Virginia College for Negroes and a recent widower, is hired. Looking to change his environment, Charles decides to integrate Wheeling after he hears the school board is looking for "one" African American.

Charles accepts an invitation extended by the Congregational minister to help a group of delinquent boys. Charles is frustrated by his failure to reach the boys but is not surprised. He feels he is viewed differently from other blacks. Charles believes he is being assigned the role of the model, or exemplary, black man.

Following a class with the boys, Charles tries to intervene when the boys assault a white girl but is himself assaulted. The boys kidnap Charles and the girl. When Charles refuses to "take his turn" with the girl, the boys throw Woodruff, his keys, glasses, and wallet from the car. As they drive off with the girl unconscious on the floor of the car, they taunt Charles that he is their only witness. The boys and Charles believe that because he is a black male he will be implicated in the crime.

Charles realizes he is not the perfect "one" African American for Wheeling, New York. There is no perfect "one." Charles must remain silent and flee Wheeling. As Charles drives away, he realizes that he is a "hot ho-daddy," what the boys called him during the assault. Charles realizes that that is all he will ever be in the eyes of America. Woodruff is not the exception, not different, not the "one."

SUGGESTED READINGS

Barrett, Lindon. *Blackness and Value: Seeing Double.* New York: Cambridge University Press, 1999.

Bell, Bernard. *The Afro-American Novel and Its Tradition.* Amherst: University of Massachusetts Press, 1987.

Carby, Hazel. *Reconstructuring Womanhood: The Emergence of the Afro-American Woman Novelist.* New York: Oxford University Press, 1987.

Clark, Keith. "A Distaff of a Dream Deferred? Ann Petry and the Art of Subversion." *African American Review* 26 (Fall, 1992): 495-505.

Clarke, Cheryl. "Ann Petry and the Isolation of Being Other." *Belles Letters* 5 (Fall, 1989): 36.

Hernton, Calvin. *The Sexual Mountain and Black Women Writers.* Garden City, N.Y.: Doubleday, 1987.

Holladay, Hilary. *Ann Petry.* New York: Twayne, 1996.

Madden, David. "Commentary." *The World of Fiction.* Chicago: Holt, Rinehart and Winston, 1990.

Park, You-me, and Gayle Wald. "Native Daughters in the Promised Land: Gender, Race, and the Question of Separate Spheres." *American Literature* 70, no. 3 (September, 1998): 607.

Petry, Ann. "A MELUS Interview: Ann Petry–The New England Connection." Interview by Mark Wilson. *MELUS* 15, no. 2 (Summer, 1988): 71-84.

Pryse, Marjorie, and Hortense Spillers, eds. *Conjuring: Black Fiction and Literary Tradition.* Bloomington: Indiana University Press, 1989.

–Muriel W. Brailey

Chaim Potok

BORN: New York, New York; February 17, 1929

Potok has presented issues and concerns in Jewish (especially Hasidic) identity to a large reading audience.

TRADITIONS: Jewish

PRINCIPAL WORKS: *The Chosen*, 1967; *The Promise*, 1969; *My Name Is Asher Lev*, 1972; *In the Beginning*, 1975; *Wanderings: Chaim Potok's History of the Jews*, 1975; *The Book of Lights*, 1981; *Davita's Harp*, 1985; *The Gift of Asher Lev*, 1990; *I Am the Clay*, 1992; *The Tree of Here*, 1993; *The Sky of Now*, 1995; *Zebra and Other Stories*, 1998

Chaim Potok was born and reared in New York City. His writings reveal a wealth of learning, due in part to his impressive academic credentials; he is a rabbi and holds a doctorate from the University of Pennsylvania. His eight novels, various plays, one nonfiction historical text, and two children's books are concerned with Jewish (often Hasidic) characters who are challenged by the conflicting identities of their cultures as Americans, Jews, Hasids, family members, and post-World War II citizens of the world.

The Chosen and its sequel, *The Promise*, confront issues of value and identity. The novels examine the tensions between Orthodox and Hasidic Jews. An injury in a baseball game initiates a friendship between Reuven Malter, pitcher on the Orthodox team whose father is a fervent Zionist, and Danny Saunders, batter on the Hasid team who is heir to the rebbe position of his father. *The Chosen* has an ironic conclusion; Reuven Malter decides to become an Orthodox rabbi, but Danny Saunders decides, after much family pain, to become a secular psychologist, a "tzaddik for the world," as his father finally understands.

Potok's most critically acclaimed novel, *My Name Is Asher Lev*, details the struggle for personal identity of a young Hasidic boy who struggles between his love for family and religion and his obligation as an artist to study and create. The sequel to this novel, *The Gift of Asher Lev*, did not appear until nearly two decades later. It tells of an adult Asher Lev, married and with children, who must confront again his unresolved status in the Brooklyn Hasidic community when the death of a family member requires his return.

In the early and mid-1990's, Potok moved beyond the genre of the novel to write four plays, which were locally produced in Philadelphia, and two works of children's literature (*The Tree of Here* and *The Sky of Now*), which enjoyed critical acclaim.

Chaim Potok (Jerry Bauer)

My Name Is Asher Lev

TYPE OF WORK: Novel
FIRST PUBLISHED: 1972

My Name Is Asher Lev, perhaps Potok's greatest novel, is an excellent example of the *Künstlerroman,* which is a novel about an artist's development. It confronts issues of Jewish and family identity in the post-Holocaust world. Asher Lev is a child prodigy artist, the only child of a Hasidic Jewish couple that lives in the Crown Heights section of Brooklyn. Aryeh Lev, Asher's father, serves as a personal emissary for the *rebbe* or tzaddik, the "righteous one" or religious leader of the Hasidic community.

The Orthodox Hasidic Jewish culture into which Asher is born approves of creativity only in the context of interpretation of Talmudic passages. Asher finds it difficult, and at times embarrassing, to follow his muse; he finds it natural to draw and to create pictures. Rivkeh Lev, Aryeh's mother, initially supports Asher's desire to draw, but she soon sides with her husband, who believes that drawing and the fine arts are products of a gentile culture. In the years during and immediately following World War II, Aryeh Lev travels the world to minister to Hasidic Jews who have been displaced by the Nazi Holocaust. Since Hasids believe that the Jewish state will be re-created in Israel only with the coming of the Messiah, who has not yet arrived, Hasidic Jews generally did not support the creation of the state of Israel in 1948. Aryeh travels about the world for the tzaddik, defending himself and his spiritual leader from the arguments of Zionist Jews and gentiles and attempting to do good works. He returns to a household in Brooklyn where his son is neglecting study of the Talmud because of his personal obsession with art and aesthetics.

The tzaddik, however, is wise enough to allow Asher to follow his destiny and to mediate between his conflicting identities. The tzaddik arranges for Jacob Kahn, an expatriate from the Hasidic community and a world-renowned sculptor, to serve as Asher's artistic mentor. Asher's apprenticeship as an artist culminates with a midtown New York showing of his work. Central to the showing is a pair of paintings, *Brooklyn Crucifixion I* and *Brooklyn Crucifixion II*, which show his mother, crucified in the venetian blinds of their apartment, her face split into "Picassoid" thirds, looking to the father, the son, and the street. The works assure Asher's reputation as a great artist but also assure, because of their religious content, that he will have to leave his Hasidic community in Brooklyn, as he does at the end of the novel. With the tzaddik's blessing, he goes to Paris to board with a Hasidic family and to continue to worship and define himself as a Hasidic Jew artist.

SUGGESTED READINGS

Abramson, Edward A. *Chaim Potok.* New York: Macmillan, 1986.

Berenson, Bernard. *Contemporary Jewish Fiction.* New York: Gordon & Breach, 1976.

Buber, Martin. *Hasidism and Modern Man.* New York: Humanities Press International, 1988.

Davenport, Guy. "Collision with the Outside World." *The New York Times Book Review,* April 16, 1972, 5, 18.

Idel, Moshe. *Hasidism: Between Ecstasy and Magic.* Albany: State University of New York Press, 1995.

Nissenson, Hugh. "The Spark and the Shell." *The New York Times Book Review*, May 7, 1967, 4-5, 34.

Safran, Bezalel. *Hasidism: Continuity or Innovation?* Cambridge, Mass.: Harvard University Press, 1988.

Sternlicht, Sanford V. *Chaim Potok: A Critical Companion.* Westport, Conn.: Greenwood Press, 2000.

—Richard Sax

John Rechy

BORN: El Paso, Texas; March 10, 1934

Rechy explores the intersection of Chicano, gay, and Roman Catholic identities in his autobiographical fiction.

TRADITIONS: Mexican American
PRINCIPAL WORKS: *City of Night,* 1963; *Numbers,* 1967; *This Day's Death,* 1970; *The Sexual Outlaw: A Documentary,* 1977; *Bodies and Souls,* 1983; *The Miraculous Day of Amalia Gómez,* 1991; *The Coming of Night,* 1999

With the publication of his first novel, *City of Night,* John Rechy commenced a lifelong process of self-analysis. "My life," Rechy stated, "is so intertwined with my writing that I almost live it as if it were a novel." In particular, Rechy examines the ways in which gay sexuality, Chicano and European American heritages, and the strictures of the Roman Catholic Church struggle and sometimes harmonize with one another despite incompatibilities. Rechy writes what he calls "autobiography as fiction" in order to construct parables of spiritual salvation and damnation. Alternately remote from or near to God, family, and human connection, Rechy's protagonists struggle against self-absorption and the fear of death.

Rechy's parents immigrated to the southwestern United States during the Mexican Revolution. Rechy grew up torn between his father's stern sense of defeat in the face of anti-Mexican discrimination and his mother's intense protection of her son. The combination of his father's Scottish heritage and his mother's traditional Mexican background made Rechy intensely aware of his status as a person of mixed ancestry in the El Paso of his youth.

Conflicts and pressures at home caused him to move into a narcissistic remoteness that found comfort in the emotional distance of purchased sex. Wandering the country after high school, Rechy worked as a male prostitute in New York, Los Angeles, San Francisco, Chicago, and New Orleans. These experiences as a hustler became the material for *City of Night.* This first-person narrative of sexual and spiritual salvation combines an unapologetic depiction of the sexual underground. The work features a sympathetic protagonist's search for ultimate connection and caring.

Set against either the urban indifference of Los Angeles or the unforgiving landscape of the desert Southwest, Rechy's novels explore the thematic connections between sex, soul, and self. In subsequent works–in particular, *This Day's Death* and *The Miraculous Day of Amalia Gómez–*Rechy has extended his explorations of the spirit to the particulars of Chicano family and culture.

Rechy's autobiographical fictions chart the intersections of ethnic, sexual, regional, and religious identities. He journeys across the Southwestern landscape, through sex and spirit, along the night streets of Los Angeles, and through his own memories of growing up in El Paso.

City of Night
TYPE OF WORK: Novel
FIRST PUBLISHED: 1963

Based on the author's experiences, *City of Night* explores sexuality and spirituality as they develop during the protagonist's quest for salvation. Combining Chicano heritage, autobiographical material, and a poetic rendering of the restless loneliness of America's sexual underground, *City of Night*–Rechy's first and best-known novel–investigates difficulties and rewards of an individual's search to claim the many identities that intersect in a single life.

The unnamed protagonist's "journey through nightcities and nightlives–looking for . . . some substitute for salvation" begins with his childhood in El Paso, Texas. Rechy draws on stark, lonely imagery (the fiercely unforgiving wind, the father's inexplicable hatred of his son, the mother's hungry love) to portray a childhood and adolescence denied any sense of connection and certainty. Disconnected and detached from his home, the protagonist stands before the mirror confusing identity with isolation. He asserts a narcissistic removal from the world ("I have only me!") that his quest at first confirms, then refutes.

The first-person narrative chronicles the protagonist's wanderings through New York City, Los Angeles, Hollywood, San Francisco, Chicago, and New Orleans. For Rechy, these various urban settings are "one vast City of Night" fused into the "unmistakable shape of loneliness." Working as a male prostitute, the protagonist navigates this landscape, portraying the types of sexual and spiritual desperation he encounters along the way. His journey is a pilgrimage first away from home and then back to it, as he accepts the possibility that he might come to terms with his family, his childhood, and himself.

City of Night interweaves chapters that describe the geographies of the cities the protagonist passes through with chapters that portray people condemned to these dark cities. Sometimes humorous, sometimes bitter, sometimes indifferent, these portraits of people trapped in the loneliness and cruelty of the cities mirror the protagonist's quest. He is like and unlike the denizens of this world.

In New Orleans during Mardi Gras, the protagonist encounters and rejects his first sincere invitation to love: the "undiscovered country which may not even exist and which I was too frightened even to attempt to discover." This invitation nevertheless triggers the narrator's search for redemption and salvation. The memory of his rejection of Jeremy's love haunts him. Caught up in the festivity of the carnival, surrounded by masked revelers and cathedrals, the protagonist affirms the possibility for change.

He returns to El Paso. Exposed to the West Texas wind, "an echo of angry childhood," the protagonist acknowledges uncertainty, the need for hope, and renewal. Rechy leaves the culmination of this search unresolved, a matter of existential self-definition. Combining ethnic, sexual, and spiritual identities, *City of Night* establishes important themes that Rechy explores in greater depth in later works. *City of Night* represents a pioneering look at the interdependency of multiple identities in an individual's search for meaning.

This Day's Death
TYPE OF WORK: Novel
FIRST PUBLISHED: 1970

This Day's Death, Rechy's third novel, explores Chicano identity and gay sexuality. Unlike other novels by Rechy, however, *This Day's Death* does not initially embody the two identities in one complex character. Instead, the novel shuttles—like its protagonist—between two identities (Chicano and gay) in two separate and yet interdependent situations (El Paso and Los Angeles). Known for acknowledging the autobiographical origins of his fiction, Rechy skillfully illustrates how identities develop, sometimes demanding a person's attention despite that person's effort of will to ignore or deny a given identity.

West Texas and Los Angeles are two poles of identity for Rechy; the one is bound up with his Chicano upbringing and his family, the other with sexual freedom and discovery. As the novel opens, Jim Girard is not gay. He has a fiancée and a promising career in law. His arrest on a lewd conduct charge is a mistake. He keeps his ongoing prosecution on that charge a secret from his mother, who is ill in El Paso. In the course of the novel, Jim recalls his Chicano upbringing. Jim also acknowledges and acts on previously unacknowledged desires for other men. Thus, he gradually becomes gay and Chicano, an embodiment of a complex intersection of identities and an opportunity for Rechy to explore the intertwined roots of self.

Bound up with guilt, pretense, and hypochondria, Girard's "terrible love" for his mother ties him to a childhood and a life that he recognizes as familiar but loathes. He knows that "she will brand each such day with memories he will carry like deep cuts forever." Like other mother-son relationships in Rechy's fiction, the relationship between Girard and his mother is an intense, stifling entanglement of need and rejection. Rechy utilizes the West Texas landscape (the wind, the sky, the desert) to impart a sense of loneliness and austerity that surrounds and amplifies Girard's life with his mother. This love-hate relationship becomes the foundation of the novel, ironically suggesting that identity is inextricably connected to relationship rather than to the isolation that Girard maintains at the beginning of the novel.

This Day's Death is an ironic coming-out story in which circumstances collude to reveal a gay man to himself. Found guilty of the crime, and therefore unable to pursue his career, Jim returns to the park where he was arrested and finds himself accepting, even celebrating desires he never before acknowledged. On one level, the novel advocates social reform, depicting an innocent man convicted of a crime that is not really criminal. On another level, *This Day's Death* is an analysis of the personal and bittersweet complex of experiences from which identities arise. *This Day's Death* acknowledges identities and their complexity. To be Chicano and gay is a burdensome and miraculous combination. Girard's relationship with his mother and whatever relationships he develops from his newly accepted desires will be tinged with joy and sadness, liberation and obligation. "The terrible love left empty" once his mother dies will be a necessary, affirming fact of having cared for his mother.

SUGGESTED READING

Isherwood, Charles. "Beyond the Night." *The Advocate*, no. 718 (October 15, 1996): 58-62.

Moore, Harry T., ed. *Contemporary American Novelists.* Carbondale: Southern Illinois University Press, 1964.

–Daniel M. Scott III

Ishmael Reed

BORN: Chattanooga, Tennessee; February 22, 1938

Reed has created a rich, unique literary synthesis from such diverse elements as African folktales, Caribbean ritual, and European culture.

TRADITIONS: African American, American Indian
PRINCIPAL WORKS: *The Free-Lance Pallbearers*, 1967; *Yellow Back Radio Broke-Down*, 1969; *Mumbo Jumbo*, 1972; *The Last Days of Louisiana Red*, 1974; *Flight to Canada*, 1976; *The Terrible Twos*, 1982; *Reckless Eyeballing*, 1986; *Airing Dirty Laundry*, 1993; *Japanese by Spring*, 1996; *The Reed Reader*, 2000

Ishmael Reed's writing can be said to mirror his own multiethnic descent, which includes African American, Native American, and Irish. His stepfather, Bennie Stephen Reed (an autoworker), later adopted him. He married Priscilla Rose in 1960; they were divorced in 1970. Reed has two children–Timothy and Brett–from his first marriage and a daughter, Tennessee Maria, by his second.

Early in his life his family moved to Buffalo, New York. He attended the State University of New York at Buffalo from 1956 to 1960 but was not graduated. He has published books of essays and poetry, but he is primarily known as a novelist. He has edited two multicultural anthologies: *Nineteen Necromancers from Now* (1970) and *Calafia: The California Poetry* (1979). He moved to Berkeley, California, where he taught at the University of California, and he served as a visiting professor or writer-in-residence at many other schools.

Reed's first novel, *The Free-Lance Pallbearers*, shows most of the elements for which his writing is known. It is the wildly picaresque and often scatological tale of the adventures of an African American, Bukka Doopeyduk, in Harry Sam, a city that reflects and exaggerates the most repressive aspects of Christian, European culture.

Reed's best-known novel, *Mumbo Jumbo*, uses the conventions of the detective story. Papa LaBas–whose name, typically for Reed, refers to the Voodoo god Papa Legba and French writer Joris-Karl Huysmans's decadent novel *Là-Bas* (1891; *Down There*, 1924)–investigates an alleged plague called Jes Grew, which turns out to be spontaneous joy, opposed to the grim power structure of monotheistic European culture.

Reed is widely praised for his style, his imaginative story construction, and his masterly use of elements from many cultural backgrounds, but he is often attacked by African American and feminist critics. He has continually satirized other African Americans, most notably in *The Last Days of Louisiana Red*, in which he refers to many of them as "Moochers." His criticisms of feminism, most notably in *Reckless Eyeballing*, are widely considered to be misogynist. *Japanese by Spring* satirizes the politics of the university.

Ishmael Reed (James Lerager)

God Made Alaska for the Indians
TYPE OF WORK: Essays
FIRST PUBLISHED: 1982

God Made Alaska for the Indians, a collection of essays, is a short book, but it manages to pack into its 130 pages many of the widely varied interests of one of the most interesting multicultural figures on the American literary scene. Reed is primarily thought of as an African American writer, but he is also much aware of his Native American ancestry. This dual viewpoint informs the title essay, a lengthy account of political and legal conflicts over the use of Alaskan lands. Reed sympathizes with the Sitka Tlingit Indians, but he realizes that the question is complicated, with other tribes opposing them.

Reed is, as always, critical of the white establishment, and he demonstrates that supposedly benign conservationist forces such as the Sierra Club can be as uncaring of the interests and customs of the indigenous population as any profit-maddened capitalist corporation. An afterword informs the reader that the Sitka Tlingits finally won.

"The Fourth Ali" covers the second fight between Muhammad Ali and Leon Spinks, late in Ali's career. There is little description of the actual fight, and one learns little more than that Ali won. Reed emphasizes the fight as spectacle, describing the followers, the hangers-on, and Ali's near-mythic role.

In the brief "How Not to Get the Infidel to Talk the King's Talk," Reed demolishes the theory that the supposed linguistic flaws of Black English keep African Americans from social advancement by pointing to the success of such verbally challenged European Americans as Gerald R. Ford and Nelson A. Rockefeller.

"Black Macho, White Macho" attacks some of the male-supremacist views Reed has been accused of holding, pointing out that such views are particularly dangerous in those with access to atomic weapons. "Race War in America?" makes some strong points about racial attitudes in the United States, in the then-pressing context of worry about the minority government in South Africa. In "Black Irishman" Reed, who has always refused to consider himself anything but an African American, looks at his Irish ancestry.

Perhaps the most interesting essay in the book is the last, "American Poetry: Is There a Center?" Reed recounts the controversies over a poetry center set up in Colorado by an Asian religious leader. The center's supporters made claims that it represented a focal point of all that is good in American poetry. Reed replies with his uncompromising view that the genius of American art can be found in the works of all races and cultures.

New and Collected Poems
TYPE OF WORK: Poetry
FIRST PUBLISHED: 1988

Reed is primarily known as a novelist. Most critical works about him deal with his fiction, and the leading books about contemporary African American poetry mention him only in passing. His poetry, however, repays reading and study—for the light it casts on his novels, for its treatment of the Hoodoo religion, and for the same verbal facility and breadth of reference that is praised in his fiction.

New and Collected Poems includes the earlier works *Conjure* (1972), *Chattanooga* (1973), and *A Secretary to the Spirits* (1977). *Conjure*, Reed's first and longest book of poems, is a mixed bag. Filled with typographical tricks that Reed later all but abandoned, it also has moments of striking wit, like the comparison of the poet to a fading city in "Man or Butterfly" or the two views of "history" in "Dualism: In Ralph Ellison's *Invisible Man*."

Conjure largely deals with the Hoodoo religion, Reed's idiosyncratic combination of ancient Egyptian and contemporary North American elements with the Caribbean religion of vodun, or Voodoo, itself a mix of Yoruba and Christian elements. In "The Neo-HooDoo Manifesto," Reed invokes American musicians, from jazz and blues greats to white rock and rollers, as exemplars of a religious approach based on creativity and bodily pleasure. Hoodoo is polytheistic, excluding only those gods who claim hegemony over the others. Reed's main disagreement with vodun springs from its acceptance of the "dangerous paranoid pain in the neck . . . cop-god from the git-go, Jeho-vah." The history of Hoodoo is outlined in Reed's novel *Mumbo Jumbo* (1972). Its view of all time as synchronous informs the setting of *Flight to Canada* (1976), in which airplanes coexist with plantation slavery, but the fullest expression of Hoodoo's spirit and aesthetic is given in *Conjure*.

Chattanooga is named for Reed's hometown, and the title poem is a paean to the area where Reed grew up and its multicultural heritage. "Railroad Bill, a Conjure Man" is a charming account of how the hero of an old-fashioned trickster tale deals with Hollywood. *A Secretary to the Spirits* is a short book with a few impressive works in it, notably, the first poem, "Pocodonia," expanding what seems to have been a traditional blues song into something far more complex and strange.

The work since *A Secretary to the Spirits* appears in the last section of *New and Collected Poems*, "Points of View." The quality is mixed, but the outrage and the wit that characterize so much of Reed's work can be found in this last section, as in "I'm Running for the Office of Love."

SUGGESTED READINGS

Clark, Tom. *The Great Naropa Poetry Wars.* Santa Barbara, Calif.: Cadmus, 1980.

Dick, Bruce Allen, ed., with Pavel Zemliansky. *The Critical Response to Ishmael Reed.* Westport, Conn.: Greenwood Press, 1999.

Elias, Amy. "Oscar Hijuelos's *The Mambo Kings Play Songs of Love,* Ishmael Reed's *Mumbo Jumbo,* and Robert Coover's *The Public Burning.*" *Critique: Studies in Contemporary Fiction* 41, no. 2 (Winter, 2000).

Fox, Robert Eliot. *Conscientious Sorcerers: The Black Postmodernist Fiction of LeRoi Jones/Amiri Baraka, Ishmael Reed, and Samuel R. Delany.* Westport, Conn.: Greenwood Press, 1987.

Martin, Reginald. *Ishmael Reed and the New Black Aesthetic Critics.* New York: St. Martin's Press, 1988.

—Arthur D. Hlavaty

Adrienne Rich

BORN: Baltimore, Maryland; May 16, 1929

Rich is an articulate, conscious, and critical explorer of such subjects as feminism and lesbianism.

TRADITIONS: Jewish

PRINCIPAL WORKS: *A Change of World*, 1951; *The Diamond Cutters*, 1955; *Snapshots of a Daughter-in-Law*, 1963; *Necessities of Life*, 1966; *Leaflets*, 1969; *The Will to Change*, 1971; *Diving into the Wreck*, 1973; *Of Woman Born*, 1976; *The Dream of a Common Language*, 1978; *On Lies, Secrets, and Silence*, 1979; *A Wild Patience Has Taken Me This Far*, 1981; *Your Native Land, Your Life*, 1986; *Blood, Bread, and Poetry*, 1986; *Time's Power*, 1989; *An Atlas of the Difficult World: Poems, 1988-1991*, 1991; *What Is Found There*, 1993; *Dark Fields of the Republic: Poems, 1991-1995*, 1995; *Midnight Salvage: Poems, 1995-1998*, 1999

As a child, Adrienne Rich was encouraged to write poetry by her father. At Radcliffe College, she continued to study the formal craft of poetry as practiced and taught by male teachers. In 1951, Rich's first volume of poetry, *A Change of World*, was selected for the Yale Series of Younger Poets. Rich was praised as a fine poet and as a modest young woman who respected her elders. The poems in her first two collections are traditional in form, modeled on the male poets Rich studied.

At twenty-four, Rich married a Harvard professor. She had three children by the time she was thirty. The conflict between the traditional roles of mother and wife and her professional accomplishments left her frustrated. *Snapshots of a Daughter-in-Law* begins to express a woman's point of view. Rich moved to New York City in 1966 and became involved in civil rights and antiwar campaigns. In 1969, she separated from her husband, who committed suicide in 1970. During the 1970's, Rich became a radical feminist, active in the women's rights movement. The collections published during these years express these political themes.

Rich came out as a lesbian in 1976, and her collection *The Dream of a Common Language* includes explicitly lesbian poems. In the early 1980's, she moved to western Massachusetts with her companion, Michelle Cliff. Her essays and poetry with political themes were sometimes criticized as more didactic than artful. Rich continued to evolve politically and artistically. She moved to California, writing and teaching at Stanford University. Her books published in the 1990's confront the relationship of poetry and politics and issues of contemporary American life. Adrienne Rich's life and work have sought to balance the conflicting demands of poetry, which is her vocation, with the ideology of engagement that her life has brought to her art.

Poetry

FIRST PUBLISHED: *A Change of World*, 1951; *Snapshots of a Daughter-in-Law*, 1963; *Diving into the Wreck*, 1973; *The Dream of a Common Language*, 1978; *The Fact of a Doorframe: Poems Selected and New, 1950-1984*, 1984; *An Atlas of the Difficult World: Poems, 1988-1991*, 1991; *Dark Fields of the Republic: Poems, 1991-1995*, 1995

Rich's poetry traces the growth of a conscious woman in the second half of the twentieth century. Her first two books, *A Change of World* and *The Diamond Cutters* (1955), contain verses of finely crafted, imitative forms, strongly influenced by the modernist poets. *Snapshots of a Daughter-in-Law* is a transitional work in which Rich begins to express a woman's concerns. Her form loosens as well; she begins to experiment with free verse.

The collections *Necessities of Life* (1966), *Leaflets* (1969), and *The Will to Change* (1971) openly reject patriarchal culture and language. Experiments with form continue as she juxtaposes poetry and prose and uses multiple voices. With *Diving into the Wreck* Rich's poetry becomes clearly identified with radical feminism and lesbian separatism. A theme of the title poem is the need for women to define themselves in their own terms and create an alternative female language. *The Dream of a Common Language* was published after Rich came out as a lesbian and includes the explicitly sexual "Twenty-one Love Poems."

By the time of the publication of *A Wild Patience Has Taken Me This Far* (1981), the influence of Rich's poetry extended beyond art and into politics. As a woman in a patriarchal society, Rich expresses a fundamental conflict between poetry and politics, which occupies her poetic voice. The collections *Your Native Land, Your Life* (1986),

Adrienne Rich (Library of Congress)

Time's Power (1989), and *An Atlas of the Difficult World* address new issues while continuing to develop Rich's feminist concerns. The long poem "Sources" addresses Rich's Jewish heritage and the Holocaust. "Living Memory" addresses issues of aging. In *Dark Fields of the Republic*, Rich continues to develop her preoccupations with the relationship of poetry and politics and grapples with issues of contemporary American society.

Most critics have characterized Adrienne Rich's work as an artistic expression of feminist politics. Some critics feel that the politics overwhelm the lyricism of her art. It is generally accepted that she is an important and innovative voice in evolving political and artistic issues, especially feminism.

SUGGESTED READINGS

Cooper, Jane Roberta, ed. *Reading Adrienne Rich: Reviews and Re-visions, 1951-81.* Ann Arbor: University of Michigan Press, 1984.

Keyes, Claire. *The Aesthetics of Power: The Poetry of Adrienne Rich.* Athens: University of Georgia Press, 1986.

Martin, Wendy. *An American Triptych: Anne Bradstreet, Emily Dickinson, Adrienne Rich.* Chapel Hill: University of North Carolina Press, 1984.

Werner, Craig Hansen. *Adrienne Rich: The Poet and Her Critics.* Chicago: American Library Association, 1988.

Yorke, Liz. *Adrienne Rich: Passion, Politics, and the Body.* Thousand Oaks, Calif.: Sage Publications, 1997.

—Susan Butterworth

Mordecai Richler

BORN: Montreal, Quebec, Canada; January 27, 1931

Challenging the myths of his culture, Richler exposes the rottenness at the heart of the human condition.

TRADITIONS: Jewish

PRINCIPAL WORKS: *The Acrobats*, 1954; *Son of a Smaller Hero*, 1955; *A Choice of Enemies*, 1957; *The Apprenticeship of Duddy Kravitz*, 1959; *The Incomparable Atuk*, 1963; *Cocksure*, 1968; *St. Urbain's Horseman*, 1971; *Joshua Then and Now*, 1980; *Solomon Gursky Was Here*, 1989; *Barney's Version*, 1997

Mordecai Richler was born in a Jewish section of Montreal. His education at Jewish parochial schools reinforced his Jewish identity, and the French language that he spoke identified him as French Canadian. Richler would embrace neither identity comfortably.

He began writing seriously when he was fourteen. At about the same time, he rejected the family expectation that he become a rabbi and ceased his religious training. After high school, Richler attended Sir George Williams University in Montreal for two years, then grew restive and left for Paris in 1951 to join such other aspiring writers as Mavis Gallant and Terry Southern. The separation from his beginnings helped to sharpen the perspective on his heritage. He knew that escape from the past is impossible and even undesirable. After two years, an invitation to become writer-in-residence at his alma mater attracted him back to Montreal.

The Acrobats introduced concerns that would recur in much of Richler's later fiction: the place of Jews in contemporary society, the need for values, and the exercise of personal responsibility. Deciding that he would make his living solely by writing, Richler moved to England, where his next six novels were published. Most of these novels revealed their author as a severe, often shocking critic of the Jewish ghetto (*Son of a Smaller Hero*), of Jewish greed and ruthlessness (*The Apprenticeship of Duddy Kravitz*), of Canadian nationalism (*The Incomparable Atuk*), and of the North American entertainment industry (*Cocksure*). The writing often reflects a certain degree of ambivalence about the author's ethnic identity, with the need to reject dominating the inclination to affirm.

When Richler returned to Canada–to "the roots of his discontent"–in 1972, his many years of "exile" in Europe had heightened his own sense of self as a Jewish Canadian writer. Richler has not always seen himself as others saw him: abrasive, arrogant, and perverse. Richler has been described as an anti-Canadian Canadian and an anti-Semitic Jew. Richler sees himself as a moralist who writes out of a sense of "disgust with things as they are," who debunks the bankrupt values that characterize his culture and his ethnic community. His most recent books establish him as a more evenhanded critic of Jewish and Canadian identity, one who affirms the need for the bonds of family and community in an unstable, corrupt world.

Son of a Smaller Hero
TYPE OF WORK: Novel
FIRST PUBLISHED: 1955

Son of a Smaller Hero is the story of an angry young man's confused search for his identity. In what is generally regarded as an apprentice work, Richler presents a fairly realistic story of a rebellious and rather self-centered hero who struggles to escape the restrictive identity that his ethnic community and his society would place on him.

Noah Adler is a second-generation Canadian, born and raised in the Montreal Jewish ghetto. His family's strife and the religious and social stric-

Mordecai Richler (Christopher Morris)

tures of his milieu, which he finds stifling, impel him to leave in search of freedom and selfhood in the gentile world. That world, too, fails to fulfill the hero's quest. Through a literature class, Noah meets Professor Theo Hall, who befriends him and takes him into his home. Soon, Hall's wife, Miriam, does more than befriend their boarder and eventually leaves her husband to live with Noah. The romance, so passionately pursued by Noah at first, fades rather quickly when he discovers that the possessive love of and responsibility for a woman can turn into its own kind of ghetto.

In addition, the ghetto of his upbringing still has its hold on him. When his father dies in a fire, Noah abandons Miriam and returns to his family, no longer the adolescent rebel that he was. Neither has he become a quiescent conformist. When the Jewish community attempts to raise his feckless father to sainthood, he demurs. When his rich Uncle Max greedily tries to exploit the dead father's new status, Noah resists. When Noah discovers his grandfather's secret, repressed, lifelong love for a gentile woman he met years before in Europe, this clarifies Noah's own predicament. The ways of his family and of his ghetto community cannot be his. When Noah's ambitious mother becomes increasingly emotionally demanding, Noah knows that he cannot stay.

The story ends as it began: Noah leaves home, this time for Europe. He turns his back on his ailing, grasping mother and on his lonely, isolated grandfather. He turns his back on his restrictive ethnic community. The search for self continues, but it is a search permeated with ambivalence. Noah has found that he cannot affirm his identity apart from community, family, and place. His confusion and torment stem from his problem that he can neither embrace nor finally reject community, family, or place. He chooses to escape them for the time being, but his search for an independent identity leads finally to a sense of futility.

SUGGESTED READINGS

Coles Editorial Board. *"The Appenticeship of Duddy Kravitz" and Other Works: Notes.* Toronto: Coles, 1997.

Davidson, Arnold E. *Mordecai Richler.* New York: Frederick Ungar, 1983.

Ramraj, Victor J. *Mordecai Richler.* Boston: Twayne, 1983.

Sheps, G. David, ed. *Mordecai Richler.* New York: McGraw-Hill, 1971.

Woodcock, George. *Mordecai Richler.* Toronto: McClelland and Stewart, 1971.

–Henry J. Baron

Tomás Rivera

BORN: Crystal City, Texas; December 22, 1935
DIED: Fontana, California; May 16, 1984

Rivera's writings sparked an explosion of work about the Chicano identity and focused attention on the experiences of migrant workers.

TRADITIONS: Mexican American

PRINCIPAL WORKS: *Always and Other Poems*, 1973; *. . . y no se lo tragó la tierra/and the earth did not part*, 1971, rev. ed., 1977 (also translated as *and the earth did not devour him*, 1987); *The Harvest: Short Stories*, 1988; *The Searchers: Collected Poetry*, 1990

Tomás Rivera was the first winner of the Quinto Sol literary prize for the best Chicano work. His death cut short a life full of achievements and promise. Rivera was born to a family of migrant farmworkers in south Texas, and much of his writing is derived from his childhood experiences in a poor, Spanish-speaking, nomadic subculture.

Rivera began college in 1954, with concerns for his people motivating him to become a teacher. He earned his bachelor's degree in 1958 and two master's degrees, in 1964 and 1969, from Southwest Texas State University. He received his Doctorate in Romance Literatures in 1969 from the University of Oklahoma. His career as a college teacher and administrator included appointments in Texas at Sam Houston State University, Trinity University, and the University of Texas at San Antonio and at El Paso.

In 1979, Rivera became the youngest person and the first member of a minority group to be appointed chancellor of a campus of the University of California. Rivera spent his last five years at the helm of the University of California at Riverside.

Rivera's poems and short stories are included in many anthologies of Chicano or Latino literature. He is recognized as one of the first to give voice to the silent Latino underclass of the American Southwest. His works explore the difficulties of growing up, of sorting truth from myth, and of finding one's identity and self-esteem in the midst of oppressive poverty. The struggle to overcome internal and external difficulties is portrayed vividly in his novel *and the earth did not part* and in such stories as "Eva and Daniel," "The Harvest," and "Zoo Island."

and the earth did not part

TYPE OF WORK: Novel
FIRST PUBLISHED: . . . *y no se lo tragó la tierra/and the earth did not part*, 1971 (rev. ed. 1977; also translated as *and the earth did not devour him*)

And the Earth Did Not Part, Rivera's only published novel, exerted a great influence on the blossoming of Chicano literature. The book explores the psychological and external circumstances of a boy who is coming of age in a Mexican American migrant family. The novel is a collection of disjointed narratives, including twelve stories and thirteen vignettes, told with various voices. This unusual structure evokes impressions of a lifestyle in which the continuity of existence is repeatedly broken by forced migration, in which conflicting values tug at the emerging self, and in which poverty creates a deadening sameness that erases time.

The story begins with "The Lost Year," which indicates the boy has lost touch with his identity and with the reality of events. Several sections portray the dismal, oppressed condition of migrant farmworkers. "Hand in His Pocket" tells of a wicked couple—immigrants who prey on their own people. In "A Silvery Night," the boy first calls the devil, then decides that the devil does not exist. Religious awakening continues in the title chapter, in which the boy curses God and is not punished—the earth remains solid.

The nature of sin, the mystery of sex, and the injustices and tragedies visited upon his people are all confusing to the boy. Brief moments of beauty are eclipsed by injuries and horrible deaths. A mother struggles to buy a few Christmas presents for her children and is thwarted by the disturbing confusion and noise of the town. In a swindle, a family loses their only photograph of a son killed in the Korean War. Bouncing from place to place in rickety trucks, the workers lose all sense of continuity. The boy becomes a man, hiding under his house. The final scene offers a glimmer of hope, as he climbs a tree and imagines that someone in another tree can see him.

The simple language and humble settings make the book accessible, but the novel's unique structure and symbolism present challenges to the reader. *and the earth did not part* has been reprinted several times, and a retelling in English (*This Migrant Earth*, 1985) was published by Rolando Hinojosa. A film version, *and the earth did not swallow him*, was released in 1994.

SUGGESTED READINGS

Foster, David William. *Handbook of Latin American Literature*. New York: Garland, 1992.
Lattin, Vernon E., Rolando Hinojosa, and Gary D. Keller, eds. *Tomás Rivera, 1935-1984: The Man and His Work*. Tempe, Ariz.: Bilingual Review Press, 1988.
Olivares, Julian, ed. *International Studies of Tomás Rivera*. Houston, Tex.: Arte Público Press, 1986.

_____, ed. *Tomás Rivera: The Complete Works.* Houston, Tex.: Arte Público Press, 1991.

Rivera, Tomás. *The Man and His Work.* Edited by Vernon E. Lattin, Rolando Hinojosa, and Gary D. Keller. Tempe, Ariz.: Bilingual Review Press, 1988.

—Laura L. Klure

Richard Rodriguez

BORN: San Francisco, California; July 31, 1944

Rodriguez's autobiography explores the identity of one whose roots can be traced to two cultures.

TRADITIONS: Mexican American
PRINCIPAL WORKS: *Hunger of Memory: The Education of Richard Rodriguez,* 1982; *Days of Obligation: An Argument with My Mexican Father,* 1992

Richard Rodriguez's *Hunger of Memory* is a collection of essays tracing his alienation from his Mexican heritage. The son of Mexican American immigrants, Rodriguez was not able to speak English when he began school in Sacramento, California. The Catholic nuns who taught him asked that his parents speak English to him at home so that he could hear English spoken all the time. When his parents complied, Rodriguez experienced his first rupture between his original culture and his newly acquired culture. That initial experience compelled him to see the difference between "public" language–English–and "private" language–Spanish. To succeed in a world controlled by those who spoke English, to succeed in the public arena, Rodriguez learned that he had to choose public language over the private language spoken within his home. Hence he opted for alienation from his Mexican heritage and roots, a choice that he viewed with resignation and regret.

His educational journey continued as he proceeded to earn a master's degree and then to become a Fulbright scholar studying English Renaissance literature in London. At that time, he decided to leave academic life, believing that it provided an advantage to Mexican Americans at the expense of those who did not possess this hyphenated background.

Rodriguez proceeded to become an opponent of affirmative action, and details his opposition to this policy in *Hunger of Memory*. Another policy to which he voices his opposition is bilingual education. Believing that "public educators in a public schoolroom have an obligation to teach a public language," Rodriguez has used various opportunities–interviews, his autobiography, television appearances–to emphasize his view of the relationship between a person's identity in a majority culture and his or her need to learn the language of that culture.

Another component of Rodriguez's identity that he has explored through various means is his relationship with the Roman Catholic Church. Having been raised in a traditional Catholic home, he was accustomed to the symbols and language of the Catholic Church as they were before the changes that resulted from the Second Vatican Council, which convened in 1962. After this council, the rituals of the Church were dramatically simplified and the liturgy was changed from Latin to vulgar tongues, such as English. According to Rodriguez, these changes in the Roman Catholic Church challenged the identity of people whose early sense of self was shaped by traditional Catholicism.

A thoughtful and articulate writer regarding the tensions experienced by Mexican Americans growing up in America and by a Catholic struggling with the changes in the Catholic Church, Richard Rodriguez has given voice to the frequently unspoken difficulties of possessing a complex identity.

Hunger of Memory
TYPE OF WORK: Memoir
FIRST PUBLISHED: 1982

Hunger of Memory: The Education of Richard Rodriguez is a memoir that explores Rodriguez's coming-of-age in an America that challenges him to understand what it is to be a Mexican American and what it is to be a Catholic in America. At the heart of this autobiography is Rodriguez's recognition that his is a position of alienation, a position that he accepts with resignation and regret. As the title of this collection of autobiographical pieces suggests, he remembers his early childhood with nostalgia, while acknowledging that his coming-of-age has resulted in his displacement from that simple, secure life.

The most critical aspect of his education and his development of an adult self is language. He explores his first recollection of language in the opening essay, which describes his hearing his name spoken in English for the first time when he attends a Catholic elementary school in Sacramento, California. He is startled by the recognition that the impersonality and public quality of this announcement herald his own adoption of public language—English—at the expense of his private language—Spanish. Rodriguez has begun to be educated as a public person with a public language.

This education, as he recalls it, occurred before the advent of bilingual education, an event that Rodriguez soundly criticizes. In his view bilingual education prevents children from learning the public language that will be their passport to success in the public world, and he uses his own experience—being a bilingual child who was educated without bilingual education as it was introduced into the American school system in the 1960's—as an example.

Rodriguez offers himself as another example in criticizing affirmative action programs. Turning down offers to teach at various postsecondary educational institutions that he believed wanted to hire him simply because he was Latino, Rodriguez began what has been his persistent criticism of affirmative action policies in America.

Still another object of his criticism in *Hunger of Memory* is the Roman Catholic Church and its changed liturgy, language, and rituals. Recalling the religious institution that had shaped his identity, he regrets the changes that he believes have simplified and therefore diminished the mystery and majesty that he associates with the traditional Catholic Church. He is nostalgic about what has been lost while accepting the reality of the present.

In providing an account of his education, Rodriguez also provides an account of his profession: writing. From his early choice of a public language to his later choice to write about this decision, he paints a self-portrait of a man whose love of words and ideas compels him to explore his past. Rodriguez accepts the adult who writes in English and who writes about the person whose identity is defined by his struggle to find his own voice.

SUGGESTED READINGS

Rodriguez, Richard. "Mexico's Children." *The American Scholar* 55, no. 2 (Spring, 1986): 161-177.

Zwieg, Paul. *"Hunger of Memory: The Education of Richard Rodriguez."* *The New York Times Book Review*, February 28, 1982, 1.

—Marjorie Smelstor

Ninotchka Rosca

BORN: Manila, Philippines; 1946

Rosca was the first Filipina to publish a serious political novel in the United States.

TRADITIONS: Filipino American
PRINCIPAL WORKS: *Bitter Country and Other Stories*, 1970; *The Monsoon Collection*, 1983; *Endgame: The Fall of Marcos*, 1987; *State of War*, 1988; *Twice Blessed*, 1992

Ninotchka Rosca accepted as her pen name that of the Russian radical played in an American film by Greta Garbo. Rosca thought of herself as a militant liberal among the students at the University of the Philippines. Her columns as associate editor of *Graphic* magazine after 1968 reinforced her image as a controversial figure. Her first fiction complained about the political passivity of the educated elite, and she remained a friend of those former classmates who joined the New People's Army against the rule-by-decree of President Ferdinand Marcos. In 1973, shortly after Marcos declared martial law, she was arrested and placed for several months in Camp Crame Detention Center. She used her experience there to provide realistic detail for nine stories about parallels between military detention and a nation run under rules of "constitutional authoritarianism." *The Monsoon Collection* was published in Australia in order to safeguard its author.

Rosca found her role as a nationalist difficult when loyalty was defined as adhering to Marcos's rule. By 1977, Rosca had gone into political self-exile among relatives connected with the University of Hawaii at Maona, where she taught. Later she moved to New York City to be closer to opportunities within the publishing industry, despite her misgivings that several American presidents had sponsored Marcos's rise to power on the premise that he was anti-Communist. After his forced flight from the Philippines in February, 1986, she returned briefly to Manila and later, with *Endgame*, contributed to reportage on Marcos's final days.

Although Rosca remained in the United States, her focus on the Philippines did not falter. She became the U.S. representative of GABRIELA, an organization named after Gabriela Silang, an eighteenth century warrior who continued the revolt against Spain after her husband's death. GABRIELA in America protects overseas workers from various kinds of abuse. She has also maintained a column of commentary in *Filipinas*, a popular magazine on the West Coast. Since the late 1980's Rosca has written novels describing the militant role of youth organizations in the Philippines.

State of War
TYPE OF WORK: Novel
FIRST PUBLISHED: 1988

State of War's dominant story line portrays a failed attempt by young radicals to assassinate Philippine dictator Ferdinand Marcos (referred to only as The Commander). The book's larger concern is with the effect of centuries of colonialism on the Filipino people's search for national identity. Portions of the novel try to reconstruct the ancestry of the principal characters during centuries of Spanish rule and fifty years of American occupation. Even after independence is achieved in 1946, freedom still is withheld from the people by troops serving The Commander. "Internal colonialism," controlled by the Filipinos' own countryman, merely replaces the tyranny that formerly came from outside. Ninotchka Rosca describes a nation forever being betrayed and, therefore, forever in the process of only beginning to find itself.

The seriousness of the assassination attempt is masked by the resplendent color and the joyful sounds of the festival that surround the attempt. Annually, in the Ati-Atihan celebration, Filipinos celebrate the clash between the Spanish and the native islanders. Anna Villaverde, who during martial law once was detained by military authorities because of her closeness to Manolo Montreal, a radical oppositionist who is assumed dead, becomes aware that Colonel Urbano Amor, her original torturer, is securing the area for The Commander's visit. Anna is protected from exposure by Adrian, a young member of the elite class. Then he is captured, and under the influence of drugs he is forced to reveal parts of the plot. Trying to compensate for this betrayal by warning Anna, he becomes crippled when the bomb intended for The Commander explodes prematurely. As for Manolo Montreal, he is not dead after all but has joined forces with his previous captors. He is prepared to betray the plans of the young conspirators, but Anna manages to kill him. What begins as a festival of song and dance ends in a bloody melee with The Commander still alive and in charge.

The only hope for social change, the novel suggests, lies in Anna and Adrian's son, who will have to become a historian of the people and storyteller of collective memories and democratic ideals. He will be expected to serve as a reminder of the recurring frustration of Filipino hopes for self-definition during centuries of foreign rule. The novel's storyline is filled with intrigue from all sides, continuously defeating the examples of reform and of resistance that, historically, only relatively few rebellious nationalists have courageously provided. A persistent "state of war," Rosca implies, has long existed, and true independence has yet to be achieved. Anna's dream of a different future among peasants, who want only a right to the land that they till, is a declaration of faith rather than of hope. Romantic as Anna's expectations of democracy might seem to be under the circumstances, the only alternative is to surrender hope for a free society. It is not in her nature to give up the beliefs that make her life worth living; and in the author, she has found an ally.

Twice Blessed
TYPE OF WORK: Novel
FIRST PUBLISHED: 1992

Twice Blessed is a comic parable. It shares with Rosca's more dramatic *State of War* (1988) a lasting concern for "a nation struggling to be born." Its method is less confrontational than Rosca's earlier work, but it goes beyond mockery of President Ferdinand Marcos and First Lady Imelda Marcos who, on the novel's publication date, were already in exile in Hawaii. The basic satire exposes a phenomenon in Filipino culture larger than the behavior of a single ruling couple: instincts of the wealthy to preserve their power through arranged marriages. This hoarding of power, Rosca has long argued as a journalist, is the source not only of vast class differences but also of elitist willingness to collaborate with foreign enemies in order to survive. Through comic irony and despite the novel's farcical features, Rosca suggests that the greed responsible for putting dynastic wealth before the welfare of the people eventually can be self-destructive.

The sibling rule of Katerina and Hector Basbas in a tropical Pacific country is reminiscent of what several commentators have called the "conjugal dictatorship" of the Marcoses. Katerina's attempts to forget her humble beginnings resemble Imelda's well-publicized delusions of grandeur, and the collapse of a heavy crane on the roof of the inaugural structure seems inspired by the fatal collapse of the Manila International Film Festival building in 1983 because of haste in its construction. In addition, Imelda not only was actually considered Ferdinand's replacement if his health failed but also ran (unsuccessfully) as a presidential candidate in 1992. These are just a few of the historical parallels borrowed by Rosca to provide realistic dimensions to a tale that otherwise might seem farfetched. Reality can be much more outlandish than fiction.

Rosca's fictional account portrays what might have resulted had Hector crashed in his airplane, been lost, and been considered dead. His twin sister Katerina seems less to grieve his possible loss than suddenly to imagine herself as his replacement. Trying to forget her lowly origins, Katerina's ambition has only been whetted by her marriage to aristocratic Armand Gloriosa. Once dreams of individual glory have been placed before the nation's needs, corruption spreads even to such opponents to oppressive government as Teresa Tikloptihod. She is the headstrong daughter of a provincial governor who at first resisted strenuously collaboration with the tyranny of Basbas. Her independent thinking washes away like sand when she allies herself with Katerina. The military, in the person of Captain de Naval, also decides to grasp this unforeseen opportunity for its own advancement. Those events recall Marcos's secretary of defense, Ponce Enrile, who, having fallen out with Marcos, tried to ensure Marcos's defeat in the 1986 election. Enrile backed Corazon Aquino, although with the intent of establishing a government run by a military junta. Even with Hector's return, coups, countercoups (such as those suffered by Aquino during her rule), and the fortification of the presidential palace follow.

If this farce were to be taken at face value, the prospects for the Philippines would be grim. Rosca's witty, colorful style, however, makes the novel seem closer to light opera. Its "music" is very different from the gongs and drums of her novel about the attempted assassination of Marcos, *State of War*. The source of Rosca's implied hope in *Twice Blessed* seems to be that when greed becomes so deeply embedded in a small class of people, alliances among even the most powerful can turn to bitter rivalry, and the system of social oppression can self-destruct.

SUGGESTED READINGS

Casper, Leonard. "Four Filipina Writers." *Amerasia Journal*, Winter, 1998, 143.

_____. *In Burning Ambush: Essays, 1985-1990*. Metro Manila, Philippines: New Day, 1991.

_____. *Sunsurfers Seen from Afar: Critical Essays, 1991-1996*. Metro Manila, Philippines: Anvil, 1996.

—Leonard Casper

Philip Roth

BORN: Newark, New Jersey; March 19, 1933

Roth's comic fiction has consistently challenged definitions of Jewish identity in late twentieth century America.

TRADITIONS: Jewish

PRINCIPAL WORKS: *Goodbye, Columbus, and Five Short Stories,* 1959; *Letting Go,* 1962; *When She Was Good,* 1967; *Portnoy's Complaint,* 1969; *Our Gang,* 1971; *The Breast,* 1972; *The Great American Novel,* 1973; *My Life as a Man,* 1974; *Reading Myself and Others,* 1975 (expanded, 1985); *The Professor of Desire,* 1977; *Zuckerman Bound,* 1985 (containing *The Ghost Writer,* 1979; *Zuckerman Unbound,* 1981; *The Anatomy Lesson,* 1983; and *Epilogue: The Prague Orgy*); *The Counterlife,* 1986; *The Facts: A Novelist's Autobiography,* 1988; *Deception,* 1990; *Patrimony: A True Story,* 1991; *Operation Shylock: A Confession,* 1993; *Sabbath's Theater,* 1995; *American Pastoral,* 1997; *The Human Stain,* 2000

Philip Roth's youth in a largely Jewish neighborhood of Newark, New Jersey, established his first subject: the ambivalence felt by American Jews on facing assimilation into American culture, which entails the loss of much, possibly all, of their distinctive Jewishness. Roth grew up in a middle-class home where, he writes, "the Jewish family was an inviolate haven against every form of menace, from personal isolation to gentile hostility." Roth has been unwilling, however, simply to depict the Jewish family as a haven. His inclination to challenge Jewish American propriety and his extravagant comic imagination have won for him a controversial place in American letters. After an education at Bucknell University and the University of Chicago, Roth earned with the publication of *Goodbye, Columbus, and Five Short Stories* the National Book Award and condemnation as an anti-Semite by some Jewish leaders.

Roth's tendency to use details from his life in his fiction has invited misinterpretations of his work as autobiography. An unhappy and short-lived marriage to Margaret Martinson, for example, was translated by Roth into *My Life as a Man,* in which Margaret's fictional surrogate attracts and devastates the protagonist in part because she is not Jewish. Roth's second wife, the Jewish actress Claire Bloom, may have provided in her English background a context for Roth's alter ego, the writer Nathan Zuckerman, to explore his identity as a Jew in *The Counterlife,* in which Zuckerman becomes involved with a Christian Englishwoman. A suicidal breakdown in 1987, caused by medication prescribed for Roth after minor surgery, appears undisguised in

Operation Shylock: A Confession, a probing quest for cultural and personal identity.

Roth's writing can be seen in stages, from the early realist fiction, to the discovery of his comic voice in *Portnoy's Complaint*, to the mid-career novels featuring Jewish writer-protagonists, to the works of the late 1980's and 1990's that either overtly recount Roth's past or collapse the distinction between fiction and reality. Throughout, however, the thread that weaves the work together is Roth's interest in exploring and exposing the Jewish American self.

Goodbye, Columbus, and Five Short Stories
TYPE OF WORK: Novella and short fiction
FIRST PUBLISHED: 1959

Roth's first published volume, *Goodbye, Columbus, and Five Short Stories*, won for the young writer not only the National Book Award in 1960 but also accusations, as a result of the book's comically piercing portraits of middle-class American Jews, of Roth's harboring self-hatred. The ambivalent exploration of Jewish American life in *Goodbye, Columbus*, and its mixed reception among Jewish readers who were sensitive to the public image of Jews established two of the central themes of Roth's fiction: a frank and often ironic look at Jewish American identity, and an intense but playful examination of the relationship between art and life.

In the novella *Goodbye, Columbus*, Neil Klugman's confrontation with his Jewish American identity is represented by his love affair with Brenda Patimkin. Brenda signifies the American Dream, her parents' suburban prosperity symbolized by a refrigerator in the basement overflowing with fresh fruit. Neil's ambivalence toward the Patimkins' conspicuous consumption and their eager assimila-

Philip Roth (Nancy Crampton)

tion into American culture is expressed by the guilt he feels when he helps himself to fruit from the refrigerator. Although Neil finally rejects Brenda, the novella closes without offering Neil a clear sense of where he might belong.

Roth poses other choices in the book's subsequent stories. Ozzie Freedman in "The Conversion of the Jews" believes he must choose between Jewish authority and the American notion of personal freedom. In outrage at his rabbi's denial that an omnipotent God could indeed have caused Mary to conceive without intercourse, Ozzie threatens to leap from the roof of the synagogue, and demands that the rabbi, his mother, and the assembled crowd kneel and affirm belief that God can do anything he wants, with the clear implication that God could have created Jesus in the manner that Christians believe. When Ozzie experiences the power of self-definition at this ironic climax, Roth suggests that Judaism, personified by the rabbi, must confront the shaping forces of the American context if it is not to lose its adherents.

In "Defender of the Faith," Sergeant Nathan Marx questions whether Jews are obligated to define themselves in relation to other Jews. After a Jewish recruit repeatedly manipulates Nathan for favors during basic training, he realizes that his greater responsibility to his fellow Jews lies in refusing to let them be different, despite the dangers that assimilation poses. As if Roth is in dialogue with himself, however, the final story in the collection reverses Nathan's decision. Eli of "Eli, the Fanatic" dons, as a challenge to his "progressive suburban community," the stale black clothes of a recent Jewish immigrant, and, with them, an identity that refuses assimilation into American life. *Goodbye, Columbus, and Five Short Stories*, then, represents Roth's first and notable attempt to explore the problem of Jewish American identity from a variety of angles and without resolution.

Portnoy's Complaint
TYPE OF WORK: Novel
FIRST PUBLISHED: 1969

Philip Roth's third novel, *Portnoy's Complaint*, takes the form of an outrageous, comic rant by Alexander Portnoy to his psychoanalyst, whose help Portnoy seeks because he feels that his life has come to be a "Jewish joke." Portnoy's impassioned, self-absorbed monologues explore his childhood and his erotic relationships. He wishes to locate the source of his pain, composed of guilt, shame, desire, and emotional paralysis, and to free himself from his past. The best-selling novel shocked readers with its obscenity, graphic sexual descriptions, and exaggerations of Jewish stereotypes.

Portnoy's early memories include his mother's intense overprotectiveness and warnings against pleasure, his father's emasculation by the gentile firm for which he works, and his own efforts to loosen the chains that bind him by breaking taboos, especially by frequent, ill-timed sexual escapades. His furious attempts at "self-loving" can be seen as symbolic expressions of self-loathing, intricately related to his position as a Jew in America. The satiric presentation of Portnoy as a figure of excess who wants to put the "id back in Yid" and the "*oy* back in *goy*," provided Roth with a way to inquire into the complacency and neuroses of assimilated Jews in gentile America.

In the postwar years, the Holocaust—the "saga of the suffering Jews"—defined Jewish American identity and encouraged Jews to assimilate inconspicuously. Portnoy's ambivalence toward this Jewish response is represented in his adolescence and adulthood by his relationships with a series of gentile women. Portnoy desires simultaneously to flaunt and to reject himself as a Jew. In each case, he uses women to transgress religious and sexual taboos, imagining that his wild and occasionally abusive relationships with them will allow him to "discover America. *Conquer* America." Yet each of these relationships results for him in intense guilt. His acknowledgement that his self-hatred makes him unable to love causes him to flail against his guilt with further transgressions, ending in more guilt, trapping him in a vicious circle.

The novel ends with Portnoy's primal scream, expressing his recognition that he cannot spring himself "from the settling of scores! the pursuit of dreams! from this hopeless, senseless loyalty to the long ago!" Portnoy, Roth's Jewish American Everyman, cannot escape his past. He struggles to discover who he is, as a Jew and as a human being.

SUGGESTED READINGS

Baumgarten, Murray, and Barbara Gottfried. *Understanding Philip Roth.* Columbia: University of South Carolina Press, 1990.

Bloom, Harold, ed. *Philip Roth: Modern Critical Views.* New York: Chelsea House, 1986.

Halio, Jay L. *Philip Roth Revisited.* New York: Twayne, 1992.

Milbauer, Asher Z., and Donald G. Watson, eds. *Reading Philip Roth.* New York: St. Martin's Press, 1988.

Pinsker, Sanford. *The Comedy That "Hoits": An Essay on the Fiction of Philip Roth.* Columbia: University of Missouri Press, 1975.

Rand, Naomi R. *Silko, Morrison, and Roth: Studies in Survival.* New York: Peter Lang, 1999.

Roth, Philip. *The Facts: A Novelist's Autobiography.* New York: Farrar, Straus & Giroux, 1988.

Searles, George J., ed. *Conversations with Philip Roth.* Jackson: University Press of Mississippi, 1992.

Walden, Daniel, ed. *The Changing Mosaic: From Cahan to Malamud, Roth, and Ozick.* Albany: State University of New York Press, 1993.

—*Debra Shostak*

Muriel Rukeyser

BORN: New York, New York; December 15, 1913
DIED: New York, New York; February 12, 1980

*Rukeyser's poems gave voice to social consciousness, embracing all ethnic
identities that she saw being treated unjustly.*

TRADITIONS: Jewish

PRINCIPAL WORKS: *Theory of Flight*, 1935; *Mediterranean*, 1938; *U.S. One*, 1938;
A Turning Wind: Poems, 1939; *The Soul and Body of John Brown*, 1940; *Wake
Island*, 1942; *Beast in View*, 1944; *The Green Wave*, 1948; *Orpheus*, 1949;
Elegies, 1949; *Selected Poems*, 1951; *Body of Waking*, 1958; *Waterlily Fire: Poems
1935-1962*, 1962; *The Outer Banks*, 1967; *The Speed of Darkness*, 1968; *Mazes*,
1970; *Twenty-nine Poems*, 1972; *Breaking Open: New Poems*, 1973; *The Gates:
Poems*, 1976; *The Collected Poems of Muriel Rukeyser*, 1978; *Out of Silence:
Selected Poems*, 1992

Muriel Rukeyser's poetic career began early with the publication of *Theory of
Flight* in the Yale Series of Younger Poets in 1935. Her poetry reflected her
intense personal passion, her call to freedom, and her search for justice.
Readers may detect the influence of Walt Whitman in her sense of American
identity as something all-embracing.

Rukeyser's sense of personal responsibility and social protest may have
been forged by her political experience. Two years before her first book of
poetry was published, while covering the Scottsboro trials for Vassar College's leftist *Student Review*, Rukeyser was arrested—and caught typhoid fever
while in jail. This event ignited her social awareness as evidenced in her
writing and subsequent actions. This particular event is recalled as "The Trial"
in *Theory of Flight*.

Wherever Rukeyser saw oppression, she became involved. To an extent,
the social and political history of the United States, as distilled through the
reactions of a female Jewish intellectual activist, may be read through Rukeyser's poems. She supported the Loyalists during the Spanish Civil War.
Later, she was jailed while protesting the Vietnam War. She rallied in South
Korea against the death sentence of the poet Kim Chi-ha. The event then
became the focus of her poem, "The Gates."

Bringing the perspective of her Jewish upbringing to her poetry, Rukeyser
wrote about the horrors of World War II. Though her concern about the
oppression of the Jews may have stemmed personally from her religion, she
had already demonstrated her global concern about fascism.

Rukeyser's early marriage did not last; later she became the single parent of a son. Although motherhood became a subject in her poetry and she wrote about women from a feminist perspective, Rukeyser was never as singly feminist in her poetry as others of her generation. Still, her influence as a woman writer on those who followed her was acknowledged by Anne Sexton, who named her "Muriel, mother of everyone," and who kept Rukeyser's *The Speed of Darkness* on her desk.

Muriel Rukeyser (Library of Congress)

"Ajanta"

TYPE OF WORK: Poetry
FIRST PUBLISHED: 1944, in *Beast in View*

"Ajanta" is a long poem written in five subtitled parts: "The Journey," "The Cave," "Les Tendresses Bestiales," "Black Blood," and "The Broken World." The poem, written in free verse, is given form by the progression of the journey it describes, in which the poet goes into herself in search of a sense of the unity of life. It is an exploration of her spirit, mind, and body.

"Ajanta" is named for the great painted caves in India, famous for their magnificent religious frescoes painted by Buddhist monks. Rukeyser uses this setting in her poem to suggest the sacredness of her own interior places, her

Ajanta, both psychic and physical. The figures of gods, men, and animals in the poem are accurate descriptions of the caves' artwork.

"Ajanta" opens *Beast in View*, Rukeyser's fourth book of poems. The "beast" she hunts on her spiritual voyage is not always in view–in "Ajanta" it remains hidden from her until her final reconciliation in the cave to which it has led her. The beast is her innermost self, what makes her who she is, what is vital to her being. The thematic energy of "Ajanta" is devoted to capturing the beast–herself in her own myth of herself–so that she can be a whole person again. Because the poem is about transformation, and adapting to changes in life and the world, the beast in "Ajanta" often appears in disguises. All these masks are part of the poet's personality and her changes. She seeks to unify them and accept them all.

The search for self-identity in "Ajanta," however, is not an end in itself. Beginning with descriptions of war atrocities, the poem reminds readers that to know oneself is vital also for the sake of the world in which one lives. The poet seeks the strong armor of self-knowledge, rather than the armor of rage, in order to know better how to aid the struggles of those who have been betrayed or who are suffering loss. The "world of the shadowed and alone" is a place in which the conscientious must fight for those in need and confront "the struggles of the moon." In "Letter to the Front" (also from Beast in View), Rukeyser praises the healing power that women can offer the world, especially in time of war. She envisioned female sensibilities transforming traditional man, or the traditional masculine ideal. This vision laid a path for later women poets, such as Adrienne Rich, who continue to explore similar themes.

The cave is a symbol for female sensibility, mystery, and strength. It is a dark interior, a place of hiding or hibernation, a place of meditation, a vault from which one emerges reborn, as did Jesus. It is also a source of life: Its watery, quiet space nurtures, like a womb. Its interior can be mysterious yet comforting, black, and frightening, or cool and beckoning. "Ajanta," said Kenneth Rexroth (1905-1982), is "an exploration . . . of her own interior–in every sense." That is, as a poet and a woman, Rukeyser is interested in her mind and in her body's flesh and form and how they shape her quest for fulfillment. The beauty, complexity, and energy of "Ajanta" has made it one of her most famous and powerful poems.

"Eyes of Night-Time"

TYPE OF WORK: Poetry
FIRST PUBLISHED: 1948, in *The Green Wave*

"Eyes of Night-Time" is a full-throated song about the beauty of night and darkness. This short poem in free verse expresses the poet's awe over nature's beauty at night. The first stanza describes with passionate wonder the creatures that see in the dark. In the second stanza, the poet considers what human beings may see in the darkness, or what the darkness may reveal to them.

For Rukeyser, "night-time" has strong metaphorical connections to the human spirit's darkness or hidden truths. The poem, while offering minute observations on nature at night, also deals with self-examination and attempts to comment on human nature in general.

In many of her poems, Rukeyser relies on a fabric woven of imagery and rhythm to provide formal unity. *The Green Wave* (1948), in which "Eyes of Night-Time" first appeared, contains other poems in which she experimented with her powers of observation and concentrated on new rhythms. Rukeyser preferred not to use traditional forms or patterns of fixed rhyme and meter. She wanted a poetry in which the material would generate its own form. Therefore, rhythm—the cadence, pace, and momentum of the line—was important to her. The music of the poem ought to allow it to echo and suggest—perhaps reproduce—the natural rhythms of the world she was attempting to describe.

In the poem, images of light and dark intertwine; points of light continually pierce the darkness. These emerging lights represent, as images of light often do in poetry, possible revelations of truth. The play between dark and light, shadow and eye shine, gives the poem both tension and balance. Dark things bear light: "the illumined shadow sea" and "the light of wood" are two examples.

Images of darkness inhabit every corner of "Eyes of Night-Time." The poet has studied night, and nighttime is this poem's territory. The earth's night and the human spirit's darkness, metaphorical counterparts in the poem, are fertile places the poet considers with full respect. The soul's darkest, most threatening realizations, she knows, will reveal the light (self-knowledge) that is needed to free the "prisoners in the forest . . . in the almost total dark."

Rukeyser's poem offers her ecstatic awareness of the healing power of darkness: If one goes deeply enough into one's own darkness, one finds, paradoxically, the light of truth that heals dark sufferings and misgivings. This light is the "glitter" she recognizes in the last line as "gifts" given, really, by all those people who have gone before her and all those who are alive now.

The poem is about examining oneself and one's spirit. It is also a statement on the need for human unity. "And in our bodies the eyes of the dead and the living" is a powerful way of saying that human beings inhabit not only the earth, but also one another. Like the creatures of nighttime—the cat, moth, fly, beetle, and toad—humans are interdependent and must rely on one another to survive.

SUGGESTED READINGS

Bernikow, Louise. "Muriel at Sixty-five: Still Ahead of Her Time." *MS,* January, 1979, 14-16.

Gould, Jean. *Modern American Woman Poets.* New York: Dodd, Mead, 1985.

Herzog, Anne F., and Janet E. Kaufman, eds. *How Shall We Tell Each Other of the Poet? The Life and Writing of Muriel Rukeyser.* New York: St. Martin's Press, 1999.

Kertesz, Louise. *The Poetic Vision of Muriel Rukeyser.* Baton Rouge: Louisiana State University Press, 1980.

—Holly Dworken Cooley/JoAnn Balingit

Sonia Sanchez
(Wilsonia Benita Driver)

BORN: Birmingham, Alabama; September 9, 1934

Among the black poets who emerged during the 1960's, Sanchez has stood out for her activism.

TRADITIONS: African American

PRINCIPAL WORKS: *Homecoming*, 1969; *We a BaddDDD People*, 1970; *A Blues Book for Blue Black Magical Women*, 1973; *Love Poems*, 1973; *I've Been a Woman: New and Selected Poems*, 1978; *homegirls & handgrenades*, 1984; *Under a Soprano Sky*, 1987; *Wounded in the House of a Friend*, 1995; *Shake Loose My Skin: New and Selected Poems*, 1999

Sonia Sanchez's emergence as a writer and political activist in the 1960's marked the beginning of the career of a poet, playwright, and cultural worker. Sanchez is noted as a poet and as a black activist committed to the belief that the role of the artist is functional. Sanchez's political interpretation of the situation of African Americans informs the creative forms she produces. The activist spirit has remained a constant in her work.

Sonia Sanchez's mother died when Sanchez was one year old. Her father, Wilson Driver, Jr., a jazz musician, moved the family to New York when Sanchez was nine years old; she was thrust into the jazz world of her father. She entered Hunter College and received her bachelor's degree in political science in 1955. As a graduate student, Sanchez studied with Louise Bogan at New York University. Bogan, a poet and literary critic, wrote restrained, concise, and deeply intellectual poetry, often compared to that of the English metaphysical poets. Bogan's influence upon Sanchez is most evident in the conciseness of her lyrical poetry; Bogan's encouragement caused Sanchez to pursue the life of a poet. Sanchez formed a writers' workshop and soon began reading poetry around New York City.

Sanchez's early works were published in little magazines; later they were published in black journals. *Homecoming*, Sanchez's first anthology of poetry, placed her among poets who espoused a philosophy of functional art. Functional art is characterized by a sense of social purpose, information, instruction, and inspiration.

Sanchez's improvisational style combines strategies common to black speech. This is particularly evident in her early poetry. Indirection, or signifying, is a key element of this poetic style. Another key element of Sanchez's style is her oral delivery, reminiscent of improvisation in jazz. Her creative vision is also expressed in her inventive poetic forms. Sanchez's speechlike, versatile style is evident in all of her poetry.

I've Been a Woman
TYPE OF WORK: Poetry
FIRST PUBLISHED: 1978

I've Been a Woman: New and Selected Poems is a compilation of selections from Sanchez's major works up to 1978. This collection offers a cross section of the themes that characterize Sonia Sanchez's poetic vision. Sanchez's work balances the private and the public. The private, or introspective poems, are intensely personal. The public poems cover a number of concerns. Selections from *Homecoming* (1969), *We a BaddDDD People* (1970), *Love Poems* (1973), *A Blues Book for Blue Black Magical Women* (1973), and *Generations: Selected Poetry 1969-1985* (1986) make up *I've Been a Woman.*

Themes include issues of identity among African Americans. Sanchez's work is characterized by her ability to offer clear-eyed commentary on African American conditions while offering poetry of destiny and self-determination. For example, one of Sanchez's ongoing concerns is drug addiction among African Americans. In works such as *Wounded in the House of a Friend* (1995), she focuses this concern on the devastating effects of addiction to crack cocaine.

This intermingling of themes is found in poems such as "Summary." This poem represents an example of Sanchez's technique. She combines personal and public concerns. Within this poem, Sanchez does not allow the narrator to move inward and remain there. She seems to assume an introspective position as a momentary restful pose. In this energizing space, the narrator is renewed and arrives at a political solution to problems noted in the poems.

The poems included in these sections are examples of Sanchez's virtuosity as a poet. Section 5 is devoted exclusively to Sanchez's "Haikus/Tankas & Other Love Syllables." Use of forms offers an example of the poet's technique.

This collection offers an excellent example of Sanchez's range as an artist. In the various sections of *I've Been a Woman*, the speaker of Sanchez's poetry is revealed as a quester for identity and resolution. Distinguished from male quest epics, Sanchez's quest focuses on the desire to embark on a quest not only for herself but also for other women as well. The knowledge that the quester seeks is assumed to be available in the person of an Earth Mother who can help the quester understand the relationship between past and present. Such a figure can also help the quester learn to have faith in the future.

SUGGESTED READINGS

Gabbin, Joanne Veal. "The Southern Imagination of Sonia Sanchez." In *Southern Women Writers: The New Generation*, edited by Tonnette Bond Inge. Tuscaloosa: University of Alabama Press, 1990.

Jennings, Regina B. "The Blue/Black Poetics of Sonia Sanchez." In *Language and Literature in the African American Imagination*, edited by Carol Aisha Blackshire-Belay. Westport, Conn.: Greenwood Press, 1992.

Joyce, Joyce Ann. "The Development of Sonia Sanchez: A Continuing Journey." *Indian Journal of American Studies* 13 (July, 1983): 37-71.

_____. *Ijala: Sonia Sanchez and the African Poetic Tradition*. Chicago: Third World Press, 1996.

Lynch, Doris. Review of *Wounded in the House of a Friend*, by Sonia Sanchez. *Library Journal*, March 15, 1995, 74.

Saunders, James Robert. "Sonia Sanchez's *homegirls & handgrenades:* Recalling Toomer's *Cane.*" MELUS 15, no. 1 (Spring, 1988): 73-83.

—Frenzella Elaine De Lancey

Thomas Sanchez

BORN: Oakland, California; February 26, 1944

Sanchez's novels portray the diverse, multiethnic experience of twentieth century American life.

TRADITIONS: Latino

PRINCIPAL WORKS: *Rabbit Boss*, 1973; *Zoot-Suit Murders*, 1978; *Native Notes from the Land of Earthquake and Fire*, 1979; *Mile Zero*, 1989; *Day of the Bees*, 2000

Growing up in a poor family, Thomas Sanchez was sent to a Catholic boarding school in Northern California after his mother became ill. There he developed his interest in Native American subjects, which informs his fiction. An outspoken advocate for human rights, Sanchez was a member of the Congress for Racial Equality, the United Farm Workers, and the Student Nonviolent Coordinating Committee during the 1960's. Sanchez participated in the Sacramento Valley grape strikes and the Vietnam antiwar movement. As a radio correspondent in 1973, he reported on the American Indian Movement's takeover of the Wounded Knee Reservation in South Dakota—a protest that prompted a Senate investigation into the conditions of Indian life.

In 1969, Sanchez left the United States to visit Spain, where he wrote his first novel. Rabbit Boss chronicles four generations of the Washo Indian tribe. The tribe's leader, the *Rabbit Boss*, encounters the Donner Party, a group of white settlers who became snowbound in the mountains and resorted to cannibalism. A Washo legend that whites are cannibals originates from this 1846 encounter. The cannibalism overturns the civilized white man-savage Indian dichotomy. Cultures clash again in Sanchez's next novel, *Zoot-Suit Murders*, a mystery set in a Los Angeles barrio of the 1940's. The story concerns the murder of two Federal Bureau of Investigation agents in a rioting neighborhood where the local zoot-suiters are regularly terrorized by sailors.

A Guggenheim Fellowship and the proceeds from the sale of his house allowed Sanchez to move to Key West, Florida, where he wrote *Mile Zero*. *Rabbit Boss* describes the beginning of an American campaign against indigenous people that culminated in the destructive logic of the Vietnam War. *Mile Zero* is Sanchez's attempt to connect with the post-Vietnam generation. For Sanchez, the tide of refugees fleeing Haiti and the increasing cocaine traffic through Florida stem from the same folly that fueled the United States' involvement in Vietnam. The novel's brilliant evocation of Key West and its political vision elicited favorable comparisons with the work of John Steinbeck and Robert Stone.

Sanchez writes novels infused with the richness of America's cultural heritage, so his work is difficult to categorize. His fiction has received laudatory reviews and other critical accolades, but it has yet to attract the scholarly attention it deserves. Nevertheless, Sanchez is an important contemporary critic of the United States' destructive desire for "progress" at the expense of others.

Mile Zero
TYPE OF WORK: Novel
FIRST PUBLISHED: 1989

Mile Zero, Sanchez's sweeping vision of Key West, Florida, brilliantly evokes the rich history and lyrical passion of the island. Key West is the southernmost point of the continental United States, where "Mile Zero," the last highway sign before the Atlantic Ocean, symbolizes the end of the American road. While Key West represents the end for the downtrodden Americans who gravitate there, the island promises hope for refugees fleeing Haiti's poverty across shark-ridden waters. Sanchez traces the island's shifting economy from a hub of the cigar industry to "a marijuana republic," then to "a mere cocaine principality." Sanchez laments how the drug trade has corrupted the American Dream.

Mile Zero's main character, St. Cloud, a former antiwar activist, drowns his self-doubt in Haitian rum and ponders his inability to sacrifice himself for his beliefs. He feels a strange kinship with MK, once a soldier in Vietnam and now a dangerous smuggler who has fled Key West for South America. MK's mysterious presence and the shadow of Vietnam permeate the book. St. Cloud imagines that his pacifism and MK's violence are two sides of the same coin. After Vietnam, returning soldiers and protesters both found themselves cast out of society.

When a Coast Guard cutter tows a refugee boat from Haiti into the harbor, Justo Tamarindo, a Cuban American police officer, drafts St. Cloud to help him prevent the deportation of the sole survivor, a boy named Voltaire. Voltaire's sad story reveals how America thrives at the expense of the Third World. Late in the novel, Voltaire escapes from the detention center where he is waiting to be deported. The young, malnourished boy dreams he has reached a heavenly land of plenty at a garish shopping mall before he dies a tragic death.

Meanwhile, Justo pursues Zobop, an enigmatic killer, who is roaming the island and leaving Voodoo-inspired clues everywhere. After Zobop is killed, Justo learns that the murderer sought purification by destruction. Like El Finito, a powerful, apocalyptic hurricane that threatens to destroy the island, Zobop believes everything must be wiped out before it can be renewed.

In *Mile Zero*, Sanchez signals the necessity of cultural change. Vietnam is over, Justo thinks, but the bodies of the dead refugees augur the arrival of a new devil. America is doomed if it does not change. The novel's ambiguous ending, in which Justo, who may have contracted AIDS, pulls St. Cloud out of the ocean, brings its readers to mile zero, a place that can be either an ending or a beginning.

SUGGESTED READINGS

Abeel, Erica. "A Winning Sort of Loser." *The New York Times Book Review*, October 1, 1989, 7.

Bonetti, Kay. "An Interview with Thomas Sanchez." *Missouri Review* 14, no. 2 (1991): 76-95.

Quinn, Mary Ellen. Review of *Day of the Bees*, by Thomas Sanchez. *Booklist* 96 (April 15, 2000): 1525.

Rieff, David. "The Affirmative Action Novel." *The New Republic*, April, 1990, 31-34.

—Trey Strecker

George S. Schuyler

BORN: Providence, Rhode Island; February 25, 1895
DIED: New York, New York; August 31, 1977

Schuyler, whose specialty was ridiculing bigotry, was one of the leading satirists of the Harlem Renaissance era.

TRADITIONS: African American
PRINCIPAL WORKS: *Black No More*, 1931; *Slaves Today: A Story of Liberia*, 1931; *Black and Conservative: The Autobiography of George S. Schuyler*, 1966

Born in Rhode Island and raised in Syracuse, New York, George S. Schuyler dropped out of high school to join the Army. There, as a member of the famous Twenty-fifth U.S. Infantry regiment, he served seven years before being discharged as a first lieutenant in 1919. After several odd jobs in New York City, Schuyler returned home and joined the Socialist Party, for which he held several offices.

Schuyler was later involved with Marcus Garvey's Universal Negro Improvement Association, but became disillusioned with Garvey's plan to return to Africa. Schuyler often spoke publicly on political and cultural issues, and by the 1920's, he had joined a black socialist group, Friends of Negro Freedom, and had accepted a job on the staff of the organization's official magazine, *The Messenger*. He also wrote as the New York correspondent for an African American weekly newspaper, *The Pittsburgh Courier*. He continued to live in New York and write for *The Pittsburgh Courier* until 1966.

Schuyler's literary identity evolves from his career as a journalist and from his deep

George S. Schuyler on the cover of his autobiography . (Arkent Archives)

respect for his mother's ideas and values. The product of a middle-class family, Schuyler comments in his autobiography, *Black and Conservative*, that his mother taught him to consider all sides of a question and to establish and stand by principles of personal conduct whether others agreed or not. True to his mother's teaching, Schuyler seldom opted for the popular road. His public actions and political views were often regarded as extremely conservative and iconoclastic.

His cynical view of race in America led to razor-sharp attacks upon racial patriots (black leaders he perceived as self-interested and bigoted) and upon white supremacists, who, he believed, exploited racism for economic reasons. In his autobiography he asserts that blacks never thought themselves inferior to whites; rather, blacks "are simply aware that their socio-economic position is inferior, which is a different thing." In chiding race organizations as perpetuating the problems of racism, Schuyler contended that ridding the country of racial hatred would absolutely disrupt the national economy.

His irreverent attacks on the traditional values and cherished beliefs of black and white society earned him much notoriety during his forty-year career, which spanned from the Harlem Renaissance to the 1960's.

Black No More
TYPE OF WORK: Novel
FIRST PUBLISHED: 1931

Schuyler's *Black No More: Being an Account of the Strange and Wonderful Workings of Science in the Land of the Free* offers a bitingly satirical attack upon America's color phobia. His targets included bigoted whites who see the perpetuation of racism as a matter of economic and political interest, black leaders who waffle between appealing to white financial backers and appeasing their black constituents, and all who cloak their ignorance and hatred with racial rhetoric.

The plot of *Black No More* centers upon Schuyler's speculation of what might happen if America were to find a means to rid itself of the "Negro problem." In an effort to uplift his race, Dr. Junius Crookman, a respected black physician, invents a process by which black people can inexpensively turn themselves permanently white. The success of his process leads him to open up numerous Black No More clinics across America to handle the throngs of hopeful clients.

His first and most eager customer is Max Disher, who sees "chromatic enhancement" initially as a chance to get a white woman and eventually to run various fund-raising shams under the auspices of the Knights of Nordica, led by the Imperial Grand Wizard, Reverend Givens. As a white man, Max takes a new name, Matthew Fisher. He soon is proving his talents as a brilliant organizer, political manipulator, and white supremacist working for "the cause." Ironically, the woman of his Harlem dreams and eventual wife, Helen, turns out to be the daughter of Reverend Givens.

Matthew's schemes initially are simply quick-money ploys that amusingly take advantage of the Knights of Nordica's ignorance and obsession for racial supremacy. As the plot moves along, however, Matthew begins to sound too sincere in his racist rhetoric and becomes obsessed with earning money and political power. An old friend, Bunny Brown, arrives to keep Matthew in line. With the numbers of blacks steadily dwindling, thanks to Crookman's clinics, Matthew and Bunny plot to expose and destroy the institution of racism in America, along with its vested leaders.

The novel concludes in a calamity as the national presidential race becomes a matter of reciprocated political tricks. The former blacks are whiter than whites, the two most notorious bigots in the book go up in flames, and Matthew's wife gives birth to a mulatto child.

Schuyler, through frequent barbs and sarcastic commentaries, exposes the hypocrisy of both white and black leaders. There are numerous thinly disguised caricatures of the black leaders of the time of the novel: W. E. B. Du Bois, Marcus Garvey, C. J. Walker, James Weldon Johnson, and many others. Schuyler's satire contends that blacks are motivated by the same economic and political interests as whites, and once given the opportunity, will resort to the same means to preserve those interests.

SUGGESTED READINGS

Davis, Arthur P. "George Schuyler." In *From the Dark Tower.* Washington, D.C.: Howard University Press, 1974.

Gayle, Addison, Jr. *The Way of the World: The Black Novel in America.* Garden City, N.J.: Anchor Press, 1975.

Goode, Stephen. "Color Bind." *Insight on the News* 16 (February 7, 2000): 26.

Schuyler, George. *Black and Conservative: The Autobiography of George S. Schuyler.* New Rochelle, N.Y.: Arlington House, 1966.

—Betty L. Hart

Delmore Schwartz

BORN: Brooklyn, New York; December 8, 1913
DIED: New York, New York; July 11, 1966

Schwartz's work affirms the power of the independent mind against materialism.

TRADITIONS: Jewish

PRINCIPAL WORKS: *In Dreams Begin Responsibilities*, 1938; *Genesis, Book I*, 1943; *The World Is a Wedding*, 1948; *Vaudeville for a Princess and Other Poems*, 1950; *Summer Knowledge: New and Selected Poems*, 1959; *Successful Love and Other Stories*, 1961

The saga of Delmore Schwartz's life reflects the Jewish American experience of the 1930's. Schwartz was the son of Romanian immigrants, and his career unfolded against the backdrop of political and social tensions of the Depression. Thus, much of his writing articulates the drama of alienation; poetic realism and psychological intensity are common characteristics. The shadow of Fyodor Dostoevski looms over Schwartz's literary figures—human archetypes of internalized chaos and ritualistic narcissism. Schwartz is often associated with the confessional school of his generation; the school includes John Berryman, Randall Jarrell, Theodore Roethke, Anne Sexton, and Robert Lowell. He fits squarely into the Jewish intellectual milieu of the post-World War I era, which produced many luminaries.

Schwartz grew up in Brooklyn, New York, and completed his education at New York University. In 1935, he entered Harvard University to study philosophy and, despite impressive achievements, left after two years, without receiving an advanced degree. Throughout his life he held numerous university and college teaching positions but was reluctant to commit himself to an academic career. His writings suggest a bohemian strain in his personality that drove him toward self-discovery instead of the regularity of a permanent job.

The publication of *In Dreams Begin Responsibilities* galvanized Schwartz's career. Within several years, he was recognized as a seminal figure. In 1943, he became an editor of the *Partisan Review*. The publication of *The World Is a Wedding*, a collection of semiautobiographical stories, and *Summer Knowledge* led to numerous awards and several distinguished lectureships.

Schwartz's volatile personality is apparent in the disenchanted loneliness of his artistic imagery, vividly depicted by Saul Bellow in *Humboldt's Gift* (1975), in which Von Humboldt Fleisher's self-destruction is modeled after Schwartz's pathetic decline. He often hurt those who loved him best, and this led to the dissolution of two marriages, insomnia, acute paranoia, heavy drinking, drug abuse, and failing health. From 1962 to 1965, he was a visiting professor of English at Syracuse University. He was popular with students, but his poetic talents had clearly deteriorated. Many of his later works seem like old pictures reframed, although he retained the brilliant flashes of a virtuoso. He died isolated and alone.

In Dreams Begin Responsibilities
TYPE OF WORK: Poetry, short fiction, and drama
FIRST PUBLISHED: 1938

The short story "In Dreams Begin Responsibilities," which lends its title to this collection of prose, poetry, and drama, was apparently written over a weekend in July, 1935. Vladimir Nabokov recognized its merit and recommended it as the lead piece in the *Partisan Review*. Schwartz's literary career was launched. The enigmatic title suggests that destiny is located in dreams, what Schwartz would later call in his fictional autobiography *Genesis* (1943) "a fixed hallucination." The attempt to realize dreams in poetry and to acknowledge the past as prologue to the future draws its inspiration from the artistic context established by William Butler Yeats and T. S. Eliot—perhaps the most powerful forces to influence Schwartz's writing.

The narrator witnesses the events leading up to his father's marriage proposal. The narrator watches a series of six film episodes depicting Sunday afternoon, June 12, 1909, in Coney Island, New York. The climactic moment when his mother accepts proves unbearable to the eventual offspring of this union and, in the darkened, womblike theater, he screams in protest against his future birth. An authoritative usher, representing the narrator's superego, reminds him that he has no control over his birth, and hence the outburst is futile. The scene closes when a fortune-teller predicts an unhappy marriage, ending in divorce.

The theme of the anguished child continues in the five-act-long poem "Coriolanus and His Mother," in which the protagonist shifts his allegiance from Rome to a barbarian cause. Based on William Shakespeare's play, the drama unfolds before a boy, the poet's alter ego, and five ghosts: Karl Marx, Sigmund Freud, Ludwig van Beethoven, Aristotle, and a small anonymous presence, perhaps Franz Kafka, chronicler of the absurd. This "dream of knowledge" play is a parable about self-destructive tendencies—anger, insolence, pride.

The management of identity is a theme carried through many of the thirty-five poems collected under the heading "Experimentation and Imitation." For example, rebel spirits such as Hart Crane, Robinson Crusoe, Wolfgang Amadeus Mozart, and Charlie Chaplin inhabit the vaudevillian circus atmosphere of the poetry, captured in the phrases "the octopus in love with God" ("Prothalamion"), "Now I float will-less in despair's dead sea ("Faust in Old Age"), and "the radiant soda of the seashore fashions" ("Far Rockaway").

"Dr. Bergen's Belief," a short play, is a lamentation on the death by suicide of the doctor's daughter. After meditating on the promise of an afterlife and God's providence—"the dream behind the dream, the Santa Claus of the obsessed obscene heart," the doctor and a second daughter leap to their deaths. Schwartz's lurid inventiveness and capricious style conjure a world of comic shame and imminent dread. *In Dreams Begin Responsibilities* represents an attempt to mold commonplace happenings into mystical shapes.

SUGGESTED READINGS

Ashbery, John. *The Heavy Bear: Delmore Schwartz's Life Versus His Poetry, a Lecture Delivered at the Sixty-seventh General Meeting of the English Literary Society of Japan.* Tokyo: English Literary Society of Japan, 1996.

Atlas, James. *Delmore Schwartz: The Life of an American Poet.* New York: Farrar, Straus & Giroux, 1977.

Breslin, Paul. "Delmore Schwartz." In *American Writers,* edited by A. Walton Litz. New York: Charles Scribner's Sons, 1981.

Kloss, Robert J. "An Ancient and Famous Capital: Delmore Schwartz's Dream." *Psychoanalytic Review* 65, no. 3 (1978): 475-490.

McDougall, Richard. *Delmore Schwartz.* New York: Twayne, 1974.

Philips, William. "Delmore." *Partisan Review* 61, no. 2 (Spring, 1994): 199-201.

Schwartz, Delmore. *Delmore Schwartz and James Laughlin: Selected Letters.* Edited by Robert Phillips. New York: W. W. Norton, 1993.

—Robert Frail

Ntozake Shange
(Paulette Williams)

BORN: Trenton, New Jersey; October 18, 1948

Shange's novels, plays, and poems speak for African American girls and women.

TRADITIONS: African American

PRINCIPAL WORKS: *for colored girls who have considered suicide/when the rainbow is enuf: a choreopoem*, pr., pb. 1976; *Nappy Edges*, 1978; *Sassafrass, Cypress, and Indigo*, 1982; *See No Evil: Prefaces, Essays, and Accounts, 1976-1983*, 1984; *Betsey Brown*, 1985; *Liliane: Resurrection of the Daughter*, 1994

Ntozake Shange, born Paulette Williams, was raised in an African American middle-class family in Trenton, New Jersey. Her mother was a social worker, and her father was a surgeon—the same occupations held by the parents in Shange's novel *Betsey Brown*. Also like Betsey, young Paulette was encouraged to get an education and was introduced to leading figures of African American music and literature. Unlike Betsey, however, the writer remembers herself as always obedient and "nice."

Not until she was in her thirties did she allow herself to express the anger always lurking beneath her polite surface. Depressed over a failed marriage, and frustrated over the roadblocks of racism and sexism she encountered as she attempted to establish a career, she began to explore anew her own identity as an African American woman. She took the African name Ntozake Shange, which means "she who comes with her own things" and "she who walks like a lion."

Her first major piece of writing remains her most important. The play *for colored girls who have considered suicide/when the rainbow is enuf* won international acclaim for its innovative combining of poetry, drama, and dance to tell the stories of seven women. Still performed, the play was one of the earliest writings in any genre to deal with the anger of black women.

The success of the play gave Shange the financial freedom to explore less financially profitable outlets of expression. She began writing and publishing poetry, and collaborating with musicians and choreographers on improvisational pieces performed in bars and small theaters. She also has taught creative writing and women's studies courses at various colleges across the United States, and has occasionally turned her pen to writing prose fiction, especially for and about adolescent girls.

Shange has often spoken of the responsibilities that inform her writing. As an adolescent she could not find fiction about people like her. As a young woman she did not know how to understand her own pain. She writes many of her works to pass on to younger black women the insights she has gained through her experiences.

Betsey Brown
TYPE OF WORK: Novel
FIRST PUBLISHED: 1985

Betsey Brown tells the story of its thirteen-year-old title character's struggles with adolescence, with discovering who she is and who she might become. Shange wrote the novel specifically to provide reading matter for adolescent African American girls. In her own youth, Shange could find no books to help her sort out her life: Books about young women were written by whites for whites, and most books by blacks were by and about men.

Betsey Brown is the oldest of five unruly children in a middle-class family. Like most adolescent girls, she feels separated from the rest of her family: They do not understand her; they do not appreciate her. Betsey's father wants her to grow up to lead her people to freedom. He wakes the children every morning with a conga drum and chanting and then leads them through a quiz on black history. All of the children can recite poetry by Paul Laurence Dunbar and Countée Cullen; they know the music of Dizzy Gillespie, Chuck Berry, and Duke Ellington. Betsey herself was once rocked to sleep by W. E. B. Du Bois. Betsey's mother fears that this exposure will limit her children instead of expanding them. She would like the children to grow up with nice middle-class manners and tastes. In many ways, she has denied her own heritage, her own identity. Eventually, she leaves the family for a time.

The story is firmly rooted in its specific time and place. In 1959, St.

Ntozake Shange (Jules Allen) Louis took its first steps

toward integrating its public schools, and the Brown children are among the first black children bussed to formerly all-white schools. The father has tried to prepare the children by giving them a firm sense of self and heritage. He is eager for them to enter the struggle for civil rights, even as the mother fears that they will be in danger if they become too involved.

A central issue of the novel is the importance of passing down one's cultural heritage. It is not until the mother decisively embraces her heritage that she can again join the family. While she is absent, the housekeeper assumes her role as mother and guide and teaches Betsey and the other children how to follow the dreams of both parents. They learn to stand up for themselves and honor their culture and history and also to be well-mannered and self-sufficient. When Jane returns, it is to a new Betsey, one who has taken the first steps in forging her adult identity.

for colored girls who have considered suicide/when the rainbow is enuf

TYPE OF WORK: Drama
FIRST PRODUCED: 1976; first published, 1976

For colored girls who have considered suicide/when the rainbow is enuf: a choreopoem, Shange's first work, tells the stories of seven women who have suffered oppression in a racist and sexist society. The choreopoem is an innovative combination of poetry, drama, music, and dance. For Shange, the combination is important. She learned about her identity as a woman through words, songs, and literature; she learned about her identity as an African through dance.

The seven women are not named; they are meant to stand for the women who make up the rainbow. They are called "lady in brown," "lady in red," and so on. Each tells her own story. The stories are interwoven together. As the women tell their stories, they reflect on what it means to be a woman of color, what chances and choices they have. These women are in pain; they are angry. They have been abused by their lovers, their rapists, their abortionists, and they have been driven to the brink of despair. What strength they have left they find in music and in each other.

Many have criticized the play for being too negative toward black men, but Shange has always attempted to direct the focus of the discussion back on the women. The play is about the women, about who they are and what they have experienced. To insist on a "balanced" view of the men in their lives is to deny these women's experiences. These women deserve a voice. The play, she insists, does not accuse all black men of being abusive. These women are not rejecting men or seeking a life without men. The women desire men and love them, and ache for that love to be returned.

Although the stories these women tell are tales of struggle, the play is ultimately uplifting. The seven women grieve, but they also celebrate their lives, their vitality, their colorfulness. As the play ends, the women recite, one at a time and then together: "i found god in myself/ & i loved her/ i loved her fiercely." These women are not entirely powerless; they have the power of their own voices. They find the courage to tell their stories and thus triumph.

SUGGESTED READINGS

Lester, Neal A. *Ntozake Shange: A Critical Study of the Plays.* New York: Garland, 1995.

Lyons, Brenda. "Interview with Ntozake Shange." *Massachusetts Review* 28 (Winter, 1987): 687-96.

Olaniyan, Tejumola. *Scars of Conquest/Masks of Resistance: The Invention of Cultural Identities in African, African-American, and Caribbean Drama.* New York: Oxford University Press, 1995.

Shange, Ntozake. "An Interview with Ntozake Shange." Interview by Neal A. Lester. *Studies in American Drama, 1945-Present* 5, no. 1 (1990): 42-66.

_____. "At the Heart of Shange's Feminism: An Interview." Interview by Neal A. Lester. *Black American Literature Forum* 24 (Winter, 1990): 717-730.

_____. *See No Evil: Prefaces, Essays, and Accounts 1976-1983.* San Francisco: Momo Press, 1984.

Sharadha, Y. S. *Black Women's Writing: Quest for Identity in the Plays of Lorraine Hansberry and Ntozake Shange.* New Delhi, India: Prestige Books, 1998.

Tate, Claudia, ed. *Black Women Writers at Work.* New York: Continuum Press, 1983.

—Cynthia A. Bily

Leslie Marmon Silko

BORN: Albuquerque, New Mexico; March 5, 1948

Silko's short stories and novels represent some of the finest writing of what has been called the Native American Renaissance.

TRADITIONS: American Indian
PRINCIPAL WORKS: *Ceremony*, 1977; *Storyteller*, 1981; *Almanac of the Dead: A Novel*, 1991; *Sacred Water*, 1993; *Gardens in the Dunes*, 1999

The tensions and cultural conflicts affecting many of Leslie Marmon Silko's characters can be seen as fictional renderings of Silko's experience. Born of mixed European American and Navajo blood, Silko spent her formative years learning the stories of her white ancestors and their relationship with the native population into which they married. Her great-grandfather, Robert Marmon, had come to the Laguna pueblo, New Mexico, in the early 1870's as a surveyor and eventually married a Laguna woman. Even more important to Silko's development as a writer was the later generation of Marmons—half European American and half Native American—who continued to transmit the oral traditions of the Laguna pueblo people. One such source was the Aunt Susie of Silko's autobiographical writings. The wife of Silko's grandfather's brother, she was a schoolteacher in the Laguna pueblo during the 1920's and years afterward passed on to the young Silko the oral heritage of her race. So intimate was Silko's imagination with the elements of Laguna culture that her father's family photographs serve as visual commentary on the sketches and stories of *Storyteller*.

Like the Inuit woman in *Storyteller*, Silko attended the local school operated by the Bureau of Indian Affairs, but she remained there only a short time, moving on to Catholic schools in Albuquerque, eventually receiving a B.A. in English from the University of New Mexico in 1969. Like her ancestors, she taught school at Navajo Community College in Tsaile, Arizona, where she wrote *Ceremony*, her first novel. One of the most well-known of her works and one of the best novels written by a Native American, the book tells the story of Tayo, a World War II veteran, who tries to cope with the conflicts of his mixed-blood heritage.

Her short stories were beginning to appear in the early 1970's, and she quickly gained a reputation as one of the leading writers in the Native American Renaissance. The term is applied to the literary movement beginning in the 1960's that features works by Native American writers using tribal customs and traditions as literary material. Stories such as "Yellow Woman," in which a mortal is seemingly abducted by spiritual beings, and "Uncle Tony's Goat," which retells an old Laguna beast fable, are typical of Silko's handling of traditional indigenous material. One of her best stories, "Lullaby," treats the conflict of an elderly Navajo couple as they seek to come to terms with the dominant culture and how that conflict strengthens their traditional values.

Storyteller
TYPE OF WORK: Autobiography, poetry, short fiction
FIRST PUBLISHED: 1981

A collection of autobiographical sketches, poems, family photographs, and short stories, *Storyteller* fuses literary and extraliterary material into a mosaic portrait of cultural heritage and of conflict between the two ethnic groups composing her heritage, the European American and the Native American.

The title story, "Storyteller," presents that conflict from the point of view of a young Inuit woman who is fascinated with and repulsed by white civilization. Set in Alaska—the only major work of the author not in a Southwestern setting—the story follows her thoughts and observations as she spends her days amid these contrasting cultures. The old man with whom she lives and who has used her sexually—"she knew what he wanted"—is the storyteller. Now bedridden with age and the cold, subsisting on dried fish, which he keeps under his pillow, the old man narrates a tale, carefully, insistently, about a hunter on the ice facing a challenge from a bear.

Between the beginning and end of his own tale, the Inuit woman's story unfolds. She went to the government school, but largely out of curiosity, and although she remembers being whipped by one of the teachers, her fascination with whites—the "Gussucks," as she calls them—only deepened when she observed their oil rigs, their large yellow machines, and their metal buildings. Gradually she learns that the Gussucks are not so much to be respected or feared but rather scorned because of their insensitivity and greed. The old man calls them thieves, and she herself laughs at the smug confidence they place in their machines, which are almost useless in the Alaskan cold.

Her physical curiosity about the Gussucks leads to her being sexually exploited by one of them, and the turning point of the story occurs when the Inuit woman learns that a Gussuck storekeeper was responsible for the death of her parents by giving them nonpotable alcohol in exchange for their rifles. In revenge, she lures the storekeeper onto the ice, where he falls through and drowns.

At the conclusion, the old man, now on his deathbed, finishes his tale of the hunter and the bear. The two stories, the old man's and the Inuit woman's, thus comment on each other. The woman's vengeance bears a double victory, one the triumph of her people, the other a vindication of her sexuality over its abuses by whites. Yet the old man's story ends menacingly for the hunter, suggesting that the Native American's fate is–like the hunter–perilous amid the alien culture that both attracts and repels.

SUGGESTED READINGS

Antel, Judith A. "Momaday, Welch, and Silko: Expressing the Feminine Principle Through Male Alienation." *American Indian Quarterly* 12, no. 3 (1988): 212-220.

Barnett, Louise K., and James L. Thorson, eds. *Leslie Marmon Silko: A Collection of Critical Essays.* Albuquerque: University of New Mexico Press, 1999.

Danielson, Linda. "Storyteller: Grandmother's Spider Web." *Journal of the Southwest* 30, no. 3 (1988): 325-355.

Hoilman, Dennis. "'A World Made of Stories': An Interpretation of Leslie Silko's *Ceremony.*" *South Dakota Review* 17, no. 4 (1979): 54-66.

Jaskoski, Helen. *Leslie Marmon Silko: A Study of the Short Fiction.* New York: Twayne, 1998.

Larson, Charles. *American Indian Fiction.* Albuquerque: University of New Mexico Press, 1978.

Lincoln, Kenneth. *Native American Renaissance.* Berkeley: University of California Press, 1983.

Rand, Naomi R. *Silko, Morrison, and Roth: Studies in Survival.* New York: Peter Lang, 1999.

–Edward A. Fiorelli

Isaac Bashevis Singer

Born: Leoncin, Poland; July 14 or November 21, 1904
Died: Surfside, Florida; July 24, 1991

Singer, who was awarded the Nobel Prize in Literature in 1978, is perhaps the most influential, prolific, and admired Jewish American author of the twentieth century.

Traditions: Jewish

Principal works: *Der Sotn in Gorey*, 1935 (*Satan in Goray*, 1955); *Di Familie Muskat*, 1950 (*The Family Moskat*, 1950); *Mayn Tatn's Besdin Shtub*, 1956 (*In My Father's Court*, 1966); *Gimpel the Fool and Other Stories*, 1957; *Shotns baym Hodson*, 1957-1958 (*Shadows on the Hudson*, 1998); *Der Kunstnmakher fun Lublin*, 1958-1959 (*The Magician of Lublin*, 1960); *Der Knekht*, 1961 (*The Slave*, 1962); *Short Friday and Other Stories*, 1964; *Sonim, de Geshichte fun a Liebe*, 1966 (*Enemies: A Love Story*, 1972); *A Crown of Feathers and Other Stories*, 1973; *Passions and Other Stories*, 1975; *Old Love*, 1979; *The Death of Methuselah and Other Stories*, 1988; *Meshugah*, 1994

The son and grandson of rabbis, Isaac Bashevis Singer was born into a pious Hasidic household in Poland, which he would imaginatively portray in his memoir *In My Father's Court*. He began his literary career writing for a Hebrew newspaper and proofreading for a journal that his brother, novelist Israel Joshua Singer, coedited. In 1925, Singer made his fiction debut with a prize-winning short story, "In Old Age." In 1932, he began co-editing *Globus*, which serialized *Satan in Goray*, his novel of messianic heresy.

In 1935, Singer emigrated to New York, where he wrote for the *Jewish Daily Forward*. Several years went by before Singer found the full strength of his writer's voice. He believed that an author needed roots, but he had lost his. Never easily placed within any tradition, Singer wrote first in Yiddish and then translated his work into English. His decision to write in Yiddish, which he knew was a dying language, was linked to his identification with a world that was destroyed by the Nazis.

Singer's work not only recalls that lost world, but his questions about the meaning of life reflect modern existential concerns. In *Enemies: A Love Story*, Herman Broder protests against suffering and the anguish of abandonment. Harry Bendiner of the story "Old Love" dreams of meditating in a solitary tent with the daughter of a dead love on why people are born and why people must die. *Neshome Ekspeditsyes* (1974; *Shosha*, 1978) concludes as two friends, reunited after the Holocaust, sit in a darkening room, waiting, as one says with a laugh, for an answer. It seems that Singer's characters all await a moment of revelation that will be more than a faint glimmer in a darkened room.

"A Crown of Feathers"

TYPE OF WORK: Short fiction
FIRST PUBLISHED: 1973, in *A Crown of Feathers and Other Stories*

"A Crown of Feathers" is the title story of a collection which won the National Book Award for 1973. Like many of Singer's stories, it depicts an individual pulled between belief and disbelief, between the religious and the secular, and between self and others. The story concerns an orphan, Akhsa, whose own emerging identity becomes entangled with the conflicting values of her wealthy grandparents.

Her grandfather is a traditionally religious man, a community leader in the Polish village of Krasnobród, while her grandmother, from the sophisticated city of Prague, is more worldly and possibly, it is learned after her death, a follower of false messiahs. These differences, presented very subtly at first, become more pronounced when, after her grandparents' deaths, Akhsa internalizes their warring voices.

Each voice accuses the other of being a demon, while both battle over Akhsa's soul. Her grandmother assures her that Jesus is the Messiah and encourages Akhsa to convert. As a sign, she has Akhsa rip open her pillowcase, where she finds an intricate crown of feathers topped by a tiny cross. Akhsa converts, makes an unhappy marriage with an alcoholic Polish squire, and sinks into melancholy. Her despair is not mere unhappiness, but a continuing crisis of faith. A demon tells her, "The truth is there is no truth," but her

Isaac Bashevis Singer (©The Nobel Foundation)

saintly grandfather appears and tells her to repent.

Her grandfather's advice leads Akhsa to return to Judaism and to seek out and marry the man her grandfather had chosen for her years before. This embittered man, however, humiliates her mercilessly. On her deathbed, Akhsa tears open her pillowcase and finds another crown of feathers, this one with the Hebrew letters for God in place of the cross. "But, she wondered, in what way was this crown more a revelation of truth than the other?"

Akhsa never grasps with certainty the truth she has sought, nor is she ever able, like Singer's Gimpel the Fool, to accept the ambiguity of uncertainty. Akhsa's conversion and subsequent exile, her repentance and journey back to her grandfather's faith—her entire life—have constituted an agonized quest for truth. Torn between two voices of authority, Akhsa has never been certain of her own voice, has never understood her own wants, needs, or beliefs. While Gimpel, when finding his vocation as wandering storyteller, ultimately finds a faith to which he can firmly adhere, Akhsa finds neither self nor truth. Moving from one pole of certain faith to its opposite, and back again, Akhsa never accepts Singer's own truth, which is that "if there is such a thing as truth it is as intricate and hidden as a crown of feathers."

"Gimpel the Fool"

TYPE OF WORK: Short fiction
FIRST PUBLISHED: "Gimpel Tam," 1945 (English translation, 1953)

The publication of "Gimpel the Fool," in a translation from the Yiddish by Saul Bellow, launched Singer's career. During the 1950's and thereafter, his work appeared widely in English, and throughout the history of Singer studies, "Gimpel the Fool" has held a place of honor. Gimpel belongs to a brotherhood of literary characters—that of the schlemiels. In this work, Singer explores the nature of belief, which, in the modern, secular world, is often considered foolish.

Gimpel believes whatever he is told: that his parents have risen from the dead, that his pregnant fiancée is a virgin, that her children are his children, that the man jumping out of her bed is a figment of his imagination. Gimpel extends his willingness to believe to every aspect of his life, because, he explains: "Everything is possible, as it is written in the Wisdom of the Fathers, I've forgotten just how."

When, on her deathbed, his wife of twenty years confesses that none of her six children are his, Gimpel is tempted to disbelieve all that he has been told and to enact revenge against those who have participated in his humiliation. His temptation is a central crisis of faith. His faith in others, who have betrayed him, is challenged, as is his faith in himself and in God, because among the stories he has believed are those pertaining to the existence of God. Gimpel's belief has always been riddled with doubt; only after he concretizes his spiritual exile by becoming a wanderer does he resolve his faith.

In Singer's fictional worlds, God is the first storyteller who, through words, spoke or wrote the world into being. Belief in God is linked to belief in stories. Thus, when Gimpel is tempted to disbelieve in God, he responds by becoming a wandering storyteller. In so doing Gimpel links himself with the great storyteller and transforms what was once simple gullibility into an act of the greatest faith. As a storyteller, Gimpel opens himself fully to the infinite possibilities of the divine word as it is transformed into the world. At the end, Gimpel still yearns for a world where even he cannot be deceived. He never finds this world. Despite the void he may face, he chooses to believe, and he finds, in his final great act of suspending disbelief, a faith to which he can firmly adhere.

SUGGESTED READINGS

Alexander, Edward. *Isaac Bashevis Singer: A Study of the Short Fiction.* Boston: Twayne, 1990.

Farrell, Grace. "Suspending Disbelief: Faith and Fiction in I. B. Singer." *Boulevard* 9, no. 3 (Fall, 1994): 111-117.

Farrell Lee, Grace. *From Exile to Redemption: The Fiction of Isaac Bashevis Singer.* Carbondale: Southern Illinois University Press, 1987.

Fiedler, Leslie. "Isaac Bashevis Singer: Or, The American-ness of the American Jewish Writer." In *Fiedler on the Roof: Essays on Literature and Jewish Identity.* Boston: David R. Godine, 1991.

Friedman, Lawrence S. *Understanding Isaac Bashevis Singer.* Columbia: University of South Carolina Press, 1988.

Hadda, Janet. *Isaac Bashevis Singer: A Life.* New York: Oxford University Press, 1997.

Pinsker, Sanford. *The Schlemiel as Metaphor.* Carbondale: Southern Illinois University Press, 1991.

Siegel, Ben. *Isaac Bashevis Singer.* Minneapolis: University of Minnesota Press, 1969.

Wisse, Ruth R. *The Schlemiel as Modern Hero.* Chicago: University of Chicago Press, 1971.

Wood, Michael. "Victims of Survival." *The New York Review of Books,* February 7, 1974, 10-12.

—Grace Farrell

Cathy Song

BORN: Honolulu, Hawaii; August 20, 1955

Song, who was the first Asian American writer to win, in 1982, a Yale Younger Poets Award, has established a formidable reputation as a chronicler of personal experience in multiplicity.

TRADITIONS: Chinese American, Korean American
PRINCIPAL WORKS: *Picture Bride*, 1983; *Frameless Windows, Squares of Light*, 1988; *School Figures*, 1994

Having grown up in the culturally and ethnically diverse society of Hawaii in a family that had been there for at least two generations, Cathy Song does not write about racial or ethnic anxieties or the pains of being an outsider in an Anglo world. Her poems reflect a family that has been close and nurturing. The title of her first book, *Picture Bride*, refers to her Korean grandmother, who immigrated to Hawaii to marry a man who knew her only from a photograph. Song's paternal grandfather was also Korean; her mother is Chinese. Song's original title for the book, "From the White Place," refers to the paintings of Georgia O'Keeffe, which she encountered while at Wellesley College, from which she was graduated in 1977. She went on to receive a master's degree in creative writing from Boston University in 1981. Her vivid imagery and interest in the subject of perspective indicate her fascination with visual art. The dominant strain in *Picture Bride* is the connection between the first-person speaker and her relatives. Song's poems show little interest in political or social issues per se. Song's appreciation of her Asian heritage, however, appears powerfully in poems such as "Girl Powdering Her Neck," which concerns a painting by the eighteenth century Japanese artist, Kitagawa Utamaro, and ends with a haiku: "Two chrysanthemums/ touch in the middle of the lake/ and drift apart."

Song appears as a somewhat distant narrator in poems such as "Chinatown" and "Magic Island," which are found in *Frameless Windows, Squares of Light*. These poems concern the immigrant experience, which she knows only secondhand. The deft beauty of a poem such as "Magic Island" does not compare with the personally felt experience of "Living Near the Water," in which the poet watches her father give his dying father a drink of water. Her own children appear in these poems: Her blond son in "Heaven," for example, thinks, "when we die we'll go to China."

The blended worlds of Cathy Song are celebrated in her third book, *School Figures*, which opens with a poem on Ludwig Bemelmans's Madeline series of children's books. "Mother on River Street" depicts the poet's mother and aunts eating at a Vietnamese restaurant and recalling Sei Mui, who, as a girl, fell out of Mrs. Chow's car. In the title poem, Western painters such as Piet Mondrian and Pieter Bruegel merge with Katsushika Hokusai. Song's poems portray not a simple multiculturalism but rather–as in "Square Mile," in which she sees her son sitting in the same classroom she once sat in and herself on the same hill her father once was on–a profound and affectionate personal unity.

Picture Bride
TYPE OF WORK: Poetry
FIRST PUBLISHED: 1983

The content and form of *Picture Bride*, Song's first book of poems, reflect intimately the personal background and interests of its author. Therefore, many of these poems have their locations in Hawaii, where she was born and reared, and the continental United States, where she attended university and married. Song's poems are valuable repositories of an Asian American woman's sensibilities as they experience the intricate varieties of familial and personal relationships–as daughter, wife, mother, lover, and friend. Art, too, is an informing interest of Song's, especially that of the Japanese ukiyo-e master Utamaro and that of the American feminist painter Georgia O'Keeffe, whose life and works lend inspiration and shape to this book of poems.

Picture Bride is organized into five sections, each deriving its title from a painting by O'Keeffe. The book begins with an initial statement of themes and an imagistic setting of scenes in "Black Iris" (familial relationships and home); continues with the development of these themes and scenes in "Sunflower"; moves into a contemplation of the effort and achievement of art in the central "Orchids"; renders scenes suggesting a darker, perhaps Dionysian, side to art and life in "Red Poppy"; and proceeds to a final affirmation of the validity and variety of human creativity and productivity in "The White Trumpet Flower." The central section of the book also contains the key poem "Blue and White Lines After O'Keeffe," whose speaker is Song's imaginative re-creation of Georgia O'Keeffe and which is itself divided into five subsections with subtitles that replicate the titles of the sections of the book itself.

The title poem, "Picture Bride," is a young Korean American woman's meditation on the feelings, experience, and thoughts of her immigrant grandmother, who came to Hawaii to be married to a worker in the sugarcane fields. This piece strikes a chord present in many of the book's poems: a woman's (and especially an ethnic woman's) experience of family. Because Song's feminism is so imbued with ethnicity, some readers may prefer to call her work "womanist," the term coined by African American author Alice Walker in *In Search of Our Mothers' Gardens* (1983). That Song should choose to meditate on her grandmother in "Picture Bride" may seem natural enough to contemporary American readers, but in terms of traditional Confucian and Asian hierarchy, Song should have memorialized and venerated her male ancestor. Instead, the grandfather is devalorized into a mere "stranger." Therefore, Song's choice of subject in this poem is itself a break from traditional Asian patriarchy and a declaration of allegiance to a feminist hierarchy of family history.

Many of Song's poems elude a rigid thematic categorization that would separate, for example, poems of women's experience from those about ethnicity or from those about art. In fact, these themes are sometimes organically and inextricably intertwined. For example, one will happen on poems about ethnic women's experience and about women artists/artisans, such as "The Seamstress," whose speaker is a Japanese American woman who makes dolls and creates wedding gowns but who seems condemned to remain in the background, a silent spinster (and spinner), or "For A. J.: On Finding That She's on Her Boat to China," which addresses an Asian ballerina manquee returning to Asia to become a materfamilias.

Women's experience, ethnicity, and art are therefore the main spheres of interest in *Picture Bride*, while the works of feminist artist O'Keeffe provide it with an encompassing structure and indwelling spirit.

SUGGESTED READINGS

Fujita-Sato, Gayle K. "'Third World' as Place and Paradigm in Cathy Song's *Picture Bride." MELUS* 15 (Spring, 1988): 49-72.

Gaffke, Carol T., and Anna J. Sheets, eds. *Poetry Criticism: Excerpts from Criticism of the Works of the Most Significant and Widely Studied Poets of World Literature.* Vol. 21. Detroit: Gale Research, 1998.

Lim, Shirley. "Reconstructing Asian-American Poetry: A Case for Ethnopoetics." *MELUS* 14, no. 2 (Summer, 1987): 51-63.

_____. Review of *Picture Bride*, by Cathy Song. *MELUS* 10, no. 3 (Fall, 1983): 95-99.

Sumida, Stephen H. "Pictures of Art and Life." *Contact II* 7, nos. 38-40 (1986): 52-55.

Wallace, Patricia. "Divided Loyalties: Literal and Literary in the Poetry of Lorna Dee Cervantes, Cathy Song, and Rita Dove." *MELUS* 18, no. 3 (Fall, 1993): 3-19.

—Ron McFarland/Laura Mitchell and C. L. Chua

Gary Soto

BORN: Fresno, California; April 12, 1952

Soto's poems, short stories, memoirs, young adult novels, and children's stories bring to life the joys and pains of growing up in the barrio.

TRADITIONS: Mexican American

PRINCIPAL WORKS: *The Elements of San Joaquin*, 1977; *Where Sparrows Work Hard*, 1981; *Black Hair*, 1985; *Living up the Street: Narrative Recollections*, 1985; *Small Faces*, 1986; *Who Will Know Us*, 1990; *Baseball in April, and Other Stories*, 1990; *A Summer Life*, 1990; *Home Course in Religion*, 1991; *Pacific Crossing*, 1992; *The Pool Party*, 1993; *Too Many Tamales*, 1993; *New and Selected Poems*, 1995; *Nickel and Dime*, 2000

Gary Soto was born to American parents of Mexican heritage and grew up in the Spanish-speaking neighborhoods in and around Fresno, California. Soto's father died when Soto was five years old; he and his siblings were reared by his mother and grandparents. After being graduated from high school in 1970, Soto attended the University of California at Irvine, where he later earned an M.F.A.

Soto's life provides much of the material for his writing. He uses his cultural heritage and neighborhood traditions as the setting for stories and poems about growing up poor and Chicano. In *The Elements of San Joaquin*, his first book, he focuses on Fresno of the 1950's. He chronicles the lives of migrant workers, of oppressed people caught in cycles of poverty and violence. In the later poetry collection, *Who Will Know Us*, Soto draws again on his life. In "That Girl," for example, he is the young "Catholic boy" at the public library, while in "Another Time," he is an adult reconsidering the death of his father.

Soto turns to prose with *Living up the Street: Narrative Recollections*, a volume of twenty-one autobiographical stories. His talent in this work is in the minute: Soto is concerned with the small event, with the everyday. In this book he explores racism through vignettes from his own life. Rather than tackle racism in the abstract, he instead offers the concrete: the fight after being called a "dirty Mexican," the anger after an Anglo child wins a beauty contest. Soto also writes books for children and young adults. His matter-of-fact use of Spanish expressions as well as his references to the sights and sounds of the Latino community provide young readers with a sense of cultural identity.

Perhaps Soto's greatest success is his ability to assert his ethnicity while demonstrating that the experiences of growing up are universal. His bittersweet stories remind his readers of their passages from childhood to adulthood, of their search for identities that began up the street.

A Summer Life

TYPE OF WORK: Short fiction
FIRST PUBLISHED: 1990

A Summer Life is a collection of thirty-nine short vignettes based on Soto's life that chronicle his coming-of-age in California. The book is arranged in three sections covering Soto's early childhood, preadolescence, and the time prior to adulthood. Soto is the writer of the everyday. In the first section, his world is bounded by his neighborhood and his eyes see this world in the sharp, concrete images of childhood. In "The Hand Brake," for example, he writes, "One afternoon in July, I invented a brake for a child's running legs. It was an old bicycle hand brake. I found it in the alley that ran alongside our house, among the rain-swollen magazines, pencils, a gutted clock and sun-baked rubber bands that cracked when I bunched them around my fingers."

Soto's Latino heritage forms the background. Soto identifies himself with this community in the descriptions he chooses for the everyday realities: his grandfather's wallet is "machine tooled with 'MEXICO' and a *campesino* and donkey climbing a hill"; his mother pounds "a round steak into *carne asada*" and crushes "a heap of beans into *refritos.*"

Gary Soto (M. L. Martinelle)

Soto's experiences include the sounds of Spanish and the objects of the barrio, but they seem universal. At heart, the book is a child's movement toward self-awareness. Through *A Summer Life*, Soto paints his growing self-consciousness and increasing awareness of life and of death. "I was four and already at night thinking of the past," he writes, "The cat with a sliver in his eye came and went. . . . the three sick pups shivered and blinked twilight in their eyes . . . the next day they rolled over into their leaf-padded graves."

In the last story in *A Summer Life*, "The River," Soto is seventeen. He and his friend Scott have traveled to Los Angeles to find themselves amid the "mobs of young people in leather vests, bell-bottoms, beads, Jesus thongs, tied-dyed shirts, and crowns of flowers." As the two of them bed down that night in an uncle's house, Soto seems to find that instant between childhood and adulthood, between the past and the present: "I thought of Braley Street and family, some of whom were now dead, and how when Uncle returned from the Korean War, he slept on a cot on the sunporch. . . . We had yet to go and come back from our war and find ourselves a life other than the one we were losing." In this moment, Soto speaks for all readers who recall that thin edge between yesterday and today.

SUGGESTED READINGS

Augenbraum, Harold, and Ilan Stavans, eds. *Growing Up Latino: Memoirs and Stories*. Boston: Houghton Mifflin, 1993.

Bruce-Novoa, Juan. *Chicano Authors: Inquiry by Interview*. Austin: University of Texas Press, 1980.

_____. *Chicano Poetry: A Response to Chaos*. Austin: University of Texas Press, 1982.

Lattin, Vernon, ed. *Contemporary Chicano Fiction: A Critical Survey*. Binghamton, N.Y.: Bilingual Press, 1986.

Martinez, Julio A., and Francisco A. Lomelí. *Chicano Literature: A Reference Guide*. Westport, Conn.: Greenwood Press, 1985.

Ponce, Mary Helen. Review of *Nickel and Dime*, by Gary Soto. *Hispanic* 13 (March, 2000): 68.

Soto, Gary, ed. *Pieces of the Heart: New Chicano Fiction*. San Francisco: Chronicle Books, 1993.

Tatum, Charles. *Chicano Literature*. Boston: Twayne, 1982.

—Diane Andrews Henningfeld

Shelby Steele

BORN: Chicago, Illinois; January 1, 1946

Steele's writings and lectures forced public debate on new ways to view radical discrimination and civil rights matters.

TRADITIONS: African American
PRINCIPAL WORKS: *The Content of Our Character: A New Vision of Race in America*, 1990; *A Dream Deferred: The Second Betrayal of Black Freedom in America*, 1998

Shelby Steele grew up in Chicago under the guidance of strong parents who provided a stable family relationship for him, his twin brother, and his two sisters. Having interracial parents, Steele was influenced by two races, although he more strongly identified with his black heritage. As a college student, he became involved in the Civil Rights movement of the 1960's, following, at different times, the leads of Martin Luther King, Jr., and Malcolm X. Steele led civil rights marches at Coe College in Cedar Rapids, Iowa, and protested that African Americans were victimized by white society.

After the completion of his education, his marriage to a white woman, and the birth of their two children, Steele developed new thoughts about African Americans in America. He came to the conclusion that opportunities are widely available to all citizens if they have personal initiative and a strong work ethic. Upon reaching this conclusion, which ran counter to his earlier ideas, Steele began to publish his ideas in major magazines and journals. His philosophy was often harshly dismissed by leaders in the Civil Rights movement, but it also garnered much praise, especially from African American political conservatives.

Steele was one of a few African Americans willing to challenge what was called the civil rights orthodoxy. When his work was published, he quickly became the subject of magazine and journal articles and was interviewed widely on radio and television, all the while drawing fire from numerous civil rights leaders.

In 1990, his first book, *The Content of Our Character*, was published. With this collection of his essays on race relations in America, Steele became recognized as a leading spokesman for political conservatives of all races. The main thesis of his book is that individual initiative, self-sufficiency, and strong families are what black America needs. Although labeled conservative by many, Steele refuses the label and calls himself a "classical Jeffersonian liberal."

Shelby Steele (Hoover Institution, Stanford University)

The Content of Our Character

TYPE OF WORK: Essays
FIRST PUBLISHED: 1990

With *The Content of Our Character: A New Vision of Race in America*, Steele created a debate on the merits of affirmative action, the direction of the Civil Rights movement, and the growing ranks of African American political conservatives. Although certainly not the first to challenge views held by African American leaders, Steele pushed his challenge onto center stage more forcefully than others had before. Coming at a time when the United States was awash in conservative radio and television talk shows, the book quickly became a source of contention among political groups of all races and philosophies. Steele, through his television appearances, became a familiar figure throughout America as he explained and defended his ideas on race problems in America.

The book, titled after a line in Martin Luther King, Jr.'s famous speech, is a collection of essays, most of which appeared earlier in various periodicals. Central to Steele's book is a call for the African American community to examine itself and look to itself for opportunities. He calls for African Americans to look not to government or white society but to itself for the solutions to its problems. Steele contends that African Americans enjoy unparalleled freedom; they have only to seize their freedom and make it work for them. He suggests that such programs as affirmative action contribute to the demoralization or demeaning of African Americans because preferential treatment denies them the opportunity to "make it on their own."

Steele, calling for a return to the original purpose of the Civil Rights movement, says that affirmative action should go back to enforcing equal opportunity rather than demanding preferences. The promised land is, he writes, an opportunity, not a deliverance. Steele's ideas were strongly challenged by African Americans who believe that affirmative action and other civil rights measures are necessary for minority groups to retain the advancements that have been forged and to assure an open path for further progress. Opposition to Steele and other African American conservatives has led to charges that traditional African American civil rights leaders' intolerance of different voices within the black community is itself a form of racism.

SUGGESTED READINGS

Anderson, Michael. Review of *A Dream Deferred*, by Shelby Steele. *The New York Times Book Review* 103 (November 22, 1998): 34.

Drake, William Avon, and Robert D. Holsworth. *Affirmative Action and the Stalled Quest for Black Progress*. Champaign: University of Illinois Press, 1996.

Little, Malcolm. *The Autobiography of Malcolm X*. New York: Ballantine, 1965.

Lokos, Lionel. *The New Racism: Reverse Discrimination in America.* New Rochelle, N.Y.: Arlington House, 1971.

Oates, Stephen B. *Let the Trumpet Sound: The Life of Martin Luther King, Jr.* New York: Harper & Row, 1982.

−*Kay Hively*

Amy Tan

BORN: Oakland, California; February 19, 1952

Tan's novels are among the first to bring literary accounts of Asian American women to a broad audience.

TRADITIONS: Chinese American
PRINCIPAL WORKS: *The Joy Luck Club*, 1989; *The Kitchen God's Wife*, 1991; *The Hundred Secret Senses*, 1995

Amy Tan was born to parents who immigrated from China to California two years before she was born, and her work is influenced by the Asian American people and community she knew in her childhood. Each of her novels features characters who have either immigrated from China or who, like Tan, are the children of those immigrants. Like many immigrants to the United States, Tan's parents had high expectations for their daughter. Tan writes: "I was led to believe from the age of six that I would grow up to be a neurosurgeon by trade and a concert pianist by hobby." In her first two novels, especially, Tan writes of the pressures her young Chinese American characters feel as they try to meet high parental expectations while also craving a normal carefree childhood.

Tan did not initially plan to be a writer of fiction. She was working long hours as a technical writer, and sought psychological therapy to help her with her workaholic tendencies. When she became dissatisfied with her therapist, who sometimes fell asleep during her sessions, she decided to use fiction writing as her therapy instead.

Tan struggled with her Chinese heritage; as a girl, she contemplated cosmetic surgery to make her look less Asian. She was ashamed of her cultural identity until she moved with her mother and brother to Switzerland, where Tan attended high school. There, Asians were a rarity, and Tan was asked out on dates because she was suddenly exotic.

Experiences from her life find their way into her novels, especially *The Joy Luck Club*. As do the characters Rose Hsu and Waverly Jong, Tan experienced the death of a brother. Waverly, like Tan, is married to a tax attorney of European descent. Tan and her husband, Lou DeMattei, married in 1974. In fact, several of Tan's Chinese American women characters are married to European American husbands.

Amy Tan's novels have all been acclaimed by critics as well-crafted works of fiction and as keyholes through which the reader can peer into a culture that has seldom been explored in American literature.

Amy Tan (AP/Wide World Photos)

The Hundred Secret Senses

TYPE OF WORK: Novel
FIRST PUBLISHED: 1995

The Hundred Secret Senses, Tan's third novel, continues her interest in Chinese and Chinese American culture, especially the strife between family members who are traditionally Chinese and those who are more Americanized. Half-

Caucasian, half-Chinese Olivia meets, at age six, her eighteen-year-old Chinese half sister, Kwan, the daughter of her father's first marriage. Kwan instigates Olivia's struggle with her Chinese identity. Olivia is alternately embarrassed, annoyed, and mystified by this sister who claims that she has daily communication with "yin people"–helpful ghosts–many of whom are the spirits of friends from Kwan's past lives. Despite her ambivalence, however, Olivia gains most of her awareness about her Chinese background from Kwan. The sisters' Chinese father has died, and Olivia is being raised in the United States by a Caucasian mother and an Italian American stepfather. After Kwan's arrival from China, the older girl is largely responsible for her sister's care. Thus, Olivia resentfully learns Chinese and learns about her Chinese heritage, including knowledge about the ghosts who populate her sister's world. Olivia is understandably skeptical about the presence of these yin people. In Olivia's culture, such ghosts are the stuff of scary films, while for Kwan, they are a part of everyday life. The title, then, refers to the hundred secret senses that, Kwan asserts, enable one to perceive the yin people. Kwan's stories about a past life are the fairy tales with which Olivia grows up.

Later, Olivia marries a half-Hawaiian, half-Caucasian man, Simon, and as the novel opens, they are beginning divorce proceedings after a long marriage. Olivia begins these proceedings in part because she believes that Simon is still in love with a former girlfriend, who died shortly before Simon and Olivia met. Olivia must develop her own sense of personal and ethnic identity in order to release this ghost from her past. She must begin to believe that she is worthy of Simon's love, and in order to discover her self-worth, she must travel to the tiny Chinese village where her sister grew up.

Although Olivia believes herself to be very American, once she, Simon, and Kwan arrive in China, she begins to feel much closer to her Chinese heritage, and in the storytelling tradition of all Tan's novels, Olivia learns about her family's past while talking to residents of the village in which Kwan grew up. Olivia also is able to confront her difficulties with Simon as a result of the trip.

The Joy Luck Club
TYPE OF WORK: Novel
FIRST PUBLISHED: 1989

The Joy Luck Club, Tan's first novel, debuted to critical acclaim. It takes its place alongside Maxine Hong Kingston's *The Woman Warrior* (1976) as a chronicle of a Chinese American woman's search for and exploration of her ethnic identity. *The Joy Luck Club* is the best-selling, accessible account of four Chinese-born mothers and their four American-born daughters. One of the women, Suyuan Woo, has died before the story opens, but the other seven women tell their own stories from their individual points of view. Critics have noted that this approach is an unusually ambitious one. Nevertheless, the novel has reached a wide audience, especially since it was made into a feature film in 1992.

At the center of the story is Jing-mei "June" Woo, who has been asked to replace her dead mother as a member of the Joy Luck Club, a group of four women who meet for food and mah-jongg. Although Americanized and non-Chinese-speaking June is initially uncertain whether she wishes to join her mother's friends, she discovers that these women know things about her mother's past that she had never imagined. Her decision to become part of the Joy Luck Club culminates in a visit to China, where she meets the half sisters whom her mother was forced to abandon before she fled to the United States. The other Chinese-born women have similarly tragic stories, involving abandonment, renunciation, and sorrow in their native country. June says of her mother's decision to begin the club: "My mother could sense that the women of these families also had unspeakable tragedies they had left behind in China and hopes they couldn't begin to express in their fragile English." Each of these women's hopes includes hopes for her daughter. Each American daughter feels that she has in some way disappointed her mother. Waverly Jong fulfills her mother's ambitions by becoming a chess prodigy, then quits suddenly, to her mother's sorrow. June can never live up to her mother's expectations, and she rebels by refusing to learn the piano. Rose Hsu turns away for a moment, and her youngest brother drowns. Lena St. Clair makes a marriage based on false ideals of equality, and only her mother understands its basic injustice. These American-born daughters insist that they are not Chinese; as June says, she has no "Chinese whatsoever below my skin." By the end of the novel, they find themselves realizing how truly Chinese they are.

The Kitchen God's Wife

TYPE OF WORK: Novel
FIRST PUBLISHED: 1991

The Kitchen God's Wife, Tan's second novel, is concerned with a young, Americanized Chinese American woman's quest to accept her heritage, and in so doing accept her family, especially her mother. The first section of the novel, told from the daughter Pearl's point of view, concerns Pearl's difficult relationship with her mother, Winnie. Pearl perceives Winnie only as an old, unfashionable woman with trivial concerns. Pearl is troubled by a secret that she believes she cannot tell her mother. Pearl has been diagnosed with multiple sclerosis but dreads her mother's reaction, her reproaches, her list of ways Pearl could have prevented her disease.

Pearl comes to recognize that her mother has secrets of her own, which

Winnie finally decides to share with her daughter. Most of the novel, which is also the part that has received the most critical praise, is Winnie's first-person account of her childhood. The reader discovers along with Pearl that her mother has not always been the penny-pinching part-owner of a dingy, outdated florist's shop. Instead, Winnie has had a life of tragedy and adventure before immigrating to the United States. She lived another life in China, complete with another husband and three long-dead children. Winnie's mother disappeared when Winnie was a child, leaving her with her father and his other wives, who promptly sent her to live with an uncle. That uncle married her to Wen Fu, a sadistic, adulterous pilot, and Winnie soon began the nomadic life of a soldier's wife during wartime. By the end of the war, Winnie found love with the man Pearl knows as her father, the Chinese American serviceman Jimmie Louie. Wen Fu had Winnie imprisoned for adultery when she tried to divorce him, then raped her upon her release. Pearl learns the secret her mother has been hiding–Jimmie Louie, who died when Pearl was fourteen, is not her biological father after all. When Pearl learns these secrets about her mother's past, she is finally able to reveal the secret of her illness.

The title refers to an altar that Pearl inherits from a woman Winnie had known in China, and it symbolizes the growing closeness that Winnie and Pearl develop after sharing their secrets. The final scene shows Winnie buying her daughter a deity for the altar. This statue, whom Winnie names Lady Sorrowfree, the kitchen god's wife, represents Winnie and her care for her daughter. By the end of the novel, Pearl achieves a greater understanding of her mother and of their often-trying relationship.

SUGGESTED READINGS

Dew, Robb Forman. Review of *The Kitchen God's Wife*, by Amy Tan. *The New York Times Book Review*, June 16, 1991, 9.

Ho, Wendy. *In Her Mother's House: The Politics of Asian American Mother-Daughter Writing*. Walnut Creek, Calif.: AltaMira Press, 1999.

Huntley, E. D. *Amy Tan: A Critical Companion*. Westport, Conn.: Greenwood Press, 1998.

Kakutani, Michiko. Review of *The Hundred Secret Senses*, by Amy Tan. *The New York Times*, November 17, 1995, p. C29.

Messud, Claire. Review of *The Hundred Secret Senses*, by Amy Tan. *The New York Times Book Review*, October 29, 1995, 11.

Pearlman, Mickey, and Katherine Usher Henderson. *Inter/View: Talks with America's Writing Women*. Lexington: University Press of Kentucky, 1990.

Schell, Orville. Review of *The Joy Luck Club*, by Amy Tan. *The New York Times Book Review*, March 19, 1989, 3.

Shapiro, Laura. Review of *The Hundred Secret Senses*, by Amy Tan. *Newsweek*, November 6, 1995, 91-92.

_____. Review of *The Kitchen God's Wife*, by Amy Tan. *Newsweek*, June 24, 1991, 63-64.

Watnabe, Sylvia, and Carol Bruchac, eds. *Home to Stay: Asian American Women's Fiction*. Greenfield Center, N.Y.: The Greenfield Review Press, 1990.

–J. Robin Coffelt

José Antonio Villarreal

BORN: Los Angeles, California; July 30, 1924

Villarreal is recognized as one of the first American writers of Mexican descent to portray the experiences of Mexican families who immigrated to the United States.

TRADITIONS: Mexican American

PRINCIPAL WORKS: *Pocho*, 1959; *The Fifth Horseman*, 1974; *Clemente Chacón*, 1984

José Antonio Villarreal's early life strongly resembles that of Richard Rubio, the hero of his first novel. Both had fathers who fought in the Mexican Revolution; both were born and raised in California. Villarreal also enjoyed, in childhood innocence, the few pleasures of the nomadic life of the migrant farmworker: living in tents, listening to Spanish stories around a campfire, absorbing Mexican lore and culture that was invisible in the white world. Like Richard, Villarreal learned English quickly but retained his fluency in Spanish. Love of language and books led him to early discovery of his desire to become a writer. Circumstances took both into the Navy in World War II. Although *Pocho* appears autobiographical in many ways, it is sometimes criticized as unrealistic in its portrayal of Richard's conscious intention to be a writer and as inattentive to the racism and injustice of American society. Villarreal rejects such pronouncements by declaring himself an American writer, not a Chicano writer. To the creator of *Pocho*, Richard's ethnic and ideological identities are only part of a greater quest for his identity as a man, an artist, and a human being.

Villarreal was graduated from the University of California at Berkeley, and since 1950 he has continued to write while supporting a family with a variety of jobs, including technical writer, magazine publisher, and teacher at a number of universities in California, Texas, and Mexico. During the Chicano movement of the 1970's, Villarreal published *The Fifth Horseman*, a novel that explores the Mexican Revolution sympathetically, suggesting its ideals are worthy of preservation in Mexican identity, although its excesses ought to be condemned.

Professional recognition and financial success have come hard to Villarreal, and perhaps as a result, the themes of work, money, and social mobility have become more dominant in his examination of the processes of acculturation. For example, *Clemente Chacón*, set in 1972, contrasts the life of the young insurance man Clemente, who hustles desperately to succeed in

American business and society, with the life of the adolescent Mario Carbajal, who hustles desperately simply to survive another day in Ciudad Juárez, Mexico. Exploitation of the poor and amoral ambition are qualities of both these characters and of their societies. Villarreal's creative focus on individual lives rather than on social institutions suggests that ultimately each person's choice is the origin of good or the origin of evil.

Pocho
Type of work: Novel
First published: 1959

Pocho is generally regarded as the first novel by an American of Mexican descent to represent the experiences of emigration from Mexico and acculturation to the United States. Although this pioneering work went out of print shortly after publication, a second edition appeared in 1970 during the Chicano Renaissance, and it has since become part of many multicultural literature classes. Set in the years between 1923 and 1942, the novel recounts the quest for personal and cultural identity by Richard Rubio, son of a soldier exiled after the Mexican Revolution and now a migrant farmworker in Santa Clara, California. As a *pocho*, a member of the first generation born in the United States, Richard grows up deeply attached to the traditions of his family and very attracted to the values and lifestyles of his American peers.

In addition to trials faced by every young person while growing up, such as the struggle with authority, the search for independence, the thirst for knowledge, and the hunger for sexual experience, Richard faces special challenges in self-definition. He confronts poverty, family instability, a blighted education system, racial prejudice, a society torn by economic crises, and world war.

Richard's passage from childhood into adulthood is given unique shape not only by the circumstances of the Depression but also by the turmoil of life as an itinerant farmworker and the powerful tensions between Mexican and American cultures. Poverty inspires his dreams of success. A life of physical labor belies his intellectual nature. He identifies intensely with his macho father but cannot abide his violence, coldness, and self-destructiveness. Drawn to the beauties of the church, he nonetheless rejects faith. He is deeply attached to his mother but finds her helplessness repugnant. Obliged to become the man of the family as a teenager, he finds that his responsibilities clash with his solitary nature, his love of books, and his emerging personal identity as a writer. His choice to join the Navy is more personal than patriotic. To resolve his conflicts he chooses exile from his shattered family, escapes from his poverty without prospects, and seeks release from the fragments of the two cultures he has not yet pieced together. He leaves to face what he knows will be a struggle for a new identity as a man, as an artist, and as an American.

SUGGESTED READINGS

Bruce-Novoa, Juan. "Canonical and Noncanonical Texts: A Chicano Case Study." In *Redefining American Literary History*, edited by A. LaVonne Brown Ruoff and Jerry W. Ward, Jr. New York: Modern Language Association of America, 1990.

_____. *Chicano Authors: Inquiry by Interview*. Austin: University of Texas Press, 1980.

Hinojosa, Rolando. "Mexican-American Literature: Toward an Identification." *Books Abroad* 49, no. 3 (Summer, 1975): 422-430.

Paredes, Raymund A. "The Evolution of Chicano Literature." In *Three American Literatures: Essays in Chicano, Native American, and Asian-American Literature for Teachers of American Literature*, edited by Houston A. Baker, Jr. New York: Modern Language Association of America, 1982.

Rocard, Marcienne. *The Children of the Sun: Mexican-Americans in the Literature of the United States*. Translated by Edward G. Brown, Jr. Tucson: The University of Arizona Press, 1989.

Ruiz, Ramón. Introduction to *Pocho*, by José Antonio Villarreal. Garden City, N.J.: Anchor Press, 1970.

Saldívar, Ramón. *Chicano Narrative: The Dialectics of Difference*. Madison: The University of Wisconsin Press, 1990.

—Virginia M. Crane

Helena María Viramontes

BORN: East Los Angeles, California; February 26, 1954

Viramontes's feminist portrayals of Latinas struggling against patriarchy and poverty condemn classism, racism, and sexism.

TRADITIONS: Mexican American

PRINCIPAL WORKS: *The Moths and Other Stories*, 1985; *Chicana Creativity and Criticism: Charting New Frontiers in American Literature*, 1987 (coeditor with María Herrera-Sobek); *Chicana (W)rites: On Word and Film*, 1995 (coeditor with María Herrera-Sobek); *Under the Feet of Jesus*, 1995; *Their Dogs Came with Them*, 2000

Helena María Viramontes's work is shaped by her feminist and Chicano identities. Viramontes presents realistic portrayals of the struggles that women, particularly Chicanas, face as they attempt to grow up, raise families, and discover their identities. As a child, Viramontes attended schools in East Los Angeles with Chicano student bodies. Her parents were hardworking people—her father was a construction worker and her mother raised nine children.

Viramontes attended Immaculate Heart College with a scholarship for underprivileged girls and was graduated in 1975. After graduating she began to send her short stories out for publication, and in 1977 one of her first stories, "Requiem for the Poor," won first prize for fiction in a literary contest sponsored by *Statement* magazine of California State University, Los Angeles. Viramontes's work continued winning awards, and in 1981 she enrolled in the creative writing program at the University of California at Irvine. Her first collection of short stories, *The Moths and Other Stories*, was published in 1985. Perhaps one of Viramontes's greatest personal achievements was receiving a National Endowment for the Arts Fellowship in 1989 to attend a workshop given by Gabriel García Márquez at the Sundance Institute.

Viramontes's work has been highly influenced by García Márquez, by Chicana feminist writers Ana Castillo and Sandra Cisneros, and by such black writers as Alice Walker, Ntozake Shange, and Toni Morrison. In *The Moths and Other Stories*, Viramontes offers her reader portrayals of women at various stages in their lives. These women face complex issues such as adolescence, sexuality, politics, family, aging, and religion and must attempt to navigate their way through problems that are often caused by the patriarchal constructs of their cultures.

The Moths and Other Stories

TYPE OF WORK: Short fiction
FIRST PUBLISHED: 1985

The Moths and Other Stories focuses on the lives of Chicana women of various ages and backgrounds. The women in Viramontes's stories often face identity crises–they struggle with religion, adolescence, sexuality, family, and aging.

"The Moths" narrates the growth of a fourteen-year-old girl who cares for her grandmother. The grandmother's home is a refuge for the young woman, whose home is ruled by her father. When her grandmother dies, the girl laments the loss of a strong female figure who has helped shape her identity. "Growing" also focuses on a young Chicana woman who struggles with adolescence. Fifteen-year-old Naomi looks forward to her first date until her parents make her take along her little sister Lucia as a chaperone. Naomi insists that dating is "different" in America, but her parents insist on their own customs and Naomi wonders about the difficulties of growing up in a new country.

In the stories focusing on young women Viramontes raises the issues of religion, reproduction, and marriage. In "Birthday" a young, unmarried woman struggles over her decision to abort a child. "The Broken Web" focuses on a young woman and her struggles with repressed family memories. Martita learns that her father, Tomas, beat and cheated on her mother, and that her mother finally snapped and killed Tomas. "The Broken Web" shows a young woman dealing with the violence of her childhood. In "The Long Reconciliation" Amanda and Chato's marriage falls apart when Amanda refuses to bring children into their meager existence. After Amanda aborts their first child, Chato refuses all sexual contact with her and their marriage ends. "The Cariboo Cafe" focuses on the struggles of a young mother. Two children are kidnapped by a woman who has lost her own child in the political problems in Central America. Eventually the woman is discovered, and the children are taken away from her. She screams for her own son, Geraldo.

The final two stories focus on older women. In "Snapshots" Olga Ruiz, a middle-aged divorcée, attempts to come to terms with her past identities. As she sifts through family photographs, she realizes how little she has left of herself–she was too busy being a good wife and mother. "Neighbors" focuses on a lonely, elderly woman. Aura has nothing but her beautiful garden and her neighbor, Fierro. When a strange woman visits Fierro, Aura is upset by the change in their relationship. In her struggles with loneliness, Aura becomes fearful, and "Neighbors" examines the loneliness, isolation, and fear of being an old, solitary woman.

Women's issues are Viramontes's focus throughout *The Moths and Other Stories*, and her narratives focusing on the struggles of primarily Chicana women are tinged with the complexities of adolescence, sexuality, marriage, poverty, and family.

Under the Feet of Jesus

TYPE OF WORK: Novel
FIRST PUBLISHED: 1995

Under the Feet of Jesus traces the day-to-day lives of a group of Chicano migrant farmworkers, revealing the struggles they must endure as they attempt to survive on low wages and in poor living conditions. Helena María Viramontes is connected to this group of people in that her parents were migrant workers, and the book is dedicated to them and to the memory of César Chávez, a man who fought for the rights of farmworkers.

The narrative focuses on a large family headed by Perfecto Flores, a man in his seventies, and Petra, a woman who is thirty-seven years younger. Perfecto and Petra travel together with Petra's children, finding fieldwork wherever they can. Estrella is Petra's eldest daughter; she is thirteen, and her voice controls much of the narrative. There are two brothers, Ricky and Arnulfo, and twin girls, Perla and Cookie. Estrella works in the fields, as do her brothers and Perfecto.

The story becomes complicated by a young man named Alejo. Alejo and his cousin Gumecindo are also migratory workers employed by the same farms as Estrella and her family. The boys earn extra money by stealing fruit from the orchards at night. One night when they are raiding the orchard, biplanes fly overhead, spraying pesticides. Although Alejo and Gumecindo attempt to run from the orchards to avoid the poisoning pesticides, Alejo is sprayed and eventually becomes very sick. Since Alejo has become friends with Estrella and her family, Petra feels obliged to care for him. She tries all her healing methods, but nothing seems to work. Alejo gets sicker each day. As he grows weaker, love between Alejo and Estrella grows.

Finally Estrella and her family have no choice but to take Alejo to the clinic. The nurse tells Estrella that Alejo must go to the hospital, and charges them ten dollars for the clinic visit. Unfortunately Perfecto only has eight dollars and some change, and their gas tank is empty. He attempts to barter with the nurse, telling her he can do chores for the clinic, but she insists that she cannot give him work. Perfecto reluctantly hands over their last nine dollars, and they leave the clinic, wondering what they are going to do. Finally Estrella goes to the car, takes out the tire iron, and walks back into the clinic. She smashes the tire iron against the nurse's desk and demands the nine dollars back. With the last of their money Perfecto fills the gas tank, and they drive to the hospital. Estrella takes Alejo into the emergency room and is forced to leave him there, knowing they cannot pay the bill but that the doctors will help him.

SUGGESTED READINGS

Garza-Falcón, Leticia Magda. *Gente Decente: A Borderlands Response to the Rhetoric of Dominance.* Austin: University of Texas Press, 1998.

Sobek, María, and Helena María Viramontes, eds. *Chicana Creativity and Criticism: Charting New Frontiers in American Literature.* Houston, Tex.: Arte Público Press, 1988.

Yarbo-Bejarano, Yvonne. Introduction to *The Moths and Other Stories,* by Helena María Viramontes. Houston, Tex.: Arte Público Press, 1985.

—Angela Athy

Gerald Vizenor

BORN: Minneapolis, Minnesota; October 22, 1934

Tribal people and tribal identity are the foci of Vizenor's life and literary work.

TRADITIONS: American Indian
PRINCIPAL WORKS: *Raising the Moon Vines*, 1964; *Darkness in Saint Louis Bearheart*, 1978 (revised as *Bearheart: The Heirship Chronicles*, 1990); *Wordarrows: Indians and Whites in the New Fur Trade*, 1978; *Matsushima: Pine Islands*, 1984; *Griever: An American Monkey King in China*, 1987; *The Trickster of Liberty*, 1988; *Interior Landscapes: Autobiographical Myths and Metaphors*, 1990; *The Heirs of Columbus*, 1991; *Manifest Manners: Postindian Warriors of Survivance*, 1994; *Hotline Healers: An Almost Browne Novel*, 1997; *Chancers*, 2000

An original voice in postmodern literature, Native American author Gerald Vizenor is a brilliant novelist, poet, and essayist, as well as an influential critic. He has received the Josephine Miles PEN award for *Interior Landscapes*, 1990, the Illinois State University/Fiction Collective Prize, 1986, and the American Book Award in 1988 for *Griever: An American Monkey King in China*.

Vizenor believes that Native American imagination foreshadows many common postmodern literary strategies regarding identity. He uses the concept of "survivance" to denote the trickster's playful attitude that undercuts domination-victimization oppositions and produces new worldviews. The trickster uses stories and humor to tease out contradictions between good and evil in the world. *The Heirs of Columbus* announces, "I am not a victim of Columbus," and uses trickster storytelling to revise the history of relations between whites and tribal peoples. Always on the move, the trickster destabilizes "pure" identities. Tribal identities pass through tribal stories.

Vizenor, who claims a mixed Native American and European American heritage, belongs to the first generation of his family born off the reservation. When he was a child, his father was murdered, and his mother left him with foster families. At eighteen, he enlisted in the Army and went to Japan. In *Interior Landscapes*, Vizenor describes his discovery of Japanese haiku as a liberating, eye-opening experience important to his development as a writer.

Besides being a writer, Vizenor worked as a social worker, a mental hospital orderly, a camp counselor, and a reporter for the *Minneapolis Tribune*, where he was a staunch advocate for human rights. He established the American Indian Employment Center in Minneapolis and directed the first Native American studies program at Bemidji State University.

The Heirs of Columbus

TYPE OF WORK: Novel
FIRST PUBLISHED: 1991

Published shortly before the quincentennial of Christopher Columbus's 1492 voyage, Vizenor's *The Heirs of Columbus* proclaims: "I am not a victim of Columbus!" The novel tells of the nine tribal descendants of Christopher Columbus, including Stone Columbus, a late-night talk radio personality, and Felipa Flowers, a liberator of cultural artifacts. For the heirs, tribal identity rests in tribal stories, and they are consummate storytellers. "We are created in stories," the heirs say, and "language is our trick of discovery." Their trickster storytelling rewrites and renews the history of white and tribal peoples. Stone tells a story, central to the novel, asserting Columbus's Mayan, not Italian, ancestry. The Mayans brought their civilization to the Old World savages long ago, Stone argues. Columbus escaped Europe's "culture of death" and brought his "tribal genes" back to his homeland in the New World. Columbus did not discover the New World; he returned to it.

Gerald Vizenor

For some readers, *The Heirs of Columbus* might recall African American novelist Ishmael Reed's *Mumbo Jumbo* (1972). Both works have a fragmented style and are concerned with the theft and repatriation of tribal property. Felipa Flowers undertakes a mission to recapture sacred medicine pouches and the remains of her ancestor Christopher Columbus from the Brotherhood of American Explorers. After Felipa's successful raid, the heirs are taken to court to tell their story. They win their court case, but Felipa is later kidnapped and murdered in London when she tries to recapture the remains of Pocahontas.

After Felipa's death, the heirs create a sovereign nation at Point Assinika, "the wild estate of tribal memories and the genes of survivance in the New World." Theirs is a natural nation, where tricksters heal with their stories and where humor rules. Stone plans "to make the world tribal, a universal identity" dedicated to healing, not stealing, tribal cultures. To this end, the heirs gather genetic material from their tribal ancestors. They devise genetic therapies that use these healing genes to combat the destructive war herbs, which have the power to erase people from memory and history. Soon, Point Assinika becomes a place to heal abandoned and abused children with the humor of their ancestors.

Stories and genes in *The Heirs of Columbus* operate according to trickster logic, which subverts the "terminal creeds" of cultural domination and signals the reinvention of the world.

Interior Landscapes
TYPE OF WORK: Autobiography
FIRST PUBLISHED: 1990

Mixed-blood Native American novelist, poet, essayist, and critic Vizenor's imaginative autobiography *Interior Landscapes: Autobiographical Myths and Metaphors*, winner of the 1990 Josephine Miles PEN Award, recounts the author's triumphs, tragedies, and confrontations with racism. Throughout his autobiography, Vizenor adopts the mythic identity of the Native American trickster, who uses humor and stories to reinvent his world. "My stories are interior landscapes," Vizenor writes, and, as trickster autobiography, these stories about Vizenor's life enable him to mold his experience of his own life.

Vizenor had a rough childhood by any standard. After his father was stabbed to death, his mother left him with foster families while she vanished for years at a time. Later, she returned and married an alcoholic who beat him. When he was eighteen, Vizenor escaped into the Army. In the Army, Vizenor traveled to Japan, one of the most important experiences of his life. Views of Mount Fuji, a romance with a Japanese woman, and his first visit to a brothel inspired him to write haiku. After his discharge from the Army, Vizenor stayed in Japan. He later returned to the United States to study at New York University and the University of Minnesota, where he discovered writers such as Lafcadio Hearn, Jack London, and Thomas Wolfe. He also studied haiku in translation. Vizenor calls his discovery of Japanese literature his "second liberation." His haikus won for him his first college teaching job, and his continuing fascination with the haiku form is demonstrated in the collections *Two Wings the Butterfly* (1962), *Raising the Moon Vines* (1964),

Seventeen Chirps (1964), *Empty Swings* (1967), and *Matsushima: Pine Islands* (1984).

Vizenor relates his experience as a community activist. As a *Minneapolis Tribune* reporter Vizenor organized civil rights protests and exposed illegal domestic operations by the Central Intelligence Agency. He wrote key articles about the funeral of Dane Michael White and the trial of Thomas James White Hawk. As a founding director of the American Indian Employment and Guidance Center, he combated the "new urban fur traders" and worked to get services for urban Indians who chose to leave the reservation.

Interior Landscapes ends in a haunted house in Santa Fe, New Mexico, where Vizenor's dreams are invaded by skinwalkers, lost souls from the world of the dead. This dream begins a meditation on the rights of remains that informs Vizenor's writing of his autobiography, a "crossblood remembrance," motivated by a trickster's desire to weave the myths and metaphors of his own life.

Wordarrows

TYPE OF WORK: Short fiction
FIRST PUBLISHED: 1978

Wordarrows: Indians and Whites in the New Fur Trade is Vizenor's collection of autobiographical short stories. It stems from Kiowa novelist N. Scott Momaday's belief that storytelling is a means of situating oneself in a particular context in order to better understand individual and collective experiences. Vizenor's stories recount cultural "word wars" in which Native Americans cannot afford to be victims in "one-act terminal scenarios," but must become survivors, relying on their own words to preserve their sacred memories and represent the bitter facts. In *Wordarrows*, the trickster, a figure from Native American oral traditions, who appears in most of Vizenor's writing, uses stories and humor to balance the forces of good and evil in the world.

Wordarrows describes the reality of urban Indians, who are denied services and shuttled between various government programs. Vizenor's persona, Clement Beaulieu, directs the American Indian Employment and Guidance Center in Minneapolis, where he is caught between politicians who want to restrict his radical activities and desperate Indians who need his help. At the center, Beaulieu encounters Marleen American Horse, who has been stereotyped as a drunken Indian. He helps her free herself from "the language of white people" so that she can create her own identity. He also meets Laurel Hole In The Day, a woman who struggles to move her family to a white neighborhood in the city. Ultimately, loneliness makes the parents turn to drink, lose their jobs, and return to the reservation.

In another story, Beaulieu and a friend visit an Indian boarding school, where the superintendent makes a boy perform a simulated tribal dance to the music of the Lord's Prayer. Outraged by the administrator's idiotic attempt to teach the child racial pride, Beaulieu fumes that white corruption of this dance makes the Indian a spectacle and erases his tribal identity.

The last section of *Wordarrows* contains four stories centering on the case of Thomas James White Hawk, a death-row inmate in South Dakota. As a staff writer for the *Minneapolis Tribune*, Vizenor covered White Hawk's hearing to commute his death sentence to life in prison. Beaulieu blames society for creating the conditions which drove White Hawk to commit his crime and argues that "a man cannot be condemned by an institution of that dominant culture which has actually led to the problems he has to live with." The "cultural schizophrenia" experienced by Beaulieu and other characters in *Wordarrows* represents the dilemma of many contemporary Native Americans.

SUGGESTED READINGS

Blaeser, Kimberly M. *Gerald Vizenor: Writing in the Oral Tradition.* Norman: University of Oklahoma Press, 1996.

Coltelli, Laura, ed. *Winged Words: American Indian Writers Speak.* Lincoln: University of Nebraska Press, 1990.

Isernhagen, Hartwig. *Momaday, Vizenor, Armstrong: Conversations on American Indian Writing.* Norman: University of Oklahoma Press, 1999.

Laga, Barry E. "Gerald Vizenor and His *Heirs of Columbus*: A Postmodern Quest for More Discourse." *American Indian Quarterly* 18, no. 1 (Winter, 1994): 71-86.

McCaffery, Larry, and Tom Marshall. "Head Water: An Interview with Gerald Vizenor." *Chicago Review* 39, nos. 3-4 (Summer/Fall, 1993): 50-54.

Velie, Alan. *Four American Indian Literary Masters: N. Scott Momaday, James Welch, Leslie Marmon Silko, and Gerald Vizenor.* Norman: University of Oklahoma Press, 1982.

Vizenor, Gerald. "Head Water: An Interview with Gerald Vizenor." Interview by Larry McCaffery and Tom Marshall. *Chicago Review* 39, nos. 3-4 (Summer-Fall, 1993): 50-54.

_____, ed. *Narrative Chance: Postmodern Discourses on Native American Indian Literatures.* Norman: University of Oklahoma Press, 1993.

—Trey Strecker

Alice Walker

BORN: Eatonton, Georgia; February 9, 1944

Walker's poetry, short stories, essays, and novels protest racism, sexism, and mistreatment of the earth while offering affirmation and hope.

TRADITIONS: African American, American Indian
PRINCIPAL WORKS: *The Third Life of Grange Copeland*, 1970; *In Love and Trouble: Stories of Black Women*, 1973; *Meridian*, 1976; *You Can't Keep a Good Woman Down*, 1981; *The Color Purple*, 1982; *In Search of Our Mothers' Gardens: Womanist Prose*, 1983; *Living by the Word: Selected Writings, 1973-1987*, 1988; *The Temple of My Familiar*, 1989; *Her Blue Body Everything We Know: Earthling Poems, 1965-1990*, 1991; *Possessing the Secret of Joy*, 1992; *By the Light of My Father's Smile*, 1998

Alice Walker wrote her first book of poetry and published her first short story in her final year at Sarah Lawrence College in 1968. Her works have come from her own experience and accomplishment. She grew up in poverty, in which seven brothers and sisters and her sharecropping parents shared impossibly cramped quarters and worked for profit that was never their own. She experienced the inspiration of Martin Luther King, Jr. She was asked to sit in the back of the bus on her way to Spelman College. She saw the failure of her college to offer courses in African American authors. This experience prompted her to write and to teach courses on black women writers whose works both African Americans and other Americans need to read.

Walker, like the character Meridian in her second novel, considered physical violence a solution to the inequities with which she and other Americans were expected to live. She studied the Cuban Revolution and its effects. She, like Meridian, found herself unable, however, to perpetuate the violence she loathed. In *The Third Life of Grange Copeland*, *The Color Purple*, and *The Temple of My Familiar* she dramatizes the conditions that occasion violence and the horrors that result from violence. In *Possessing the Secret of Joy* she graphically describes the life-crippling effects of the ritualized and con-tinued violence of female genital mutilation. Meridian chooses, as Walker has chosen, a political activism that is peaceful and positive. Meridian goes to the South to educate, enlist, and assist prospective but fearful African American voters. Walker returned to the South with a similar purpose in the mid-1960's. Walker's writing, her study of world cultures, and her speaking engagements around the world show her continued peaceful political activism.

Walker's Pulitzer Prize-winning *The Color Purple* has proven itself, thanks partly to its film adaptation, the most popular presentation of her life-affirming philosophy. It draws upon African and Native American ideas of celebration and nurturance of the earth. The novel opposes the ideas too common to the European and the European American cultures: denigration and destruction of self, others, and the earth.

The Color Purple

TYPE OF WORK: Novel
FIRST PUBLISHED: 1982

The Color Purple, awarded the Pulitzer Prize in fiction in 1983 and made into a successful film, is ultimately a novel of celebration. Initially, however, it is the tragic history of an extended African American family in the early and middle years of the twentieth century. Its tragedy is reflective of the country's and its characters' illness, and its celebration is of the characters' and the country's cure.

The story is written as a series of letters by two sisters, Celie and Nettie. The first letters reveal the fourteen-year-old Celie's miserable existence as caretaker of her parents' household. She bears two children to the man she believes to be her father (he is her stepfather), who immediately takes the children from her.

Celie is given into the same situation in marriage: She is made caretaker for the children of a deceased woman and a stand-in sexual partner for yet another woman. When Celie and Nettie's father seeks to make Nettie his next victim, Nettie follows Celie to her new home, only to be victimized there by Celie's husband.

Nettie finds a home with the minister and his wife, who have become parents to Celie's children, Adam and Olivia. The five move to Africa to bring their Christian message to the Olinka. When Shug, the woman for whom Celie is stand-in partner, enters her home, the note of harmony which will swell to the final chorus of celebration is

Alice Walker (Jeff Reinking/Picture Group)

sounded. Celie comes to love and to learn from Shug. She learns that she must enter Creation as loved creature of her Creator, who, neither white nor male, creates out of love and a desire to please "Its" creatures. Reverence for all of Creation–trees, the color purple, humanity–is the cure, finally, to her and the novel's ills. Nettie's letters show Celie that she and her minister husband have come independently, in Africa, to know the same loving Creator who loves all and repudiates no part of Creation.

Celie leaves her abuser, Albert, who is slow to learn and sing the novel's song. He finally helps to bring Nettie, Samuel, Adam, Olivia, and Tashi, Adam's wife, back to Celie. He tells Celie, as they, finally, establish a friendship, that the more he wonders at and about Creation the more he loves. Celie, now lover of self and Creation, is reunited in middle age with her sister and grown children.

Possessing the Secret of Joy
TYPE OF WORK: Novel
FIRST PUBLISHED: 1992

Possessing the Secret of Joy expresses, in fictional and direct statements, its author's resistance to the practice of female circumcision. According to Walker, in 1991 ninety to a hundred million women and girls living in African, Far Eastern, and Middle Eastern countries were genitally mutilated, and the practice of "female circumcision" in the United States and Europe was growing among immigrants from countries where it was a part of the culture.

Three characters from Walker's *The Color Purple* (1982) and *The Temple of My Familiar* (1989) assume major roles in *Possessing the Secret of Joy*. The ritual mutilation of Tashi, childhood African friend to Celie's children Adam and Olivia and later wife to Adam, is graphically described, and its physical and emotional effects are explored in this novel.

Olivia speaks first, as others speak later, of her own, Adam's, and her missionary parents' introduction to the six-year-old Tashi. Tashi was inconsolable, having just witnessed the death of her sister Dura, victim of genital mutilation. The novel's action moves back and forth between Dura's death and the trial of Tashi for the murder of M'Lissa, Dura's killer and her own mutilator. It ends with the roar of rifle fire as Tashi is punished for her crime.

The aged Carl Jung is introduced to the novel's list of characters. While he appears only briefly, his psychological and mythological probing of Tashi's and the world's problem is carried on by his female and male successors, Raye and Pierre.

The recurrent imagery of Tashi's subconscious is finally interpreted by Pierre (son of Adam, Tashi's husband) and Lisette, Jung's niece. Pierre, having grown up with his parents' accounts of Tashi's physical and emotional suffering (continual pain, impeded motion, difficult and aborted childbirth; recurrent nightmares, truncated relationships, frequent confinement to mental institutions), studies anthropology and continues his great uncle's intellectual pursuits.

In Pierre's account, the myth is simple, and it is full of Walker's condemnation of the mutilation and subjugation of women. It is a story the aging Tashi remembers overhearing in bits from covert conversations among the male African elders. The male god descends from the sky to overcome, enjoy, and rape the female earth. Challenged by the earth's response to his advance, he cuts down the source (the mound or hill) of her pleasure.

"*RESISTANCE* IS THE SECRET OF JOY!" is the novel's final statement. Adam, Olivia, Benny (mildly retarded son to Tashi and Adam), Pierre, Raye, and Mbate (servant to M'Lissa and friend to Tashi) hold it up as a banner for Tashi's viewing as she is killed for the murder of M'Lissa. The novel is Walker's act of resistance to male domination and the physical and emotional disabling of women.

SUGGESTED READINGS

Banks, Erma Davis, and Keith Eldon Byerman. *Alice Walker: An Annotated Bibliography*. New York: Garland, 1989.

Bass, Margaret Kent. "Alice's *Secret.*" *CLA Journal* 38, no. 1 (September, 1994): 1-11.

Bloom, Harold, ed. *Alice Walker: Modern Critical Views*. New York: Chelsea House, 1989.

Christophe, Marc-A. "*The Color Purple:* An Existential Novel." *CLA Journal* 36, no. 3 (March, 1993): 280-291.

Dieke, Ikenna, ed. *Critical Essays on Alice Walker*. Westport, Conn.: Greenwood Press, 1999.

Marvin, Thomas F. "Preachin' the Blues: Bessie Smith's Secular Religion and Alice Walker's *The Color Purple.*" *African American Review* 28, no. 3 (Fall, 1994): 411-422.

Taylor, Carole Anne. "Humor, Subjectivity, Resistance: The Case of Laughter in *The Color Purple.*" *Texas Studies in Literature and Language* 36, no. 4 (Winter, 1994): 462-483.

Walker, Alice, and Parmar, Pratibha. *Warrior Marks: Female Genital Mutilation and the Sexual Blinding of Women*. New York: Harcourt, Brace Jovanovich, 1993.

Winchell, Donna Haisty. *Alice Walker*. New York: Twayne, 1992.

–Judith K. Taylor

Booker T. Washington

BORN: Near Hale's Ford, Virginia; April 5, 1856
DIED: Tuskegee, Alabama; November 14, 1915

Washington's autobiography brought national attention to the need for education for African Americans at a time when most schools were segregated.

TRADITIONS: African American
PRINCIPAL WORKS: *Up from Slavery: An Autobiography*, 1901; *My Larger Education*, 1911; *The Man Farthest Down*, 1912

Booker T. Washington rose to national prominence early in the twentieth century for promoting mutual interests as the foundation for better race relations. His views were rejected as limited and harmful by African American activists in the 1960's because he concentrated on economic rather than social equality. His achievements have been given renewed consideration in light of historical perspective.

Washington was born on a Virginia plantation, the son of a white plantation owner and a slave woman. At the end of the Civil War, he moved with his mother and his stepfather to Malden, West Virginia, where he worked in the salt mines and grew up in poverty. Determined to get an education, he made a five-hundred-mile journey, mostly by foot, to Virginia's Hampton Institute, a school set up to educate poor African Americans.

These early experiences influenced Washington's dedication to an ethic of self-help and self-discipline as the means of achievement, principles that became the foundation for his educational philosophy. In 1881, he became the first principal of a fledgling school in Tuskegee, Alabama, established to give industrial training to African Americans. At Tuskegee, Washington took a pragmatic approach to education, stressing personal cleanliness, correct behavior, and industrial education to improve students' economic condition. In a Deep South state where legal restrictions relegated African Americans to second-class citizenship and where injustice and lynching were common, Washington successfully recruited students, promoted education, and raised funds. As Tuskegee prospered, Washington emerged as a national spokesman for race relations.

His circle of influence widened after his 1895 address at the Cotton States and International Exposition in Atlanta. Later called the Atlanta Compromise by his critics, the speech argued in favor of economic gains, while ignoring the white community's denial of black political rights. As a man who understood his times, Washington believed that a materialistic society even-

Booker T. Washington (Library of Congress)

tually would respond to economic equality, that social equality would follow. After his address, his fame increased; he was invited to the White House, was awarded an honorary degree from Harvard University, and won the financial support of leading industrial figures for Tuskegee Institute.

In the last years of his career, however, he was sharply criticized by younger, intellectual African Americans who rejected his policies. Washington's contributions are nevertheless remarkable. His autobiography, *Up from*

Slavery, is an inspiring record of achievements in the face of overwhelming social handicaps, and even his sharpest critics pay tribute to Washington's singleness of vision.

Up from Slavery
TYPE OF WORK: Autobiography
FIRST PUBLISHED: 1901

Up from Slavery: An Autobiography is an account of Washington's life, which began in slavery and ended with his being a renowned educator. It is written in a simple style with an optimistic tone that suggests to African Americans that they can succeed through self-improvement and hard work. Although *Up from Slavery* has been ranked along with Benjamin Franklin's *Autobiography of Benjamin Franklin* (1791) as a classic story of personal achievement, critics disagree about its central theme. Some scholars complain of its conciliatory stance, while others see the work as a justification for black pride.

The book opens with Washington's boyhood hardships, beginning with his life as a slave on a Virginia plantation where the lack of a family name and a history that would give identity to his existence was painful and difficult to understand. He mentions the slaves' fidelity and loyalty to the master, but he stresses the brutality of the institution: A lack of refinement in living, a poor diet, bad clothing, and ignorance were the slave's lot.

A struggle for literacy is the focus in the intermediate chapters. Leaving the plantation with his mother and stepfather after the Civil War, Washington moved to West Virginia to work in salt and coal mines, where he learned letters while doing manual labor and used trickery to escape work and get to school on time. His situation improved after he was employed as a house servant by a Mrs. Ruffner, who taught him the value of cleanliness and work, lessons he put to good use when he sought admission to Hampton Institute, a Virginia school for poor African Americans. There Washington received an education that led to a teaching job. Throughout these chapters, he gives the impression that his early hardships were a challenge that gave impetus to his later success. He stresses the dignity of labor and the importance of helping others as the means of getting ahead.

Beginning with chapter seven, Washington discusses his work at Tuskegee Institute, where classes were first taught in a stable and a hen house, and he takes pride in the growth of the school from an original enrollment of thirty students to a large body of students from twenty-seven states and several foreign countries. His educational theories conform to his belief in manual labor rather than intellectual pursuit, and he stresses economic growth as the important goal.

The later portion of the book is primarily a chronicle of fund-raising and an account of grants and gifts. His image as a national leader is firmly established, and he includes newspaper comments on his speeches as well as answers to the critics regarding his Atlanta address. In "Last Words," Washington expresses his hope for an end to racial prejudice.

SUGGESTED READINGS

Adeleke, Tunde, ed. *Booker T. Washington–Interpretative Essays.* Black Studies 4. Lewiston, N.Y.: Edwin Mellen Press, 1998.

Harlan, Louis T. *Booker T. Washington: The Making of a Black Leader, 1856-1901.* New York: Oxford University Press, 1983.

_____. *Booker T. Washington: The Wizard of Tuskegee, 1901-1915.* New York: Oxford University Press, 1983.

Hawkins, Hugh, ed. *Booker T. Washington and His Critics.* Lexington, Mass.: D. C. Heath, 1974.

Mansfield, Stephen. *Then Darkness Fled: The Liberating Wisdom of Booker T. Washington.* Nashville: Cumberland House, 1999.

Mathews, Basil. *Booker T. Washington.* College Park, Md.: McGrath, 1969.

Riley, D. D. *The Life and Times of Booker T. Washington.* London: Fleming H. Revell, 1916.

Spencer, Samuel. *Booker T. Washington and the Negro's Place in American Life.* Boston: Little, Brown, 1955.

–Joyce Chandler Davis

Wendy Wasserstein

BORN: Brooklyn, New York; October 18, 1950

Wasserstein's plays have helped define the feminist experience of the baby boom generation.

TRADITIONS: Jewish

PRINCIPAL WORKS: *Any Woman Can't,* pr. 1973; *Uncommon Women and Others,* pr. 1975; *Isn't It Romantic,* pr. 1981, pr. 1983 (revised version), pb. 1984; *The Heidi Chronicles,* pr., pb. 1988; *The Sisters Rosensweig,* pr. 1992, pb. 1993; *An American Daughter,* pr., pb. 1998

Wendy Wasserstein attended college at Mount Holyoke. Her first play to gain critical attention, *Uncommon Women and Others,* relates the experiences six alumni from that all-female college have upon being graduated from their supportive environment and entering the "real world," where their abilities and identities as intelligent women were often denigrated or denied.

Wasserstein was raised by an extraordinary and flamboyant mother, Lola, and a quieter, though no less supportive, father, Morris. She used them as models for the pushy Jewish parents in *Isn't It Romantic,* which is about a woman who chooses to remain single rather than marry the Jewish doctor of her mother's dreams. This play entertainingly dramatizes how liberated women hoped to attain equality and fulfillment.

The Heidi Chronicles won the Pulitzer Prize in drama in 1989. This play explores the life of a feminist art historian from grade school dances, through woman's consciousness-raising, the acquired immunodeficiency syndrome (AIDS) crisis, her problems with men, and her eventual decision to adopt a child. Wasserstein, who considered herself a "professional malcontent," was suddenly inundated with flowers and awards. The play was hailed as a milestone in feminist playwriting, documenting a generation's sadness after the disappointing outcome of the women's movement.

Along with Wendy, Lola and Morris reared three other children, all of whom have been exceptionally successful in the high-pressure fields of business and banking. Wasserstein uses the worlds her siblings inhabit, and the bondings they formed as adults, to good effect in *The Sisters Rosensweig.* The play shows how Jews still perceive themselves as outsiders in modern society. Wasserstein, having enjoyed the success of *The Heidi Chronicles,* specifically set out to create a hopeful, romantic ending to this crowd-pleasing work, the most highly structured of her plays.

While critics have occasionally been less than kind to Wasserstein, seeing her scripts as period pieces, she deserves attention as a feminist pioneer. Her plays dramatize a unique perspective on the women's movement; they also describe the search for religious identity.

The Heidi Chronicles

TYPE OF WORK: Drama
FIRST PRODUCED: 1988; first published, 1988

The Heidi Chronicles, which won the Pulitzer Prize in drama in 1989, focuses on the women's movement of the late twentieth century from the point of view of Heidi Holland, feminist art historian. The two acts each open with a prologue about overlooked women painters. The action of the play begins at a dance in 1965 where Heidi meets Peter Patrone, who charms her with his wit. They promise to know each other all their lives.

Several years later during a Eugene McCarthy rally, Heidi encounters Scoop Rosenbaum. Scoop is obnoxious and extremely arrogant, and he has a tendency to grade everything, yet Heidi leaves the party to go to bed with him. At a consciousness-raising session a lesbian explains to Heidi that in feminism, "you either shave your legs or you don't." Heidi considers body hair in the range of the personal, but she participates in the group, detailing her pathetic attachment to Scoop. Distraught, she begs the women to tell her that all their daughters will feel more worthwhile than they do.

Next, Heidi attends a rally at the Chicago Art Institute, protesting the opening of a major retrospective containing no women artists. Peter arrives and confesses his homosexuality. Act 1 closes with Scoop's wedding to another woman. Although he claims to love Heidi, Scoop does not promise her equality. At the wedding he knowingly marries a woman he considers his lesser. By act 2 Heidi has written her book, *And the Light Floods in from the Left*. She attends a baby shower for Scoop's wife held on the same day as the memorial service for John Lennon. In 1982, Heidi appears on a talk show with Peter, now a popular pediatrician, and Scoop, owner of Boomer magazine. The men continually interrupt her. Later, when Heidi tries to tell an old friend how unhappy she is, the woman is too involved with her own career to care.

In 1986, Heidi gives an address to the alumni of her alma mater, divulging how sad she is. She feels stranded, and she thought the whole point of the feminist movement was that they were all in it together. In 1987, Peter explains that her kind of sadness is a luxury after all the memorial services for those who have died of acquired immunodeficiency syndrome (AIDS). The play's final scene occurs in 1989, when Scoop comes to meet Heidi's adopted child. He has sold *Boomer* and is planning to run for Congress. Heidi hopes that Scoop's son and her daughter will someday find a truer equality. The final image of the play is Heidi and child in front of a banner displaying a major Georgia O'Keeffe retrospective.

By turns heartwrenching and hilarious, the play captures the angst, admittedly sometimes whiny, of a generation of women who could not understand why the world would not accept them as they were and as they wanted to be.

The Sisters Rosensweig
TYPE OF WORK: Drama
FIRST PRODUCED: 1992; first published, 1993

The Sisters Rosensweig, a play intended to echo Russian playwright Anton Chekhov's *Tri sestry* (1901, revised, 1904; *The Three Sisters,* 1920), is set in August of 1991 as the Soviet Union is dissolving. To celebrate Sara Goode's birthday, her two sisters, Pfeni Rosensweig and "Dr." Gorgeous Teitelbaum, come to England. Also invited are Sara's teenage daughter, Tessie; Pfeni's lover, the bisexual play director, Geoffrey Duncan; Sara's aristocratic lover, Nicholas Pymn; and Tessie's working-class Catholic boyfriend, Tom.

As the play opens, Tessie is listening to recordings of Sara's college chorus for a school project. Pfeni, a globe-trotting feminist journalist, arrives and embraces Geoffrey, whose friend, Mervyn Kant, "world leader in synthetic animal protective covering"–a fake furrier–meets them at Sara's house. Mervyn becomes smitten with Sara and invites himself to dinner.

Dr. Gorgeous, a radio personality who funded her trip from Newton, Massachusetts, by leading a tour for the Temple Beth El sisterhood, enters, her feet aching from cheap shoes. Before dinner Nicholas baits Mervyn about his Jewishness, and Tom and Tessie, who want to go to the celebration in Lithuania, are entranced by Mervyn's political views. After dinner Sara and Mervyn discuss their similar American pasts until he charms her into bed. When Mervyn asks for a song, however, Sara refuses. In act 2 Gorgeous arranges for Geoffrey to entertain her sisterhood. Then everyone questions Sara about Mervyn until she gets annoyed, offends Gorgeous, and sends Mervyn away. When Geoffrey returns he tells Pfeni he misses men. Pfeni replies, "So do I" and allows him to depart.

Pfeni turns to Sara for comfort. Gorgeous enters wearing new, expensive, accidentally broken, shoes. Pfeni suggests Gorgeous's husband should buy her replacements and Gorgeous reveals she now supports her family. The sisters share revelations and finally relax together.

Mervyn, responding to a call from Sara, returns. He delivers a designer suit to Gorgeous, a gift from her sisterhood. Gorgeous is ecstatic, but will return it and use the money for her children's tuition. Pfeni decides to return to work, and leaves. Sara and Mervyn agree to continue their relationship. Tessie avoids the Lithuanian celebration, realizing she would be an outsider, and cajoles her mother into joining her in song.

While Wasserstein's play was a Broadway success, reviews were frequently lukewarm. Although blessed with witty dialogue, the sisters often seem like caricatures. Yet this is less a character drama than an exploration of issues, specifically those relating to identity, the fears common to middle-aged women, and the self-loathing, self-loving attitudes Jews have toward their culture. Not a classic like Chekhov's masterpiece, Wasserstein's play is nevertheless a triumph of substance and style over structure.

SUGGESTED READINGS

Arthur, Helen. "Wendy Wasserstein's *The Heidi Chronicles.*" Review of *The Heidi Chronicles*, by Wendy Wasserstein. *The Nation* 261, no. 12 (October 16, 1995): 443-445.

Barnett, Claudia. *Wendy Wasserstein: A Casebook.* New York: Garland, 1999.

Ciociola, Gail. *Wendy Wasserstein: Dramatizing Women, Their Choices and Their Boundaries.* Jefferson, N.C.: McFarland, 1998.

Finn, William. "Sister Act." *Vogue* 182, no. 9 (September, 1992): 360.

Hoban, Phoebe. "The Family Wasserstein." *New York* 26 (January 4, 1993): 32-37.

Shapiro, Walter. "Chronicler of Frayed Feminism." *Time*, March 27, 1989, 90-92.

—Shira Daemon

James Welch

BORN: Browning, Montana; November 18, 1940

Welch's poems, novels, films, and nonfiction present the viewpoint of Native Americans.

TRADITIONS: American Indian

PRINCIPAL WORKS: *Winter in the Blood*, 1974; *The Death of Jim Loney*, 1979; *Fools Crow*, 1986; *The Indian Lawyer*, 1990; *Killing Custer: The Battle of the Little Bighorn and the Fate of the Plains Indians*, 1994 (with Paul Stekler); *The Heartsong of Charging Elk*, 2000

James Welch received his Indian bloodline from his mother, of the Gros Ventre tribe, and from his father, of the Blackfeet tribe. Although his parents had as much Irish as Indian ancestry, for the most part he grew up in Indian territory. He attended Indian high schools in Browning and in Fort Belknap, Montana.

In 1965, while Welch was a student at the University of Montana, his mother, a stenographer at the reservation agency, brought home copies of annual reports from the Fort Belknap Indian agents for 1880, 1887, and 1897. These documents excited Welch, for they offered statistics on the numerical decline of Indians and showed agents' purposeful efforts to control Indians. Of greater interest was evidence that an agent had reported communication with Chief Sitting Bull who had been for a time within a few miles of the house where Welch lived. This revelation ignited Welch's interest in the history of his people.

"I wanted to write about that Highline Country in an extended way," says Welch in describing the impetus for *Winter in the Blood*. Welch captures the feeling of vast openness of Northeastern Montana's rolling plains. The novel is about a young Indian who lacks purpose in life until he discovers how Yellow Calf saved and protected an Indian maiden, an intriguing, heroic tale of his Indian grandparents. The novel's locale is Welch's parents' ranch, and it suggests Welch's own discovery of Indian forebears.

In *The Death of Jim Loney*, Welch portrays a young Indian tied by heritage to his reservation, unable to find opportunity there, endlessly drinking at lonely bars. Welch says that he writes only of situations that he has witnessed on Indian reservations. Lack of opportunity on the reservation, asserts Welch, leads Indians whom he has known to alcoholic despair. In *Killing Custer*, Welch portrays his people not as savages but as people justly defending their land, livelihood, and lives from military massacre. Welch re-creates nineteenth and twentieth century Indians living on the Western plains; he engages the reader in their viewpoint.

Fools Crow

TYPE OF WORK: Novel
FIRST PUBLISHED: 1986

Fools Crow dramatizes Native American life on the plains of eastern Montana toward the end of the era of the free, nonreservation tribe. This novel follows an Indian coming to manhood, his free life, his romantic marriage, his daring attack on an enemy, his struggle with the dilemma of whether to fight the white man and be slain or to submit to humiliating poverty and confinement on a reservation. Welch inherited sympathy for Native Americans from his Gros Ventre mother and from his Blackfoot father. His mother showed Welch documents from the Indian agency where she worked. The tales of his paternal grandmother concerning the awful massacre at Marias River, Mon-

tana, provided basic material and a viewpoint from which to write. Welch's grandmother, a girl at the time of the massacre, was wounded but escaped with a few survivors. She spoke only her tribal language.

In *Fools Crow*, White Man's Dog yearns to find respect. At eighteen he has three puny horses, a musket without powder, and no wife. He joins in a raid, in which he proves himself. He woos beautiful Red Paint. His young wife fears he may be killed yet yearns for his honor as a warrior; in a war raid, he outwits and kills the renowned Crow chief, thereby winning the mature name of Fools Crow. Names such as that of his father, Rides-at-the-door, and of the medicine man, Mik-Api, suggest

James Welch (Marc Hefty)

an Indian culture. The people pray to The Above Ones–the gods–and to Cold Maker, winter personified. These gods sometimes instruct warriors such as Fools Crow in dreams.

Fools Crow follows Raven–a sacred messenger–to free his animal helper, a wolverine, from a white man's steel trap. Later the Raven requires that Fools Crow lure to death a white man who shoots animals and leaves the flesh to rot. Smallpox ravages the teepees. Settlers push into the treaty territory, reducing buffalo, essential for food, shelter, and livelihood. Fools Crow finds a few of his people running in the northern winter away from the army slaughter of an entire village. In a vision experience, he sees his people living submissively with the powerful whites. Hope for his people resides in such children as his infant son Butterfly.

SUGGESTED READINGS

Barry, Nora. "A Myth to Be Alive: James Welch's *Fools Crow*." *MELUS* 17 (Spring, 1991): 3-20.

Bevis, William. "Dialogue with James Welch." *Northwest Review* 20 (1982): 163-185.

Gish, Robert F. "Word Medicine: Storytelling and Magic Realism in James Welch's *Fools Crow*." *American Indian Quarterly* 14, no. 4 (Fall, 1990): 349-354.

McFarland, Ronald E. "'The End' in James Welch's Novels." *American Indian Quarterly* 17, no. 3 (Summer, 1995): 319-327.

_____, ed. *James Welch*. Lewiston, Idaho: Confluence Press, 1986.

_____. *Understanding James Welch*. Columbia: University of South Carolina Press, 2000.

Murphree, Bruce. "Welch's *Fools Crow*." *The Explicator* 52, no. 3 (Spring, 1994): 186-187.

O'Connell, Nicholas. *At the Field's End: Interviews with Twenty Pacific Northwest Writers*. Seattle: Madrona, 1987.

–Emmett H. Carroll

Ida B. Wells-Barnett

BORN: Holly Springs, Mississippi; July 16, 1862
DIED: Chicago, Illinois; March 25, 1931

Wells-Barnett's work in civil rights and in feminism was central to the struggle for African Americans' participation in American life.

TRADITIONS: African American
PRINCIPAL WORKS: *On Lynchings: Southern Horrors, A Red Record, Mob Rule in New Orleans*, 1969; *Crusade for Justice: The Autobiography of Ida B. Wells*, 1970

Ida B. Wells-Barnett was a prolific author whose work covered a wide range of subjects: civil rights, suffrage, social justice, feminism, race riots, social settlements, women's organizations, travel, and voluntary associations. Many of these works were published in newspapers, pamphlets, and journals.

From 1889 to 1892 she was the editor of a newspaper, *Free Speech*, in Memphis, Tennessee. When she wrote an editorial criticizing a white mob who lynched three men who were her friends, her newspaper was destroyed and she had to flee for her life. She continued to protest against lynching for the rest of her life. She documented the horrors of the practice in a series of writings, especially in pamphlets, and three of these pamphlets were reprinted in the book *On Lynchings*.

Wells-Barnett witnessed injustice toward African Americans in a wide range of other settings and institutions, for example, in employment, housing, voting, and politics. Many of her writings on these subjects were published in African American news-

Ida B. Wells-Barnett honored on a United States postage stamp.
(Arkent Archives)

papers that have been lost, so the full range of her thought remains to be documented. She was active in founding many civil rights organizations, such as the National Association for the Advancement of Colored People, the Equal Rights League, and the Negro Fellowship League. Two important allies on numerous issues were Frederick Douglass and Jane Addams. Wells-Barnett opposed the gradual approach to changing race relations advocated by Booker T. Washington, and this stand was courageous during the height of Washington's influence.

Wells-Barnett was a leader in women's clubs, although she fought with many white and African American women about the pace and direction of their protests. She was active for several years in the National Association of Colored Women's Clubs and founded the Ida B. Wells Clubs and the Alpha Suffrage Club, among others.

Although Wells-Barnett was born into slavery, she conquered racism, sexism, and poverty to become an articulate and forceful leader. Her autobiography documents not only these public struggles but also her personal decisions to help rear her orphaned siblings, marry, and rear five children.

Crusade for Justice
TYPE OF WORK: Autobiography
FIRST PUBLISHED: 1970

Crusade for Justice: The Autobiography of Ida B. Wells is the inspiring story of an African American feminist and civil rights leader. Wells-Barnett documents her individual struggles, her accomplishments, and her major activities to promote equality for women and African Americans. Born into slavery in 1862, she lived through the Reconstruction era after the U. S. Civil War, the battle for suffrage, World War I, and its aftermath. Wells-Barnett's reflections provide a critical review of American racial and sexual relations. She did not simply observe the American scene; she also altered it as a leader in the women's movement and the African American Civil Rights movement.

The autobiography is especially important in documenting the widespread patterns of lynchings of African American men by white mobs. In protests and writings about these horrors, Wells-Barnett fought against any acceptance of these illegal and violent acts. She struggled with many people to have her radical and unflinching stands represented. Her struggles included arguments with other leaders such as the suffragist Susan B. Anthony, the civil rights activist W. E. B. Du Bois, and the African American leader Booker T. Washington. She presents her side of these differences in the autobiography, which reflects her occasional unwillingness to compromise and her hot temper.

Wells-Barnett published in formats such as small-circulation newspapers, pamphlets, and journals, so the autobiography is vital in providing obscure information about her life and ideas. She did not complete the autobiography, however, and her daughter Alfreda Duster helped fill in many missing pieces for the publication of the manuscript almost four decades after her mother's death. In addition, Wells-Barnett lost many of her writings in two different fires, so her daughter did not have access to the full range of her mother's publications and thoughts. As a result, major areas of Wells-Barnett's life and ideas are not covered or explained. Wells-Barnett's life is remarkable in its courage and influence. She refused to be limited by her battles with personal poverty, sexism, and racism, and her valiant spirit is apparent in her life story.

SUGGESTED READINGS

Aptheker, Bettina. Introduction to *Lynching and Rape: An Exchange of Views*, by Jane Addams and Ida B. Wells-Barnett. Occasional Papers Series 25. San Jose, Calif.: American Institute for Marxist Studies, 1977.

Broschart, Kay. "Ida B. Wells-Barnett." In *Women in Sociology*, edited by Mary Jo Deegan. Westport, Conn.: Greenwood Press, 1991.

McMurry, Linda O. *To Keep the Waters Troubled: The Life of Ida B. Wells*. New York: Oxford University Press, 1998.

Miller, Ericka M. *The Other Construction: Where Violence and Womanhood Meet in the Writings of Wells-Barnett, Grimke, and Larsen*. New York: Garland, 2000.

Tucker, David M. "Miss Ida B. Wells and Memphis Lynching." *Phylon* 32 (Summer, 1971): 112-22.

Wells-Barnett, Ida B. *The Memphis Diary of Ida B. Wells*. Edited by Miriam DeCosta-Willis. Boston: Beacon Press, 1995.

—Mary Jo Deegan

John Edgar Wideman

BORN: Washington, D.C.; June 14, 1941

*John Edgar Wideman is the author of twelve books of highly
acclaimed fiction.*

TRADITIONS: African American
PRINCIPAL WORKS: *Damballah*, 1981; *Hiding Place*, 1981; *Sent for You Yesterday*,
1983; *Brothers and Keepers*, 1984; *The Homewood Trilogy*, 1985; *Fatheralong*,
1994; *The Cattle Killing*, 1996; *Two Cities*, 1998

Growing up in Homewood (the African American section of Pittsburgh) and
attending public school, Wideman was every parent's dream. Delivering
newspapers after school, he learned to manage finances. He was careful to
avoid getting in trouble. He cared about school, did his homework, and he
was smart, but his first love was basketball. These were all winning characteristics, and Wideman was successful on and off the court.

In his senior year of high
school, Wideman was the
captain of the basketball
team and the class valedic-
torian. He earned a four-
year scholarship from the
University of Pennsylvania.
The university gave Wide-
man choices that would
change his life dramati-
cally. In 1963, Wideman
was named a Rhodes
Scholar, the second black
American to receive that
honor. Wideman also be-
came a graduate of the University of Iowa Writers'
Workshop. Wideman went
on to teach at various universities.

In many ways, Wideman
has left Homewood physi-
cally, emotionally, and

John Edgar Wideman (University of Wyoming)

spiritually behind. In his writing, however, Wideman never strays far from Homewood. *The Homewood Trilogy* (comprising *Damballah, Hiding Place,* and *Sent for You Yesterday*), perhaps his most widely read fiction, may be read as Wideman's return to Homewood and his determination to find his identity. The trilogy is the story, from the times of slavery onward, of Wideman's family. The trilogy is also about how creativity and imagination are important means of transcending despair.

Brothers and Keepers is a nonfiction work about Wideman's brother, who was incarcerated for murder, and how the two brothers' lives diverged from common beginnings. The work has deep implications for the lives and living conditions of African Americans.

Brothers and Keepers
TYPE OF WORK: Novel
FIRST PUBLISHED: 1984

Brothers and Keepers, Wideman's most popular novel, is a psychologically realistic portrait of two brothers. Although they grow up in the same environment, Homewood, these brothers travel diverse paths. Wideman is a black star pulsing brilliantly in a white universe; his brother, Robby, sinks into a life of crime and drug addiction. Robby's path leads to his serving a life sentence without parole for taking part in a robbery in which a man was killed. *Brothers and Keepers* is a novel of tragic dimensions, grave despair, and spiritual survival.

This novel had to be written as much for Wideman as for Robby. It is a homecoming for Wideman—a return to the community of brotherhood, concern, and understanding. In part 1, "Visits," readers learn that although Wideman never sees his color as an obstacle to his own success, he views Robby as a black victim of society's ills: "A brother behind bars, my own flesh and blood, raised in the same house by the same mother and father; a brother confined in prison has to be a mistake, a malfunctioning of the system."

In the second part of the novel, "Our Time," Wideman describes his growth and maturation while he spends time with his brother on visits to the prison. Wideman is seen as searching for his own identity while he searches for reasons for Robby's fall from grace. Learning that he needs as much help as Robby does, Wideman gains respect for Robby's intelligence. Wideman also learns the truth about the foiled robbery attempt.

In the final section, "Doing Time," a spirituality operates to bring harmony to the two brothers. Especially moving is Robby's graduation speech as he receives his associate degree, and his promise to Wideman that he will "forever pray." From a sociological point of view, it is interesting that prison can rehabilitate someone like Robby and motivate him to work on his education. It is an equally moving experience to see Wideman connect with his own identity and return to his roots. Wideman learns that he cannot escape genetics or the ghetto. Until Robby is free, Wideman is not free.

The Homewood Trilogy

TYPE OF WORK: Novels and short fiction
FIRST PUBLISHED: *Damballah*, 1981; *Hiding Place*, 1981; *Sent for You Yesterday*, 1983; *The Homewood Trilogy*, 1985

In *The Homewood Trilogy*, which comprises the short-story collection *Damballah* and the novels *Hiding Place* and *Sent for You Yesterday*, Wideman re-creates Homewood, the black section of Pittsburgh, and describes the myriad relationships among ancestors and a living African American family in the hundred years since slavery. Damballah is an African Voodoo god, "the good serpent of the sky." The hero of the trilogy is John French, who specializes in a kind of benevolent fatherhood. Wideman's return to Homewood through these novels convinces readers of his determination to find and understand his identity through tracing his roots as deep as he can. In *Damballah* and *Hiding Place*, Wideman furnishes a family tree. Readers are told of his great-great-great grandmother, who fled through the Underground Railroad with a white man to safety in Pittsburgh. Biological roots traced, the job of understanding begins.

One sour apple on the family tree is Tommy. The character Tommy is actually Robby, Wideman's brother. Tommy and Wideman are complex dimensions in finding the identity that Wideman seeks. The main character in *Hiding Place*, Tommy, is a fugitive from history as well as the law. He is taken in by Mama Bess, who is family and who represents what family does. Family tries to put together the "scars" and the "stories" that give young people their identities. Essentially, *Hiding Place* is the story of two lost souls, Mama Bess and Tommy. Mama Bess is lost because she has lost her husband and her son; she becomes a recluse, a fugitive living on a hill overlooking Pittsburgh, away from the family. Tommy is lost because he is too headstrong to listen and finds himself on the run after a scheme to rob a ghetto hoodlum ends in murder. Tommy does not want to hear the stories and learn about the scars; he is too absorbed in preservation.

Sent for You Yesterday, through the characters of Doot and Albert Wilkes, the outspoken blues pianist, suggests that creativity and imagination are important means of transcending despair. Creativity also strengthens the common bonds of race, culture, and class. *Homewood Trilogy* is a monumental work of investigating and understanding the origins of self and identity.

SUGGESTED READINGS

Bennetts, Leslie. "Seeds of Violence." *Vanity Fair*, March, 1989, 156-161, 210-214.

Bertley, Christopher. "Brothers and Keepers." Review of *Brothers and Keepers*, by John Edgar Wideman. *Black Enterprise* 15 (May, 1985): 15.

Byerman, Keith Eldon. *John Edgar Wideman: A Study of the Short Fiction.* New York: Twayne, 1998.

Coleman, J. W. "Going Back Home: The Literary Development of John Edgar Wideman." *College Language Association* 28 (March, 1985): 326-343.

Fraser, C. Gerald. "Brothers and Keepers." Review of *Brothers and Keepers*, by John Edgar Wideman. *The New York Times Book Review*, November 10, 1985, 56.

Marcus, James. "The Pain of Being Two." *The Nation*, October 4, 1986, 321-322.

Rushdy, Ashraf H. A. "Fraternal Blues: John Edgar Wideman's *Homewood Trilogy*." *Contemporary Literature* 32 (Fall, 1991): 312-343.

TuSmith, Bonnie, ed. *Conversations with John Edgar Wideman.* Jackson: University Press of Mississippi, 1998.

Wideman, John Edgar. "Language of Home." *The New York Times Book Review*, January 13, 1985, 1-3.

Wilson, Matthew. "The Circles of History in John Edgar Wideman's *The Homewood Trilogy*." *College Language Association* 33 (March, 1990): 239-259.

—*Barbara Cecelia Rhodes*

Elie Wiesel

BORN: Sighet, Transylvania (now Romania); September 30, 1928

Wiesel, who has won the Nobel Peace Prize, is an important writer on the Holocaust.

TRADITIONS: Jewish

PRINCIPAL WORKS: *Un di Velt hot geshvign*, 1956 (*La Nuit*, 1958; *Night*, 1960); *Le Mendiant de Jérusalem*, 1968 (*A Beggar in Jerusalem*, 1970); *L'Oublié*, 1989 (*The Forgotten*, 1992); *Tous les fleuves vont à la mer: Mémoires*, 1994 (*All Rivers Run to the Sea: Memoir*, 1995); . . . *et la mer n'est pas remplie*, 1996 (*And the Sea Is Never Full: Memoirs, 1969-   *, 1999)

Elie Wiesel's sheltered, bookish adolescence was forever shattered in 1944, when the Nazis invaded Hungary and rounded up all its Jews, including the Wiesel family. The fifteen-year-old Elie was deported to Auschwitz and Buchenwald, from which he was liberated in April, 1945. The horrors he saw there, the despair he felt, the anger he directed at God were later themes in his literary and nonfiction writings.

Shortly after the war, Elie went to France, where he learned the language and developed a lifelong passion for philosophy and literature. When, in 1955, French novelist François Mauriac urged him to bear witness to the six million Jews murdered in Europe's concentration camps, Wiesel wrote the acclaimed *Night*. First published in Yiddish, then French, then English, the book began as an eight-hundred-page manuscript but was cut to about one hundred pages of terrifyingly bald description of what happened to Wiesel. *Night* is a wrenching account of evil and a terrifying indictment of God.

He next published novels presenting the anguished guilt of those who survived the mass slaughter. Central to the protagonists' conduct and outlook is the belief that every act is ambiguous and implies a loss of innocence. By rejoining the religious community, however, the survivor may finally transform despair into joy.

A Beggar in Jerusalem shows how a tormented people came of age. Celebrating Israel's victory in the Six-Day War, the novel is a memorial to the dead and an appeal for the world's beggars. Although still haunted by the Holocaust, Wiesel could thereafter address other problems confronting the next generation–from madness as an escape from persecution to silence as a means of overcoming horror.

Wiesel returns to the Holocaust and its aftermath in *The Forgotten*. The original French title refers to what is forgotten as well as to one who is forgotten; memory, remembrance, forgetting are all important leitmotifs. Through legends, stories, and eyewitness accounts, one triumphs over oblivion and, ultimately, over death. The spinner of tales survives, along with his message, however incomplete and lost in the fog of memory.

Wiesel encompasses Jewish lore, tradition, and memory, and by relating the Jews' unique experience to the universal legacy of humanity he succeeds in creating an Everyman. In recognition of his humanism and activism he received the Nobel Peace Prize in 1986.

All Rivers Run to the Sea

TYPE OF WORK: Autobiography
FIRST PUBLISHED: *Tous les fleuves vont à la mer*, 1994 (English translation, 1995)

Taking the title of his autobiography from Ecclesiastes, Wiesel presents the important people and events of his life, beginning with his childhood in Sighet, Romania, and culminating in his 1969 marriage in Jerusalem. Wiesel, through stories and remembrances, tells of a family full of piety, moral courage, and selfless devotion to Judaism. From his mother and grandmother, Elie learned goodness and love; from his grandfather, the Jewish legends he would later use in fiction and essays; from his father, rectitude and altruism. His teachers, at various times of his life, inculcated in him a reverence for learning, an exactness in biblical or philosophical discourse, and above all the joy, sadness, and truth of the old masters.

World War II and the persecution of the Jews destroyed Wiesel's idyllic world forever. He and his family were taken to Auschwitz. He later was transferred to Buchenwald. Unable to understand German cruelty, angry at those who did not intervene on the victims' behalf, angry too at

Elie Wiesel (©The Nobel Foundation)

God for letting it happen, Wiesel emerged alive after terrible trials. At age seventeen he was endowed with a special knowledge of life and death.

Shortly after his liberation from Buchenwald he went to France, where he eventually enrolled at the university, enduring hardship and contemplating suicide. Saved by Zionist fervor, he worked as a journalist for an Israeli newspaper in Paris. A crucial meeting with novelist François Mauriac in 1955 was to decide his literary career: Mauriac encouraged him to break his self-imposed silence about his experience in concentration camps and found a publisher for Wiesel's first novel, *La Nuit* (1958; *Night*, 1960), to which he contributed the foreword.

After Wiesel moved to New York to become his newspaper's American correspondent, he soon applied for U.S. citizenship. In a series of amusing anecdotes he describes his life in a Jewish American milieu. He also tells of his relations with his French publishers and of his meeting with Marion, his future wife and translator. More moving and bittersweet are his return to his native town, where relatives and friends have disappeared and only the ghosts of his youth remain; his personal and literary campaign for Russian Jewry; the fear caused by the Six-Day War of 1967, since it could have meant the end of Israel and the Jewish dream; and his prayer of thanksgiving at the newly liberated Wailing Wall.

Throughout, a celebration of life and of the great Hasidic teachers and thinkers as well as a moral and ethical strength permeates Wiesel's conduct and writings over his first forty years. In memorializing his relatives and friends and in bearing witness to their passing, he leaves his own mark behind.

A Beggar in Jerusalem

TYPE OF WORK: Novel
FIRST PUBLISHED: *Le Mendiant de Jérusalem*, 1968 (English translation, 1970)

A Beggar in Jerusalem is told in the first person by David, heir to a bloody history of anti-Semitic persecutions. It is a novel in which Jewish survivors of destruction must confront their miraculous escape. In the process, although they suffer from guilt and anger, they ultimately forge an identity based on hope.

In June, 1967, the forty-year-old David goes to fight against the united Arab armies. He wishes to die in order to finally overcome the despair caused by God's abandonment of the Jews during World War II and by his own pointless survival. At the front, he meets Katriel, and both soon agree that whoever comes back will tell the other's story. Israel wins a resounding victory in what comes to be called the Six-Day War, and as the narrative opens, there are celebrations all over the land, especially in Jerusalem. Katriel, however, does not come back.

David not only tells his comrade's story—much as King David told of Absalom—but also wonders whether he ought to live it as well. This he does, at the end, by marrying Katriel's widow, not out of love, which would imply a total gift of self and of which he does not feel himself capable, but rather out of affection and sympathy, perhaps out of friendship. The hero has realized that, beyond suffering and bitterness, he can arrive at self-discovery.

Whereas Albert Camus favored revolt in the face of the absurd, Wiesel advocates laughter. By laughing one succeeds in conquering oneself, and by dominating one's fear one learns to laugh: "Let our laughter drown all the noises of the earth, all the regrets of mankind." There is no longer a need to search for an antidote against distress, but simply to abandon oneself to the joy of an event without precedent—the reunion of Israel with Jerusalem, uniting those absent and present, the fighters and mad beggars, in similar euphoria and similar ecstasy: "I want to laugh and it is my laughter I wish to offer to Jerusalem, my laughter and not my tears."

In his tireless attempt to understand the awesome and terrifying mystery of Jewish suffering, the once-tormented David is resolutely optimistic, for the recaptured Jerusalem means the end of despair for Jews in Israel and abroad. The victory celebrations are a memorial to the dead, a song to and of life, and an appeal in behalf of history's wandering outcasts—the allegorical beggars who, after the annihilation of European Jewry, have come to Jerusalem to give God the last chance to save his people.

Night

TYPE OF WORK: Memoir
FIRST PUBLISHED: *Un di Velt hot geshvign*, 1956; *La Nuit*, 1958 (English translation, 1960)

Night, Wiesel's memoir of the Holocaust, tells of his concentration camp experience. Encompassing events from the end of 1941 to 1945, the book ponders a series of questions, whose answers, Moché the Beadle, who was miraculously saved from an early German massacre, reminds the boy, lie "only within yourself."

Moché, who teaches the boy the beauty of biblical studies, is a strange character with a clownish awkwardness, more God's madman than mentally ill; he is also a recurring figure in later Wiesel works. After Moché returns to town to describe the horrible scenes he has witnessed, no one listens to this apparently insane rambler who, like Cassandra, repeats his warnings in vain. The clown, a moving and tragic fool, is unable to convince the Jewish community of its impending doom. Despite arrests, ghettoizations, and mass deportations, the Jews still cannot believe him, even as they embark for Auschwitz.

In 1944, the young narrator is initiated into the horrors of the archipelago of Nazi death camps. There he becomes A-7713, deprived of name, self-esteem, identity. He observes and undergoes hunger, exhaustion, cold, suffering, brutality, executions, cruelty, breakdown in personal relationships, and flames and smoke coming from crematories in the German death factories. In the barracks of terror, where he sees the death of his mother and seven-year-old sister, his religious faith is corroded. The world no longer represents God's mind. Comparing himself to Job, he bitterly asks God for an explanation of such evil. The boy violently rejects God's presence and God's justice, love, and mercy: "I was alone—terribly alone in a world without God and without man."

After a death march and brutally cruel train ride, young Wiesel and his father arrive at Buchenwald, where his father soon dies of malnutrition and dysentery. As in a daze, the son waits to be killed by fleeing German soldiers. Instead, he coolly notes, on April 11, 1945, "at about six o'clock in the evening, the first American tank stood at the gates of Buchenwald."

In addition to wanting to elucidate the unfathomable secret of death and theodicy, the narrator lived a monstrous, stunted, and isolated existence as an adult. He saw himself as victim, executioner, and spectator. By affirming that he was not divided among the three but was in fact all of them at once, he was able to resolve his identity problem. The autobiography's last image shows Wiesel looking at himself in a mirror: The body and soul are wounded, but the night and its nightmares are finally over.

SUGGESTED READINGS

Berenbaum, Michael. *The Vision of the Void: Theological Reflections on the Works of Elie Wiesel.* Middletown, Conn.: Wesleyan University Press, 1979.

Estess, Ted L. *Elie Wiesel.* New York: Frederick Ungar, 1980.

Patterson, David. *In Dialogue with Elie Wiesel.* Wakefield, N.H.: Longwood Academic, 1991.

Rittner, Carol, ed. *Elie Wiesel: Between Memory and Hope.* New York: New York University Press, 1990.

Rosen, Alan, ed. *Celebrating Elie Wiesel: Stories, Essays, Reflections.* Notre Dame, Ind.: University of Notre Dame Press, 1998.

Rosenfeld, Alvin H., and Irving Greenberg, eds. *Confronting the Holocaust: The Impact of Elie Wiesel.* Bloomington: Indiana University Press, 1978.

Roth, John K. *A Consuming Fire: Encounters with Elie Wiesel and the Holocaust.* Atlanta: John Knox Press, 1979.

Sibelman, Simon P. "The Mystical Union: A Re-Examination of Elie Wiesel's *Le Mendiant de Jérusalem.*" *Literature and Theology* 7, no. 2 (June, 1993): 186-197.

_____. *Silence in the Novels of Elie Wiesel.* New York: St. Martin's Press, 1995.

Stern, Ellen N. *Elie Wiesel: Witness for Life.* New York: Ktav, 1982.

—Pierre L. Horn

August Wilson

BORN: Pittsburgh, Pennsylvania; April 27, 1945

Wilson has made an ambitious effort to create a cycle of ten plays examining African American life in each decade of the twentieth century.

TRADITIONS: African American

PRINCIPAL WORKS: *Ma Rainey's Black Bottom*, pr. 1984, pb. 1985; *Fences*, pr., pb. 1985; *Joe Turner's Come and Gone*, pr. 1986, pb. 1988; *The Piano Lesson*, pr. 1987, pb. 1990; *Two Trains Running*, pr. 1990, pb. 1992; *Seven Guitars*, pr. 1995, pb. 1996

August Wilson considers contact with one's roots to be a crucial source of strength, and his plays have explored and celebrated African American culture. Wilson's plays also acknowledge the white racism that has marked African American history. Black experience in America contains, Wilson has noted, "all the universalities." His work has received wide acclaim, winning Pulitzers and numerous other awards.

Wilson's father was a white baker from Germany, and his mother was a black cleaning woman who had moved to Pittsburgh from rural North Carolina. His father "wasn't around much," according to Wilson, and he and his brothers and sisters grew up in a financially strapped single-parent household "in a cultural environment which was black." At age twelve Wilson discovered and read through the small "Negro section" of the public library.

August Wilson (AP/Wide World Photos)

In 1965, he decided to become a writer and adopted his mother's maiden name, becoming August Wilson (which he legally formalized in the early 1970's) instead of Frederick August Kittel. He began living on his own in a rooming house in the black area of Pittsburgh, known as the Hill, while writing poetry and supporting himself in a series of menial jobs. In 1965, he also discovered the blues, which he acknowledges as "the greatest source of my inspiration." Wilson identifies three other B's as influences: Amiri Baraka, some of whose plays Wilson directed in the 1960's at the Black Horizons Theater Company that Wilson cofounded; the art of Romare Bearden, noted for his collages of black life; and the stories of Argentinean author Jorge Luis Borges. In addition, he claims that most of the plays he has seen have been by South African playwright Athol Fugard.

In 1978, Wilson moved to St. Paul, Minnesota, where, surrounded by white voices, he began to create characters who spoke a poeticized version of the black English he had heard on the Hill. Lloyd Richards—then dean of the Yale School of Drama—directed Wilson's first major dramatic success, *Ma Rainey's Black Bottom*, and began a long-term working relationship with Wilson, who sees Richards as a father figure and professional mentor, with insight into Wilson's plays because of his own roots in black culture.

After *Ma Rainey's Black Bottom* Wilson realized he had written three plays set in different decades and decided to complete a historical cycle, with a play for each decade of the twentieth century. He has used Pittsburgh as a setting for his plays after *Ma Rainey's Black Bottom* (which is set in Chicago), causing him to be compared to fiction writers James Joyce (who used Dublin) and William Faulkner (who used the area around Oxford, Mississippi).

Fences

TYPE OF WORK: Drama
FIRST PRODUCED: 1985; first published, 1985

Troy Maxson, the protagonist of Wilson's *Fences*, is the son of a frustrated sharecropper whose harshness drove off his wives and Troy. Troy has made his way north to a world where African Americans live in shacks and are unable to find work. Troy takes to stealing, kills a man, and is sent to prison, where he learns how to play baseball, which he loves and at which he excels. Segregation confines Troy, after prison, to the Negro Leagues. He is angry at the racism that frustrates his attempt at achieving the American Dream in the most American of sports, but he remains resilient. *Fences* celebrates his indomitable spirit, while acknowledging his flaws.

The play opens in 1957, when Troy is fifty-three years old. He is appealing in the zest with which he dramatizes his life. A battle with pneumonia becomes a time when he wrestles with a white-robed and hooded Death, and buying furniture on credit from a white man becomes making a deal with the devil. His friend Bono seems to acknowledge the African American tradition of these tall tales when he comments: "You got some Uncle Remus in your blood." The audience learns of Troy's admirable defiance at work in questioning the sanitation department's policy of having all the whites drive while the blacks do the lifting. Troy also has an affectionate teasing relationship with Bono and his wife Rose.

As the play continues, however, Troy erects fences between himself and those he loves. He refuses to allow his son to accept a football fellowship to college and then forces him to leave home. Troy loses contact with Bono after being promoted at work. Troy hurts his wife through an extramarital affair, and he commits his brain-damaged brother, Gabe, to a mental institution so he can collect part of Gabe's government checks.

Although Troy has tragic flaws, the ending of *Fences* is not tragic. A spirit of reconciliation is brought by Gabe, who has been allowed to leave the mental hospital to attend his brother's funeral. Gabe thinks that, when he blows his trumpet, Saint Peter will open the pearly gates and allow Troy into Heaven. Gabe's horn lacks a mouthpiece, however, and, distraught, he performs a dance, connected, presumably, to pre-Christian African ancestors. In performance, the stage is then flooded with light, indicating that the gates have opened.

Ma Rainey's Black Bottom

TYPE OF WORK: Drama
FIRST PRODUCED: 1984; first published, 1985

Set in 1927 in a Chicago recording studio, Wilson's play *Ma Rainey's Black Bottom* explores the values and attitudes toward life and music of the classic blues singer Ma Rainey. Their economic exploitation as African American musicians in a white-controlled recording industry, as well as their inferior social status in the majority white culture, become evident in the play's dialogue and action. As Ma Rainey puts it: "If you colored and can make them some money, then you all right with them. Otherwise, you just a dog in the alley."

For Rainey, the blues is "a way of understanding life" that gives folks a sense they are not alone: "This be an empty world without the blues." As such, the blues has been a source of strength for African Americans, and performers like Ma Rainey have been bearers of cultural identity. A major theme of *Ma Rainey's Black Bottom* and of other plays by Wilson is the necessity of acknowledging one's past and connecting with one's culture.

African American identity, however, with its roots in Africa and the rural South, is at times rejected by the members of Ma Rainey's band. The pianist, Toledo, for example, points out the "ancestral retention" involved in the bass player's trying to get some marijuana from another band member by naming things they have done together—in effect, an African appeal to a bond of kinship. Toledo's observation is immediately rejected by the bass player, who replies: "I ain't no African!" and by Levee, the trumpet player, who remarks: "You don't see me running around in no jungle with no bone between my nose." Levee also has a loathing for the South, which he associates with sharecropping and general backwardness. Levee's disregard for African American heritage extends to Ma Rainey's style of blues, which he calls "old jug-band st." He resents her refusal to use his jazzed-up arrangements and, at the tragic end of the play, when his hopes for a recording contract of his own are dashed, his rage is misdirected at Toledo, who happens to step on his shoe, and whom he stabs with his knife.

Two Trains Running
TYPE OF WORK: Drama
FIRST PRODUCED: 1990; first published, 1992

Memphis Lee's small restaurant is the setting of Wilson's *Two Trains Running*. Risa, a young woman who has scarred her legs with a razor to deflect the sexual interest of men, is the restaurant's cook and waitress. The rest of the African American cast are male and include, among others, Sterling, an unemployed young man recently released from prison; Holloway, a retired house painter; and Hambone, who is mentally retarded.

The gossip, debates, philosophizing, and storytelling that take place in Memphis's restaurant reflect the oral tradition of African American culture. Some critics note that the characters engaged in the talk seem detached from the racial riots, assassinations, and antiwar protests that marked the late 1960s, when the play takes place. Wilson responds by saying that he was not interested in writing "what *white* folks think of as American history for the 1960's." He was interested in making the point that "by 1969 nothing has changed for the black man."

One thing not changed by 1969 was economic injustice. Holloway notes that for centuries blacks worked hard for free, enriching white slaveholders. Once blacks have to be paid whites deny them work and call them lazy. The characters in *Two Trains Running* are directly affected by the whites' ability to make and interpret rules, to the disadvantage of blacks. When Hambone painted a fence, the white butcher who hired him offered a chicken in payment instead of the promised ham. When Sterling wins at the numbers, the whites who run the game cut his winnings in half. When Memphis's restaurant is scheduled to be taken over by the city, the whites in charge invoke a clause saying they do not have to pay his price.

Hambone dies without getting his ham, but his persistence in demanding it for more than nine years moves Memphis to donate fifty dollars for flowers for his funeral and moves Sterling to break into the butcher shop and steal a ham for his casket. By the end of the play Sterling has been transformed from a man unwilling to pay the price for love (he is reluctant to accept responsibility for others) to one who is willing to make a commitment to Risa, who seems willing to have a relationship with him. In this he has the blessing of Aunt Ester, reputedly 322 years old and an important offstage character. She symbolizes the wisdom of black experience in America, the wisdom of a people who survived against the odds. Memphis, too, has been transformed. He was run off his land in Mississippi years before, and he vowed one day to return seeking justice. "They got two trains running every day." By the play's end he wins his fight with the city, which agrees to pay more than his price for his restaurant, and he declares he will now follow through on his vow because, as he understands Aunt Ester to have told him: "If you drop the ball, you got to go back and pick it up."

SUGGESTED READINGS

Birdwell, Christine. "Death as a Fastball on the Outside Corner: *Fences'* Troy Maxson and the American Dream." *Aethlon* 8 (Fall, 1990): 16-25.

Elkins, Marilyn, ed. *August Wilson: A Casebook.* New York: Garland, 1994.

Nadel, Alan, ed. *May All Your Fences Have Gates: Essays on the Drama of August Wilson.* Iowa City: University of Iowa Press, 1994.

Pereira, Kim. *August Wilson and the African-American Odyssey.* Champaign: University of Illinois Press, 1995.

Shannon, Sandra G. *The Dramatic Vision of August Wilson.* Washington, D.C.: Howard University Press, 1995.

Wilde, Lisa. "Reclaiming the Past: Narrative and Memory in August Wilson's *Two Trains Running.*" *Theater* 22 (Fall-Winter, 1990-1991): 36-41.

Wolfe, Peter. *August Wilson.* New York: Twayne, 1999.

–Jack Vincent Barbera

Jade Snow Wong

BORN: San Francisco, California; January 21, 1922

Wong's accounts of Chinese life in America break down prejudice and create understanding among cultures.

TRADITIONS: Chinese American

PRINCIPAL WORKS: *Fifth Chinese Daughter*, 1950; *The Immigrant Experience*, 1971; *No Chinese Stranger*, 1975

Jade Snow Wong was introduced to writing by her father, who gave her a diary when she was young and encouraged her to record the important events of her life. She continued this habit into her adult life. She also received formal training in college, where she wrote many papers about her life in Chinatown.

Wong began work on her first book, *Fifth Chinese Daughter*, in 1946, at the age of twenty-four. Her goal was to create a "better understanding of the Chinese culture on the part of Americans." She wanted to show non-Chinese Americans the beauty and traditions of her culture and dispel prevalent stereotypes. Although Wong has produced two other major works, writing is not her primary occupation. Instead, she sees it as a method for exposing other Americans to her cultural heritage.

As a result of her first book, the U.S. State Department sent her on a four-month tour to speak to various audiences and to relate her experiences of breaking through race and gender barriers in America. Wong and her husband also acted as tour guides and escorted many Americans to China before her husband's death in 1985. Wong has continued this practice, leading one group a year since then. Her third book, *No Chinese Stranger*, was written in reaction to her first visit to China, in 1972, only one month after Richard M. Nixon's trip. During that trip, she learned what it is like to be part of a homogenous society, and not a minority.

Wong's works also show that each person must establish an identity regardless of race. Her wish is to share her struggles in order to encourage others who may face similar obstacles. She continues to fight prejudice and to encourage individuals to make a place for themselves in the world where they can express themselves and be recognized for who they are.

In addition to writing, Wong has expressed herself through the creation of pottery, which is sold in her shop. She also takes care of her children, which she says is the most important duty in her life. She claims, "Our basic and greatest value is family cohesiveness." She sees the nurturing of her family as an additional way to foster individuality and self-expression.

Fifth Chinese Daughter

TYPE OF WORK: Autobiography
FIRST PUBLISHED: 1950

Fifth Chinese Daughter, Wong's autobiography, directly and honestly relates the struggles and accomplishments of an American-born Chinese girl. Although it is an autobiography, it is written in the third person, which reflects the Chinese custom of humility. This use of the third person also reminds the reader of how difficult it is for the author to express her individual identity.

The book explains Wong's desire to prove to her parents that she was "a person, besides being a female." Even as a toddler, she was taught to obey her parents and her older brother and sisters without question. She was not allowed to express her opinions; rather, she was forced to comply with the demands of the rest of her family.

When she began school, her parents expected her to earn good grades, yet they refused to praise or even encourage her when she was recognized for her school achievements. In fact, they refused to fund her college education, although they paid her brothers' expenses, because it was not considered wise to educate a girl, who would leave the family when she married. As a result, Wong was forced to work full time throughout her teenage years in order to save the money to go to college. During this time, she was exposed to the "foreign" culture of the whites living in San Francisco, and she was surprised to learn that parents in many Anglo families listened to children and respected their opinions. Further, she learned in a college sociology class that in many families, children were afforded the right to discuss with their parents what they saw as unfair. Learning about the practices of other families caused Wong to question her parents' practices for the first time.

As a result, Wong began a slow and painful struggle to earn her parents' respect while developing her own identity. Unfortunately, her parents were not the only people who would discourage her. She also had to face prejudice and stereotyping in the white world. She refused to be discouraged by this and accepted the challenges that it brought.

Eventually, Jade Snow was able to win her parents' respect. She established her own identity and her independence by beginning a business selling handmade pottery. Although her Chinatown shop was patronized only by white customers, her ability to attract many customers was recognized by her family and by members of Wong's community. The pottery shop venture finally allowed her to find "that niche which would be hers alone."

SUGGESTED READINGS

Hong, Maria, ed. *Growing Up Asian American: An Anthology*, Morrow, 1993.
Lim, Shirley Geok-lin. "Twelve Asian American Writers: In Search of Self-

Definition." In *Redefining American Literary History*. New York: The Modern Language Association of America, 1990.

Ling, Amy. *Between Worlds: Women Writers of Chinese Ancestry*, Pergamon Press, 1990.

_____. "Chinese American Women Writers: The Tradition Behind Maxine Hong Kingston." In *Redefining American Literary History*. New York: Modern Language Association of America, 1990.

—Amy Beth Shollenberger

Jay Wright

BORN: Albuquerque, New Mexico; May 25, 1935

Wright's intellectually demanding poetry illuminates the African American experience by exploring the philosophies and religious cosmologies that underlie historical events and personal spiritual development.

TRADITIONS: African American

PRINCIPAL WORKS: *Death as History*, 1967; *The Homecoming Singer*, 1971; *Soothsayers and Omens*, 1976; *Dimensions of History*, 1976; *The Double Invention of Komo*, 1980; *Explications/Interpretations*, 1984; *Elaine's Book*, 1986; *Selected Poems of Jay Wright*, 1987; *Boleros*, 1991

Jay Wright was reared in New Mexico and Southern California. Wright became fluent in English and Spanish and knowledgeable regarding African American, Hispanic, and Native American ways of looking at the world. Extended travels in Mexico and Europe in later years also expanded his cultural literacy and empathy. His poetry expresses his interest in understanding all of the many different cultures that have contributed to modern global identity.

After high school in San Pedro, California, Wright played minor league baseball and served in the U.S. Army. He earned a degree at the University of California at Berkeley in 1961, studied briefly at Union Theological Seminary, and received a master's degree from Rutgers University in 1966. Though he taught at Tougaloo College, Talladega College, and Yale University in the late 1960's and early 1970's, Wright did not pursue a regular academic career. Married in 1971 to Lois Silber, Wright settled in New Hampshire to continue his research and writing.

Wright's serious devotion to poetry and his prolific production brought him numerous awards, including a National Endowment for the Arts Fellowship in 1968, a Guggenheim Fellowship in 1974, and the prestigious MacArthur Fellowship in 1986. These awards allowed Wright time to study and to write. The study of comparative religion, philosophy, and anthropology is central to Wright's poetic work, which explores the history of slavery in the New World by investigating the mythologies and cosmologies of the African, European, and Native American peoples.

Poetry

FIRST PUBLISHED: *Death as History,* 1967; *The Homecoming Singer,* 1971; *Sooth-sayers and Omens,* 1976; *Dimensions of History,* 1976; *The Double Invention of Komo,* 1980; *Explications/Interpretations,* 1984; *Elaine's Book,* 1986; *Selected Poems of Jay Wright,* 1987; *Boleros,* 1991

In the early 1970's, when many African Americans adopted such aspects of traditional African culture as wardrobe and hairstyle, Jay Wright chose to explore the complex mythologies of the West African Dogon and Bambara peoples. Early poems in *The Homecoming Singer* are often biographical, but later poetry, drawing upon Wright's study of anthropological works, approaches these African cosmologies with the gravity that English-language poets previously have accorded to biblical and ancient classical sources. A full appreciation of *The Double Invention of Komo* depends upon the reader's willingness to investigate these sources, but many of Wright's shorter poems in *Explications/Interpretations* and other books are accessible to more casual attention. In every case, Wright views poetry as a personal means of learning about spiritual and communal realities. "My speech is a plumb line/ to the echo of the earth" he writes in "Inscrutability."

Raised in New Mexico and Southern California, Wright was directly influenced by African American, Hispanic, and Native American culture and his literary search for identity avoids the binary black-white focus of much African American literature. In his notes to *The Double Invention of Komo,* Wright asserts that "history and poetry have the same creative ground" and are tools for individual discovery that "permit a man to know himself." As a result, Wright's poetry is an ambitious and demanding intellectual exercise, demonstrating his belief that traditional African cosmologies and rituals effectively define the relationship of the individual to society and the natural world in ways that are unavailable through European philosophy. Well-read in religion and modern science, Western and non-Western philosophy, Wright requires his readers to see each of these as equally complex and valid approaches to understanding reality. *The Double Invention of Komo* is a cross-cultural epic that dramatizes a Bambara initiation ritual, recording Wright's intellectual quest and introducing his readers to a syncretic view of the world.

Wright is primarily a religious poet—in the sense that his works seek to engage the spiritual dimension of human life—and even his scintillating love poems seek "the gift of being transformed." What there is of social commentary in his work may be found in his suggestion that actively pursuing an understanding of spirituality may be the most effective way to deal with social problems. He writes in "Journey to the Place of Ghosts," "It is time for the snail's pace/ of coming again into life,/ with the world swept clean,/ the crying done." In Wright's poetry, even the most minute achievement of personal intelligence counts more than Western notions of material progress.

SUGGESTED READINGS

Barrax, Gerald. "The Early Poetry of Jay Wright." *Callaloo* 6 (Fall, 1983): 85-101.

Kutzinski, Vera M. *Against the American Grain: Myth and History in William Carlos Williams, Jay Wright, and Nicolas Guillén.* Baltimore: The Johns Hopkins University Press, 1987.

Okpewho, Isidore. "From a Goat Path in Africa: An Approach to the Poetry of Jay Wright." *Callaloo* 14 (1991): 692-726.

Stepto, Robert B. "After Modernism, After Hibernation: Michael Harper, Robert Hayden, and Jay Wright." In *Chant of Saints: A Gathering of Afro-American Art, Literature, and Scholarship*, edited by Michael S. Harper and Robert B. Stepto. Champaign: University of Illinois Press, 1979.

Welburn, Ron. "Jay Wright's Poetics: An Appreciation." *MELUS* 18 (1994): 51-70.

—Lorenzo Thomas

Richard Wright

BORN: Natchez, Mississippi; September 4, 1908
DIED: Paris, France; November 28, 1960

Wright portrays African Americans entrapped in forms of neo-slavery;
he earned national and international acclaim.

TRADITIONS: African American
PRINCIPAL WORKS: *Uncle Tom's Children*, 1938; *Native Son*, 1940; *Twelve Million Black Voices: A Folk History of the Negro in the United States*, 1941; *Native Son: The Biography of a Young American, a Play in Ten Scenes*, pr. 1941; *Black Boy: A Record of Childhood and Youth*, 1945; *The Outsider*, 1953; *Black Power: A Record of Reaction in a Land of Pathos*, 1954; *The Color Curtain: A Report of the Bandung Conference*, 1956; *White Man, Listen!*, 1957; *The Long Dream*, 1958; *American Hunger*, 1977; *Rite of Passage*, 1994

Richard Wright rose from abject poverty to become one of America's foremost writers. His topics consistently focus on the freedom and self-governance of African Americans in texts before 1950. He chronicled his Southern experiences from 1908 to 1927 in *Black Boy*, and his Northern experiences from 1927 to 1937 in *American Hunger*. Wright met with success once he moved to New York City in 1937. He won a literary prize in 1938 that earned him a contract with a major publisher, which published *Uncle Tom's Children*. A Guggenheim Fellowship in 1939 enabled Wright to complete *Native Son*; with that work alone, he earned acclaim as the leading African American writer of his time. The novel is Wright's moral indictment of America for perpetrating neo-slavery among African Americans. In *Native Son*, the ghetto produces Bigger Thomas, who dies as a result of his accidentally killing a white woman. The 1940's brought personal crises to Wright. He faced America's continuous racial discrimination toward him and toward interracial couples once he married Ellen Poplar in 1941. Ongoing rifts with the Communist Party also added to Wright's tensions. In 1946, he renounced America for France, as did other expatriates who sought freedom abroad. The 1950's marked the emergence of Wright's global consciousness and his writings concerning Western imperialism. His immersion in French existentialism provided the means to assess the effects of Western imperialism on Asian, African, and Spanish cultures. *The Outsider* became the seminal existentialist novel in African American letters. Wright became an existentialist humanist, transformed from what he identified as an "American Negro" to a "Western man of color" and freedom activist. Wright was prolific as well as a writer of high quality; his writings continued to be published after his death in 1960.

American Hunger

TYPE OF WORK: Autobiography
FIRST PUBLISHED: 1977

American Hunger, the second part of Wright's autobiography, focuses on his life in Chicago, Illinois, from 1927 to 1937. The book was written in 1944. The northern experience recurs as a new slave narrative. It demonstrates how modern African Americans were deceived. Wright opens the text in 1927, when nineteen-year-old Richard, his alter ego, arrives in Chicago with his Aunt Maggie. Wright juxtaposes the terms "strange" and "familiar" to express Richard's dismay at seeing African Americans openly consort with whites in public facilities. He learns quickly that appearances are deceptive.

Wright employs literary naturalism to illustrate racial and environmental barriers erected by whites to imprison African Americans in modern slavery. Richard discovers that migrants have traded Southern plantations for urban ghettos. They live in the black belt of Chicago and remain racially and economically disfranchised. Richard's economic status soon imitates that of his impoverished southern experience. Richard earns low wages at menial jobs during the following six years. The intermittent checks from his postal service job or the relief agency barely sustain Richard's family.

Consistent with *Black Boy*, Richard becomes the outsider, in conflict with his family, community, and professional affiliations. A major source of conflict is his independent thinking. His attempts at writing cause alarm to his Aunt Maggie, who believes that fiction writing and book reading serve no value unless Richard is studying law. Richard's white employer cannot understand why an African American dishwasher would read newspapers. Once Richard joins professional writing groups, between 1933 and 1935, he discovers that his intelligence poses a threat to members of the John Reed Club of the Communist Party, the Southside Writers' Group, and the Federal Theatre Project. They attack him for being an "intellectual" just as Southerners attacked the "smart Ne-

Richard Wright (Library of Congress)

gro." The Communists even label Richard a Trotskyite or traitor, and physically assault him at the May Day parade of 1936.

His freedom from slavery culminates with Richard's resignation from the Communist Party. He takes physical flight to New York in 1937. In his ongoing quest for freedom, his psychological emancipation is the real moral to his narrative. It coincides with the successful publication of fiction, which frees Richard to write "art for art's sake," not propaganda, and to accelerate his "war with words."

Black Boy
TYPE OF WORK: Autobiography
FIRST PUBLISHED: 1945

Black Boy: A Record of Childhood and Youth stands as a classic African American autobiography. It tells of Wright's escape from figurative slavery in the South to freedom in the North. The text opens in 1912 on Wright's earliest memory at age four. Richard is living in Jackson, Mississippi, in the crowded home of his grandparents. The household includes Richard, his mother, father, brother, and his uncle, and it replicates the subhuman living conditions of slaves.

Richard's father is illiterate and an unskilled laborer; in search of work, he moves his family to another state, which initiates Richard's life of emotional and physical instability. These disruptions occur in three cycles. From age four to age twelve, Richard moves frequently from Mississippi to Tennessee to Arkansas and back again. From age twelve to age seventeen, he remains in Jackson. From age seventeen to age nineteen, he escapes, first to Tennessee and then to Illinois. Before age twelve, Richard suffers abandonment by his father, life in an orphanage, street life, heavy drinking, and the illness of his mother.

Wright employs the literary technique of naturalism to portray the racial and environmental factors that create a hostile world for Richard. Whites consider African Americans to be inferior because of their skin color, and Richard hears of violent acts against African Americans in the form of murders, lynchings, and beatings. He personally experiences verbal threats, physical assaults, and animal attacks. Whites pay African Americans low wages to keep them economically enslaved and unable to escape the mandated segregated housing, which is substandard. Richard consistently suffers from hunger, poor housing, insufficient clothing, and erratic schooling.

Richard grows up an isolated figure because he does not fit the servile demeanor required of African Americans to live in the South. He rejects religion since he cannot understand how a white God allows his mother, family, and community to suffer. In turn, they assail his reading and writing of fiction, which his grandmother charges is "Devil's work." The school principal even denounces Richard when he refuses to deliver the stock valedictory speech of humility at his graduation ceremony from ninth grade. Whites, too, attack Richard for being a "smart Negro" when he undertakes menial jobs in private homes or at businesses during his stay in the South.

Richard resists these oppressive forces in his quest for knowledge and for freedom. At nineteen, he discovers the writer H. L. Mencken, and decides that he, too, wants to become a writer to "wage war with words." *Black Boy* concludes in 1927, with Richard's flight to the North in the tradition of former slaves before him.

SUGGESTED READINGS

Fabre, Michel. *From Harlem to Paris: Black American Writers in France, 1840-1980.* Champaign: University of Illinois Press, 1991.

_____. *The Unfinished Quest of Richard Wright.* New York: William Morrow, 1973.

_____. *The World of Richard Wright.* Jackson: University Press of Mississippi, 1985.

Hakutani, Yoshinobu. *Critical Essays on Richard Wright.* Boston: G. K. Hall, 1982.

Rampersad, Arnold, ed. *Richard Wright: A Collection of Essays.* Englewood Cliffs, N.J.: Prentice Hall, 1995.

Stepto, Robert T. *Behind the Veil: A Study of Afro-American Narrative.* 2d ed. Champaign: University of Illinois Press, 1979.

Weiss, M. Lynn. *Gertrude Stein and Richard Wright: The Poetics and Politics of Modernism.* Jackson: University Press of Mississippi, 1998.

Wright, Richard. *Conversations with Richard Wright.* Edited by Keneth Kinnamon and Michel Fabre. Jackson: University Press of Mississippi, 1993.

—Virginia Whatley Smith

Mitsuye Yasutake Yamada

BORN: Kyushu, Japan; July 5, 1923

Yamada's contribution to American women's writing is in her furthering of the cause of human rights.

TRADITIONS: Japanese American
PRINCIPAL WORKS: *Camp Notes and Other Poems*, 1976; *Desert Run: Poems and Stories*, 1988

Mitsuye Yasutake Yamada spent most of her formative years in Seattle, Washington, until a few months after the outbreak of World War II, when her family was removed to a concentration camp at Minidoka, Idaho. Her poems in *Camp Notes and Other Poems* recount this experience. Her need to integrate her art, her beliefs, and her commitment to human rights stems largely from the impact this event had on her.

Yamada earned a bachelor's degree in English and Art at New York University and a master's degree in literature at the University of Chicago. She had a distinguished career as a teacher, working for many years at a community college in Cypress, California, and serving as writer-in-residence at Pitzer College and San Diego State University.

In her writings, Yamada has characteristically focused on her bicultural heritage, women, and human rights. During the early 1960's she began working as a volunteer with Amnesty International, and her continuing commitment to human rights through that organization eventually led to her service on the national board of Amnesty International USA and participation in international committees seeking increased Asian involvement in human rights work. She made several trips to South Korea, Japan, and other countries in Asia on behalf of Amnesty International.

Commitment to diversity in all areas of life has led Yamada to multidisciplinary as well as multicultural commitments. While a community college professor she team-taught an interdisciplinary course in biology and poetry which involved field trips to research and experience the wilderness areas of California. Out of this experience came many of the poems in Yamada's second collection, *Desert Run*. This book returns to the themes of alienation, human rights, and protest against injustice that reverberate through the earlier collection. In *Desert Run*, seeing the desert from a new perspective enables a healing process to take place. The title poem, "Desert Run," makes the comparison explicitly as the speaker returns in memory to an earlier, enforced encampment on the desert, where armed guards stood watch over

American men, women, and children, and contrasts it with the silence, agelessness, and demanding beauty of the desert as seen on a class camping trip. Other poems celebrate the beauty of seemingly insignificant flowers and, especially, the strength and endurance of desert plants such as cacti and lichens.

Another avenue of Yamada's activism is her formation of a writers' group, MultiCultural Women Writers. This loosely formed association works to raise support and awareness of diversity in the arts and has published an anthology, *Sowing Ti Leaves: Writings by Multi-Cultural Women* (1992), coedited by Yamada, which has gone through several editions.

Camp Notes and Other Poems
Type of work: Poetry
First published: 1976

The poems in *Camp Notes and Other Poems* originated in the experience of a concentration camp. Yamada and her family were interned with other Japanese Americans from the West Coast during World War II. Yamada spent April, 1942, through September, 1943, at the internment camp near Minidoka, Idaho. Inmates could have few possessions; Yamada brought a tablet of paper on which she recorded her reflections on life in the camp. To the poems from this period she later added others concerning the time preceding and the time following the camp experience.

At the beginning of the book are poems about ancestors and parents: great-grandmother's box of treasured souvenirs, a young bride in a new and precarious environment, a folktale related by a sophisticated father. Following the poems about internment are poems related to the poet's later life. These poems frequently have themes that are a feature of the center section about the internment: justice, equity, and generosity. These themes are continuing threads in these poems, which occasionally have a feminist perspective.

The middle, or "Camp Notes," section contains the angriest poems. With irony, the speaker in the poems expresses and conquers the rage, humiliation, and despair of unjust captivity. A photographer's instruction to "smile" as internees are collected at staging points, the bus ride to the camps, a guard tower seen through the eyes of a child, makeshift furniture of packing crates and straw mattresses, stuffing rags into cracks in the shacklike barracks during a dust storm—each of these moments is crystallized. The poem titled "Curfew" ends in a particularly vivid commentary: After quoting the "block head" giving orders for lights out, the speaker simply remarks, "There must be no light." One of the briefest poems, "In the Outhouse," is also one of the most powerful. The stench of the outhouse becomes a metaphor for the entire camp and the mentality that created it; fear and racism relegate a whole group of people to the domain of "refuse" and "outsider." Many of the poems focus on the absurdity and duplicity of the language and thinking used to justify the camps. In "Desert Storm" the speaker notes the euphemisms that attempted to disguise injustice, noting how the reality of imprisonment was "sanitized" by the term "relocation." The speaker notes in "The Trick Was" that the "mind was not fooled."

Camp Notes and Other Poems is actually a cooperative and family project. Yamada's husband, Yoshikazu Yamada, contributed the calligraphs that translate titles and text for some of the poems. Her daughters, Jeni and Hedi, produced illustrations for some pages. Yamada also includes a translation of one of her father's poems, written while he was interned apart from his family in a different camp.

SUGGESTED READINGS

Jaskoski, Helen. "A MELUS Interview: Mitsuye Yamada." *MELUS* 15, no. 1 (1988): 97-108.

Schweik, Susan. "A Needle with Mama's Voice: Mitsuye Yamada's *Camp Notes* and the American Canon of War Poetry." In *Arms and the Woman: War, Gender, and Literary Representation*, edited by Helen M. Cooper, Susan Merrill Squier, and Adrienne Auslander Munich. Chapel Hill: University of North Carolina Press, 1989.

Yamada, Mitsuye. "A MELUS Interview: Mitsuye Yamada." Interview by Helen Jaskoski. *MELUS* 15, no. 1 (1988): 97-108.

Yamada, Mitsuye, and Sarie Sachie Hylkema, eds. *Sowing Ti Leaves: Writings by Multi-Cultural Women*. Irvine, Calif.: MultiCultural Women Writers, 1991.

—Helen Jaskoski

Hisaye Yamamoto

BORN: Redondo Beach, California; 1921

Yamamoto, an accomplished short-story writer, was one of the first Japanese American writers to gain recognition after World War II.

TRADITIONS: Japanese American
PRINCIPAL WORKS: *Seventeen Syllables and Other Stories*, 1988

Born of Japanese immigrant parents, Hisaye Yamamoto began writing in her teens. As a second-generation Japanese American, she was especially interested in the interaction between the Japanese traditions passed on to her and the American experience she encountered. She once cited that her main reason for writing was a desire "to reaffirm certain basic truths which seem to get lost in the shuffle from generation to generation, so that we seem destined to go on making the same mistakes over and over again."

Interest in literary subjects was strong among the generation born in Japan, many of whom wrote traditional Japanese poetry, which appeared in Japanese-language periodicals. The second generation tended to express its literary leanings in English. Yamamoto contributed regularly to *Kashu Mainichi* in Los Angeles and associated herself with the League of Nisei Writers and Artists.

In 1942, President Franklin D. Roosevelt ordered that all people of Japanese descent living on the West Coast be evacuated to internment camps. Interned at Poston, Arizona until 1945, Yamamoto became a columnist and sometime editor for the camp newsletter. She published her first mystery, "Death Rides the Rails to Poston." The experience of internment looms large in postwar Japanese American writing. In "I Still Carry It Around," Yamamoto describes internment as a painful collective wound.

From 1945 to 1948, she worked for the *Los Angeles Tribune*, a black weekly, thus extending her experience of multiculturalism, before deciding to turn to writing full time. In 1950, she received a John Hay Whitney Foundation Opportunity Fellowship. Three of her short stories received critical attention: "High-Heeled Shoes," dealing with sexual harassment; "The Brown House," dealing with interethnic and interracial encounters; and "Epithalamium," dealing with romance. Yamamoto's themes are multiple, but she is especially sensitive to the life allotted to Japanese American women.

Marriage in 1955 and four subsequent children (added to one she had already adopted) curtailed her literary output, but she did not cease to write and to influence other writers. In 1988, Kitchen Table Press published *Seven-*

teen Syllables and Other Stories, a collection of fifteen of her short stories, making her work easily available.

"Seventeen Syllables"

TYPE OF WORK: Short fiction
FIRST PUBLISHED: 1949

"Seventeen Syllables," Yamamoto's most acclaimed short story, combines a number of themes that appear frequently in her fiction. These themes include the difficulties faced by Japanese immigrants to the United States, the cultural separation between these immigrants and their children, and the restrictions experienced by Japanese American women within traditional Japanese culture. Important for an understanding of the story are some facts about the Japanese immigrant experience in America. Although the United States welcomed Japanese immigrants after 1885, immigration was stopped with the Asian Exclusion Act of 1924. Many of the first Japanese immigrants were unmarried men, who saved their earnings and sent back to Japan for brides they knew only through letters and photograph... Many of these married couples proved incompatible and were forced to make the best of an unsuitable marriage, keeping their problems concealed from the children. The Alien Land Act of 1913 prohibited Japanese immigrants from buying or leasing land for a period of more than three years. Since one-half of the immigrants lived in rural areas, the law forced families to move constantly and dispersed them often. A Japanese woman frequently had no other woman in whom to confide. In spite of these hardships, literature flourished and many immigrants wrote traditional Japanese poetry.

Yamamoto's story deals with these concerns through a device used often by Yamamoto, the double plot. On one level the plot concerns the adolescent Rosie Hayashi and her secret plan to meet Jesus Carrasco, a member of a Mexican family hired for the harvest. Rosie's inability to speak much Japanese and her failure to understand the interest her mother, Tome, takes in writing *haiku*, which she submits weekly to a Japanese-language paper in San Francisco, highlight the cultural and intergenerational differences between them. In the midst of the tomato harvest, when all workers are desperately needed, the editor arrives with a prize for Tome's poetry, a print by Hiroshige. Angry, her husband burns the picture. Tome reveals to Rosie that she has married her husband as an alternative to suicide. Rejected by a well-to-do lover, she had given birth to a stillborn son. An aunt in the United States arranged the marriage. Disappointed and disillusioned, Tome asks Rosie to promise never to marry at a time Rosie is experiencing the blissful promise of young romance. The story is a carefully nuanced and technically sophisticated combination of ethnic, feminist, and intergenerational concerns.

SUGGESTED READINGS

Cheung, King-Kok. *Articulate Silences: Hisaye Yamamoto, Maxine Hong Kingston, Joy Kogawa.* Ithaca, N.Y.: Cornell University Press, 1993.

_____. "Double-Telling: Intertextual Silence in Hisaye Yamamoto's Fiction." *American Literary History* 3, no. 2 (1991): 277-293.

_____, ed. *Seventeen Syllables.* New Brunswick, N.J.: Rutgers University Press, 1994.

Kim, Elaine H. *Asian American Literature: An Introduction to the Writings and Their Social Context.* Philadelphia: Temple University Press, 1982.

Nesbitt, Anna Sheets. *Short Story Criticism: Criticism of the Works of Short Fiction Writers.* Vol. 34. Detroit: Gale Group, 2000.

Yogi, Stan. "Legacies Revealed: Uncovering Buried Plots in the Stories of Hisaye Yamamoto." *Studies in American Fiction* 17, no. 2 (1989): 169-181.

—*Christine R. Catron*

Indexes

Author Index

Title Index

Ethnic Identity List